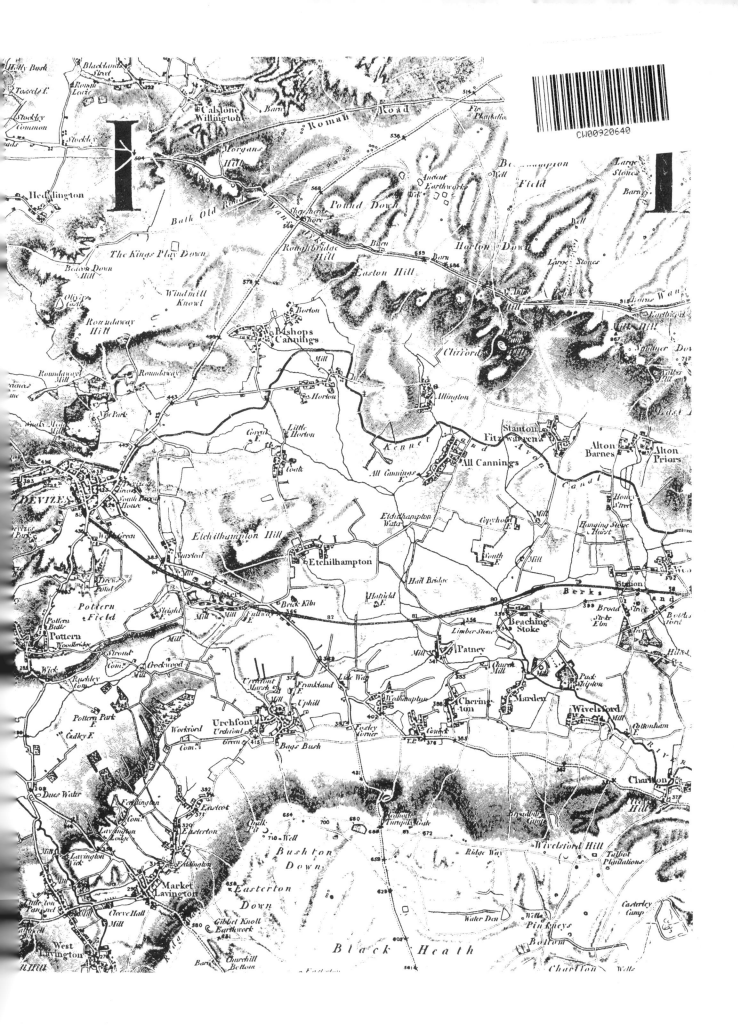

GWR
to
DEVIZES

Looking west across Devizes station in 1921, showing the fully-extended platforms, station lamps and flowerbeds. (LGRP)

GWR
to
DEVIZES

From Holt Junction I took the rails
Through Semington, Seend and Sells;
Bromham & Rowde soon passed by
With its Mill and its crane touching the sky.
Over the canal at Foxhangers and on
Towards Fish Bridge, majestic and strong,
Slowing now as Caen Hill rises
Thick smoke swirling, pulling in to Devizes.
A short rest here at Platform 1,
The journey continues, for some it's begun.
Carriages are lit as we enter the tunnel,
Dark at one end and light at the funnel.
The romantic Pans Lane is left in the cutting,
The meadows in Stert with hedges abutting.
Lydeway went by and now I was certain
The station was near for Patney & Chirton.

Rod Priddle & David Hyde

Millstream Books

Preface

The Devizes Branch was born on 1st July 1857 and died on 16th April 1966. It was a short line, just 13 miles in distance, running from the village of Holt near Trowbridge, through the town of Devizes, to the village of Patney. With the exception of Devizes station and Pans Lane Halt, also in Devizes, the other five stations on the line all served small Wiltshire villages.

It is hoped that this book will provide something for everybody who has an interest in railways past, for we have tried to include not just pictures of trains but an insight into the infrastructure of the line, the people and local businesses who used it, as well as the not-to-be-forgotten men and women who worked it. The historical facts and figures have been kept to a minimum as they have been comprehensively covered in Nigel Bray's earlier publication, *The Devizes Branch* .

The production of this book at this time came about because it was felt that the line was already becoming a distant memory. Many of the railway staff who were there at the time of closure are no longer with us and those that remain are beginning to run out of steam, so it was important to capture their knowledge, recollections and the photographs of them in their working environment as a record for the future.

We hope you enjoy this relaxing journey through the centre of Wiltshire, along the Devizes Branch from Holt Junction to Patney & Chirton.

The name plate of Castle Class No.5050 Devizes Castle, built in May 1936. The name was changed in August 1937 to Earl of St Germans. Subsequent locomotives named Devizes Castle were: No.5075, built in August 1938 and renamed Wellington in October 1940; and No.7002, built in June 1946, fitted with a double chimney in July 1961, and withdrawn in March 1964. (Keith Buckle)

First published 1996 by Millstream Books, 18 The Tyning, Bath BA2 6AL
Set in 11 point Palatino and printed in Great Britain by The Amadeus Press, Huddersfield

ISBN 0 948975 43 1

©Rod Priddle and David Hyde 1996

Contents

The Devizes Branch passed into a tunnel directly beneath De____ Castle, shown atop its mound in this 1925 GWR Publicity Department photograph. The castle is a Victorian replica, ____ the site of the early 12th-century original.

Introduction

With the arrival of the railway in Wiltshire, the prominent people of the market town of Devizes could see the benefits it would provide for them. It would improve trade and certainly provide a faster service for transporting goods than those existing by road and canal. It was hoped Devizes would be on the route to London, which in addition to trade benefits would also be a bonus for passenger traffic. From the early 1830s and into the next decade the citizens tried desperately to attract a railway to the town but to no avail and it was not until 1845 that they could see the light at the end of the tunnel, when on 30th June the independent Wiltshire, Somerset & Weymouth Railway obtained parliamentary approval for a line from Thingley Junction to Westbury, having branches to Devizes and Bradford-on-Avon, as well as from Westbury to Salisbury and to Weymouth.

It was at this time that Isambard Kingdom Brunel was appointed as the company's engineer. The financing of the WSWR came primarily from the GWR. At this stage it was intended that the Devizes Branch would have its junction at Melksham, with traffic to Bath going via Chippenham. This proposal was changed later in the year when it was decided the branch would join the main line at Staverton so making a shorter route to Bath. The route changed again in 1846 resulting in the final site for the junction, at the village of Holt.

The line from Westbury to Thingley opened on 5th September 1848 but owing to financial problems very little progress was made with the Devizes section and so the people of the town would have a further six-year wait before construction of the line was commenced in earnest, this following purchase of the WSWR by the GWR in March 1850.

The GWR needed to raise extra finance to complete the line; they were empowered to do this by an Act of Parliament passed on 31st July 1854. The day Devizes had long been awaiting eventually came on 1st July 1857 when the almost 8¼ mile broad-gauge length opened. At this time there were no other stations between Devizes and Trowbridge. This section of line continued as a branch until 11th November 1862 when Devizes ceased to be a terminus station with the opening of the Berks & Hants Extension from Hungerford to Devizes. The ambition of being on a direct route with London had now been realised and it was hoped that the town was going to find itself on the main route for traffic from the capital to the West Country. Conversion of the track from broad gauge 7' 0¼" to standard gauge 4' 8½" took place over one weekend in June 1874.

After 38 years of semi-mainline working, Devizes was once again reduced to branch line status when in 1900 a line from Patney & Chirton to Westbury was opened on 20th July for goods traffic and on 1st October for passengers. This effectively resulted in a decline of use, as traffic to the west soon operated via Lavington and Castle Cary. The branch did however see a new lease of life during both world wars when it played its part to the full in providing the military with means of transporting equipment, personnel and prisoners of war to the various camps in the area of Salisbury Plain.

Following the war years and with the growing use of motorised commercial transport and private car ownership, the branch started its decline but another brief revival occurred in 1961 when during the early morning of 21st August an embankment

Thursday was market day and many people were brought into Devizes from the surrounding villages by pony and trap, charabanc, omnibus or by train, for which the GWR issued Market Day tickets and published a special timetable listing suitable services. Many facets of country life may be seen in these GWR publicity views of June 1925 (below and opposite). One of the destinations on the charabanc is shown as Charlton & the Plain. Station Road lies between the Corn Exchange and Central Café, as was the Great Western Hotel, just out of sight.

subsidence took place on the main line between Patney and Lavington resulting in closure of the down line and a 15mph speed restriction on the up. The subsidence continued over the next couple of days so it became necessary to close the section entirely on 23rd August with trains being diverted along the branch to and from the West Country or via Swindon. The main line reopened in mid-September and hopes were that the branch might even be retained as a permanent diversionary route but this was not to happen. The end eventually came, as with many other lines, under the prunings of Dr Beeching. The official closure date was 18th April 1966 but the last train actually pulled out of Devizes on the evening of 16th April.

During the preparation of this book, many people commented on their sorrow at the loss of the line and felt what an asset it would have been today. Whilst these are heart-warming sentiments, it is doubtful if this would be so. It was lost in the post-war years because of its fall in use and it is hard to see it being capable of attracting any more use in the present climate. Would the inhabitants of Chirton or Marden trek to their outlying station at Patney in order to make the short journey to Devizes or would it be easier to use the Community Bus or their cars, and which would cost less?

The Devizes Branch *will* live again we hope - if only in the following pages.

St John's Church (above), through the medieval St John's Court. The footpath to the right beyond the iron gates led to Hillworth Road via the footbridge popular with railway photographers as it overlooked the east tunnel portal. This GWR publicity view of June 1925 was for use in brochures and carriage prints, behind the seats in compartments, alongside the maps and mirrors. Another carriage print was of the Crammer (below) – the pond beside St James's Church.

GREAT WESTERN RAILWAY.

PUBLIC RECEPTION

OF

LORD METHUEN

AT

DEVIZES.

ON FRIDAY, OCTOBER 31st, 1902,

CHEAP TICKETS

WILL BE ISSUED TO

DEVIZES

AS UNDER:—

From	Trains.		RETURN FARES.			From	Trains.		RETURN FARES.		
			1st Class.	2nd Class.	3rd Class.				1st Class.	2nd Class.	3rd Class.
	a.m.	a.m.					a.m.	a.m.			
SWINDON ...	7.35	10.55	6/11	4/5	3/6	HEYTESBURY	8.31	11.13	5/0	3/2	2/6
WOOTTON BASSETT	7.47	9.32	5/10	3/9	2/11	WARMINSTER	8.43	11.35	4/0	2/6	2/0
DAUNTSEY ...	7.59	9.45	4/10	3/2	2/5			noon.			
CHIPPENHAM ...	8.32	11.30	3/7	2/4	1/10	FROME ...	8.45	12.0	4/5	2/10	2/3
MELKSHAM ...	8.45	11.44	2/3	1/6	1/2	WESTBURY ...	9.16	12.37	3/2	2/0	1/7
BOX ...	7.18	10.28	4/2	2/6	2/1	TROWBRIDGE	9.35	12.32	2/4	1/6	1/2
CORSHAM ...	7.29	10.34	4/2	2/6	2/1			a.m.			
BATH ...	8.36	10.26	4/5	2/10	2/3	HOLT ...	9.45	11.53	1/8	1/1	1/0
BATHAMPTON ...	8.46	10.36	4/2	2/6	2/1			p.m.			
LIMPLEY STOKE ...	8.55	10.45	3/9	2/4	1/10	HUNGERFORD	9.6	12.32	5/0	3/2	2/7
FRESHFORD	8.50	10.49	3/6	2/3	1/9	BEDWYN	9.16	12.35	4/1	2/6	2/1
BRADFORD-ON-AVON	9.6	10.55	3/2	2/0	1/7	MARLBORO'	9.3	12.37	4/5	2/10	2/3
SALISBURY ...	7.50	10.50	6/11	5/3	4/2	SAVERNAKE ...	9.27	12.45	3/4	2/1	1/8
WILTON ...	7.59	10.39	6/3	5/0	3/11	PEWSEY ...	9.37	12.55	2/3	1/6	1/2
WISHFORD ...	8.6	10.45	6/3	4/7	3/6	WOODBORO'	9.46	1.5	1/6	1/0	1/0
WYLYE ...	8.15	10.56	6/3	4/0	3/2	EDINGTON	9.25	12.46	3/2	2/0	1/7
CODFORD ...	8.24	11.6	5/5	3/6	2/9	LAVINGTON ...	9.35	12.56	2/3	1/6	1/2

These Tickets will be available for return by any train having a through connection on the day of issue only. A Special train will leave Devizes at 5.30 p.m., and convey Passengers for all Stations to Newbury, connecting there with the 6.56 p.m. fast train to Reading and London. There will also be a connection to Marlborough.

Should an Excursion or Cheap Ticket be used for any other Station than those named upon it, or by any other train than as above specified, it will be rendered void, and therefore the fare paid will be liable to forfeiture, and the full Ordinary Fare will become chargeable. The Tickets are not transferable.

PADDINGTON, October, 1902.   J. L. WILKINSON, General Manager.

RD.—370. R.D'.—1580.   F. W. Starkey, Printer, Castle Street, Reading.

9

1. Holt Junction

Holt is a pleasant village close to Trowbridge on the western side of the county of Wiltshire. A fresh chapter in the history of the village began in 1848 with the arrival of the railway promoted by the Wilts, Somerset & Weymouth Railway Company. It was not, however, until 1861 that the station, comprising a single island platform, was provided. Even then it was only used as an exchange station and did not become open to local passengers until 1st April 1874. Its distance from London, as recorded in the *Railway Gazetteer*, was 94 miles.

Station Buildings

In the early days there was no access road to the station and it was necessary for passengers to cross the fields by footpath to the station yard. Assisted by a public subscription of £200, a road was eventually built in 1877 which provided much needed access for both commercial and passenger traffic. Prior to this, local businesses had to send their products by road to Trowbridge or Bradford-on-Avon for the canal route to the Midland Railway in Bath. Coinciding with the road construction, building of a goods shed was started, to accommodate the anticipated increase in trade. The road was finished on the last Tuesday in November, and the goods shed two weeks later, in December 1877. By the turn of the century the facilities at Holt had changed from a narrow platform with a hut, a signalbox and several sheds, to a station of some substance. The early platform was so narrow that a passing train on one occasion swept a passenger over the edge onto the track. After the platform was widened, the wooden hut was replaced in August 1895 by a larger wooden building with accommodation comprising a ladies waiting room and toilet accommodation, built to GWR specifications at a cost of £175. The erection of a footbridge crossing from the road to the platform also provided

A view of Holt station from the footbridge, showing the staff of J.& T.Beaven's tannery setting out on their annual trip to Weymouth in 1908. The building is in its early condition without a canopy. (P.Gooding)

This postcard view, taken soon after the previous 1908 photograph, illustrates the iron footbridge and typical goods traffic in the yard on the left, where the milk shelter was constructed in 1909.

Passengers had to use a board crossing before the footbridge was built on the same site. It is seen here in the 1950s. The complex pointwork – the 'labyrinth of points and crossings' referred to in the Wiltshire Times – gives access to the goods yard, while the bleakness of the approach road is apparent in the background.

considerable improvement. Before it was built, passengers alighting in darkness found that crossing the line and searching for the footpath could be an alarming experience, so in 1871, after an accident to a passenger, two platform lights were installed. A *Wiltshire Times* reporter wrote at the time:

> the point where the line has to be crossed is some distance from the end of the platform, the few lights of which only serve to make the darkness more visible, while the signal lights down the line act as a 'will-o-the-wisp' to lure hapless travellers the wrong way ... he has to grope his way amid a labyrinth of points and crossings and goods trucks to reach the road, with an uncontrollable feeling that at any moment he may find himself at cross-purposes with a passing train ... a modicum of safety can be obtained by keeping close to the railings ...

Although Edwin Russell, the last Station Master appointed at Holt, fought continuously for the provision of electric lighting, throughout its entire

The milk shed had been built in 1909; the canopy, with 3 hanging lamps, was added in 1913; and by the time of this c.1919 view, the platform parcels office had appeared. Note the variety of luggage trolleys on the platform. (Mowat collection)

life the station relied on oil and, later, Tilley lamps, which were a great nuisance to staff, frequently blowing out in windy conditions.

In January 1909 a covered loading bay costing £614 was added to the lengthened and slewed siding extension to the goods shed road. This bay was provided to deal with the milk and milk products traffic from the nearby Nestlé factory. The Anglo-Swiss Condensed Milk Company had purchased the former Staverton Cloth Mill in 1897 for £6,000 and had merged with Henri Nestlé Company in 1905.

Staverton Halt was opened in October of that year, 1¼ miles south of Holt. It was considered in 1912 that two factory sidings would be more beneficial than continuing with the road journey from Holt goods yard but it was to be September 1934 before a connection was laid into the factory premises, so the Holt loading bay was in use for over 20 years. On the south side of the station and alongside the Devizes line further expansion took place in 1913 with the building of two new sidings to hold 25 wagons each, the extension of an existing siding and shunting neck to take 60 wagons and also the erection of a canopy to cover over 30 feet of the passenger platform. The cost of these improvements amounted to £1,284.4s.6d.

In 1925 the Station House was built by A & W Mortimer Bros for £675. It was sited at the road entrance to the station yard and is today used as an office by the local coal merchant. Station Master Walter Bull was the first occupant. Three of the station staff and their families were housed at Foxhill Cottage, close to the station in Station Road and the fox weather vane can still be seen on the roof. At the turn of the century, the railway occupants were the families of Bryant, Cousins and Cornish.

A new parcels office was added at the Trowbridge end of the station in 1948 at a cost of £250. This included lighting, washing facilities and a parcels rack. In front of this office stood a standard corrugated iron cabin which was used for keeping platform lamps and was referred to as the lamp room.

The nameboards at Holt were of timber, at one time with cast-iron letters. The design and size of boards changed over the years as can be seen from the photographs. The board at the Devizes end of the station in 1906 was of a deep type but after 1908 it changed to a narrower board displaying the lettering HOLT JUNCTION FOR DEVIZES BRANCH. The three support posts at this end were changed from wood to metal channelling some time later. This board faced the down line platform edge and the one at the Trowbridge end faced the up line.

After leaving the platform towards Melksham and Chippenham, the Devizes line branched eastwards, passing by some trees in the fork of the junction which were known locally as the Cuckoo's Nest. The line then crossed the River Avon at Whaddon Bridge, close to the 103-mile post.

View of the station from the footbridge in the 1920s. Note that the wooden parcels office has been removed. (LGRP)

View from the approach road of the footbridge and milk shelter. Running for a waiting train over the footbridge must have been a daunting task.

The Devizes end of the platform in August 1950 showing nameboard, signalbox and lamp post for the Tilley lamp. (D.Thompson)

This three-quarter view of the station was taken on the last day of working, 16th April 1966. The site of the wooden parcels office on the platform is now occupied by a lamp hut. (R.J.Coles)

An overall view of Whaddon Bridge. (J.Sawtell)

The caisson and girder construction. (J.Sawtell)

Brunel's original structure over the river here was a wooden pile bridge with cross bracing but this was replaced in the early 1880s by a GWR caisson bridge. The main support pillars of these iron bridges consisted of large pipes cast in convenient lengths and fitted with flanges on the inside. These were bolted up, the joints stopped and their lower segments threaded; the whole assembly was 'screwed' into the river bed. Steam engines erected on temporary staging provided the power. The pipes were then pumped dry, filled with concrete, and the horizontal girders laid across to the stone abutments. There were two river and two land spans. In 1955 extensive maintenance work was carried out on the bridge, including renewal of the decking. One of the concrete-filled caissons can still be seen on the track bed near Seend.

Passenger Services

For the opening of the branch line on 1st July 1857, the people of Holt formed a procession and with flags, banners and music from a band, marched to the Junction to meet the first train, scheduled to leave Devizes at 7.45am. It was reported that it did not arrive at Holt until 9.55am, so it must have had a delayed start. It appears that many of the villagers took trips to Devizes on this first day and the Devizes passengers got off the train at Holt to join the celebrations taking place. As there were no station buildings at this time, it must be assumed that some suitable means was found to allow passengers on and off the trains.

The first timetable scheduled seven trains from Trowbridge to Devizes for weekdays, with four returning, and on Sundays there were four trains each way. Traffic had been over-estimated, however.

The schedule was soon changed to five trains each way on weekdays and none on Sundays.

While the coming of the railway was an exciting time for Holt village, it was not until 1861, with the provision of the first station that rail travel became popular. By 1862, when the line had been extended from the original Devizes terminus, seven stopping trains called at Holt in addition to the local Trowbridge and Devizes trains. The journey time from Trowbridge to Paddington, with stops at Devizes, Hungerford, Newbury and Reading, was just 3 hours 10 minutes, and it was advertised in the *Wiltshire Times* as the easiest and speediest journey. This would not have been the case in 1866, however, when the severe winter disrupted services, bringing considerable chaos to the timetable. Trains were crawling through snowdrifts and one arrival due at Trowbridge at 8.00am failed to reach there until 6.00pm. The situation was made even worse by the breakdown of telegraphic communications and it was necessary to use mounted messengers between some stations in order to maintain any form of communication. The Holt station staff worked miracles clearing the lines of snowdrifts with just shovels and hand-lamps to guide them in the dark. Some train journeys in those early days must have been more of an endurance than a pleasure. In the 1898 timetable a daily train was shown as leaving Paddington at 6.30am, running over the Berks & Hants extension via Devizes, and joining the WSWR at Holt Junction. It reached Weymouth at 1.10pm, a journey of 6 hours 40 minutes. Relaxing at the seaside must have been most welcome after leaving the train.

Business through the station prospered as was reported in the parish magazine of February 1891:

An unidentified locomotive stops by the footbridge. The postcard is dated 1906, but the scene could be as early as 1903. Note that the cowl and upper part of the left-hand chimney are still in situ but had gone by the time of the Beaven's factory outing photograph on page 11. The uppermost advertisement is also different, Pears soap having superseded Bovril (P.Gooding)

It will be interesting to our readers to learn the amount of business that was done at our station during the last year. We are indebted for the following information to our Station Master Mr Chalke. In the year 1890, 12,226 tickets were issued for which £637 was paid; 4,508 tons of goods passed through the hands of the officials for which £2,189 was paid while the sum of £294 was taken for small parcels. This surely speaks well for the trade of our parish.

At this time a local boy was issued with a season ticket which allowed him to travel to school in Trowbridge. There was a train at a convenient time in the morning but to return, he had to wait $2\frac{1}{4}$ hours after school to catch the 6.45pm to Paddington. During the 1890s, 'specials' were run from Holt to the seaside for chapel choir outings. The organiser would hire a coach, known as a 'saloon', which had long seats running down its length. The GWR had numerous saloons of this type for family and party travel. The coach would be brought from Bristol and attached to a train whose destination was usually Weston-super-Mare. At Holt other specials were the Beaven's Tannery annual outings which likewise were to a number of different seaside destinations. These annual 'Away Days', when the factory closed for the day, were the management's treat for its workers and their families. Before the train left, Mr Harry Trent, Office Manager for the company, would position himself by the footbridge and hand out florins (10p) to each person to spend at the seaside. On 4th July 1905 the trip was to Portsmouth and in 1908 to Weymouth. On a postcard sent from here to a friend by a lady from Holt, she wrote: 'Weymouth is our favourite place - tried Bournemouth once but too far to walk from the station'.

In 1905, a half day return ticket from Holt to London cost 5s. and for an evening at a theatre in the city, the return fare to Paddington was just 2s.6d. Every Thursday throughout July, August and September 1908 (July 2nd excepted), Special Day Excursions were run from Swindon to Weymouth and West Bay (Bridport). The train picking up at Holt would depart at 7.27am at a 3rd Class return fare of 3s.6d. The return train left West Bay at 7.45pm and Weymouth at 8.20pm. At this time also, Weekend Excursions from Holt could be taken to Avonmouth, Portishead, Clevedon and Weston-super-Mare, the return fare for the latter being 9s.3d for 1st Class, 5s.9d for 2nd Class and 4s.9d for 3rd Class. If on Thursdays the villagers wished to shop at Devizes Market, a Market Ticket could be brought for 11d return, 3rd Class. The departure times for this service were 9.43am and 12.00 noon. Passengers were able to return by any train on the day of issue.

MARKET TICKETS

WILL BE ISSUED

To DEVIZES on Thursdays.

FROM	At			Return Fares, 3rd Cl.	
	A.M.	A.M.	NOON.	s.	d.
Calne	7 42	10 45	...	2	4
Chippenham	8 32	11 28	...	1 10	
Melksham	8 47	11 43	...	1	3
Holt Junction	9 43	....	12 0	0 11	
Trowbridge	9 35	11 50	...	1	3
Bradford-on-Avon ...	9 7	10 58	12 16	1	1
Pewsey	9 37	11 57	...	1	3
		noon.			
Woodborough	9 46	12 5	...	0 10	
Edington and Bratton	9 20	12 50	...	1	6
Lavington	9 31	1 0	...	1	0
Patney and Chirton...	9 53	12 10	...	0	7
Seend	9 51	12 8	...	0	6
Passengers may return by any train on the day of issue.					

17

Steam railmotor No.48, with a six-wheel milk 'siphon' as tail traffic, is seen at Holt in 1906 travelling towards Trowbridge from Chippenham. Built to diagram M in April 1905, it was a 70-foot suburban type car used to serve new halts in Wiltshire and elsewhere to combat road competition. It was destroyed by fire at Chalford on 22nd December 1915. (Bob Hallam)

A similar type of suburban steam railmotor entering Holt from Chippenham. These services were introduced on the branch in October 1906 after successful use on the Stroud line. Note the original deep type of station nameboard and cast-iron lamp posts, and that the staircase of the signalbox is supported only by an iron wall bracket, without the later corner pole. (Bob Hallam)

A Cardiff to Newbury race special, via Devizes, leaves Holt headed by two Hall Class locomotives. No.5963 Wimpole Hall is the pilot from Westbury, and 6999 Capel Dewi Hall is the Cardiff locomotive. (I.Hibbard)

From the turn of the century until the start of the First World War, there was a steady increase in passenger traffic. In 1903, 12,929 tickets were issued with total receipts of £699 and in 1913, 13,474 issues were made at £698. At Christmas time 1913, a return ticket to visit a London Theatre had risen to 7s 6d compared with the 1905 price.

Between the wars, passenger traffic declined. At the end of the 1920s, annual ticket sales were over 15,000 but by the end of the 1930s they had dropped to just over 3,000. This doubled during the Second World War with the increased movement of people, and particularly of military personnel, around the country.

The years following the war still produced busy days at Holt. During the 1950s there were specials such as the Race Trains carrying the race-goers from Cardiff to meetings at Newbury. Following the departure from the station on a Saturday of the

10.30am up goods, a pilot engine from Westbury, usually a Hall Class, would arrive and be stabled in the short siding on the up side next to the main line, waiting there for the arrival of the Cardiff train travelling via the Severn Tunnel, Bath Spa and Bradford-on-Avon. The 10- and sometimes 12-coach trains, including a buffet car, were also usually headed by a Hall Class engine and on arrival at Holt, the pilot would back on to the Cardiff engine for double-headed working up in to Devizes where, on arrival at 11.45am, the pilot was removed, or at Patney & Chirton from where it would return light engine to Westbury on the main line. Those joining the train at Devizes paid 10s 6d for 1st Class and 7s 2d for 2nd Class. There was one occasion when, prior to the arrival of the Race Train, a message was received at Holt station to the affect that because of heavy fog the meeting at Newbury had been cancelled. Consequently, on

Through trains stopping at Holt in 1956 included No. 73029 B.R. Standard Class 5 on the 07.12 Weymouth to Chippenham train. Pannier 9762 is shunting the milk traffic in the 'shelter line'. (I.Hibbard)

arrival of the train from Cardiff, it fell to the station staff to inform the then irate Welsh race-goers that they would have to return to Wales. The engine ran around its train and they were soon on their way, probably to drown their sorrows in the public houses of Cardiff. This incident was recalled by Ian Hibbard, a local boy at the time. He remembers having seen this special on numerous occasions and that the Welshmen always wore their best suits but without a tie. Apparently the tradition amongst the miners was that the mine managers wore ties but the miners, to differentiate, went tie-less, although some would wear white scarves.

During this period the famous 2.35pm train from Paddington to Bristol continued its run via Devizes and Holt, providing a connection at Holt for Trowbridge, Melksham and Chippenham.

In 1961, after an embankment slip on the main line between Patney and Westbury near Lavington, the down *Cornish Riviera* was a common visitor at Holt. The train would leave Paddington in two parts; that travelling down the line via Newbury and Hungerford and entering the Devizes branch at Patney & Chirton would be headed by a diesel Warship Class, while the other part would go via Swindon. This would be steam-hauled, often by a King Class, and both trains would arrive at Holt Junction within minutes of each other.

Stan Tout, a goods shunter at Holt at the time of these diversions, recalls an occasion when a prohibited King Class engine did in fact travel over the branch. He was on duty at Holt when a telephone message was received from Rowley Reeves, the signalman in the Devizes box. He was informing Holt that the *Cornish Riviera* had just passed through Devizes station and warned them that it was headed by a King. On its arrival at Holt Junction, it stopped and the driver jumped off to inspect the engine, explaining to the Holt staff who were awaiting its appearance, that he had hit something a couple of miles back along the track. This turned out to be the platform edging at Seend station; however, no serious damage was done to the engine or the platform.

No.6968 Woodcock Hall leaving the branch with the afternoon through train from Newbury, with a 'B' set and two strengthening coaches, stopping all stations to Trowbridge. (Trevor J.Saunders)

No.4966 Shakenhurst Hall hauling the 1.45pm Weston-super-Mare to Reading train, crossing a local 3.18pm Devizes to Trowbridge service at 3.40pm, in the early 1950s. (Trevor J.Saunders)

The passenger trains on the branch in the final years were usually 2- or 3-car DMUs, seen here in one of the few photographs of the station building from the side. (J.Sawtell)

The DMU service for Devizes waits to leave. The wooden building at this northern end of the station was the Gentlemen's lavatory. The nameboard, always eye-catching, hides the milk shelter, now in use by the coal merchant. (J.Sawtell)

Freight Traffic

While passengers had been used to crossing the fields between the village and the station, they were pleased with the provision of a roadway in 1877 on which they could cover the half-mile journey in comparable comfort. At the time, with the building of the goods shed and other station facilities, freight business both in and out, started to develop. Holt had an industrial background of a similar but smaller scale to its larger neighbour Trowbridge. Major industrialists in Holt at the time of the railway's arrival, were the tannery of J. & T.Beaven, originating from the 18th century, being founded in 1783. The bed manufacturers of John Sawtell & Co. were established in 1830 on the site where the former Holt Spa once flourished. Both companies used the services of the railway and outlived it; the former continues to trade in Holt today. Sawtell's had raw materials brought in for making mattresses of hair and feather. Straw palliasses and planks of wood arrived by the wagon load and the finished goods were taken out by rail for distribution all over the country.

Transportation in the early days between the factory and station was by horse and cart, and later by GWR lorry.

Extracts from *The GWR Marshalling Instructions for Freight Trains* in the early 1900s showed:

May 1911 - 3.15pm Holt Junction to Bristol (via Camerton) wagons to be marshalled by 10.55am ex Trowbridge. Wagons to be attached at Bradford at one shunt, having been marshalled by 12.10pm ex-Melksham. To pick up traffic at Freshford at one shunt if any delay is likely to occur. To shunt Camerton Colliery and put traffic in order for 1.50pm ex Frome.

May 1918 - A special engine from Trowbridge will work the 9.52am Holt Junction to Devizes returning light to Trowbridge and the train engine of the 9.52am train will bank the 8.40am Holt to Didcot to Devizes when required and take up the shunting at the latter station.

1922 –

5.10 p.m. (New Train) Holt Junction to Devizes. Mondays to Saturdays.

	arr. p.m.	dep. p.m.	
Holt	—	5 10	Worked by engine and van of 12.1 p.m. ex Hallatrow from Holt Junction to Devizes to connect with 6.11 p.m. ex Devizes worked by Devizes shunting engine, Devizes to Patney and back as now.
Seend	C|S		
Devizes	5 37	6 11	
Patney	6 26	6†40	
Devizes	6†50	—	
Devizes	—	5†45	Engine of 12.1 p.m. ex Hallatrow (conveys van to Holt Junction).
Holt Junction	6† 5	6†20	
Trowbridge	6†28	—	

1922 –

11. 0 p.m. Devizes to Freshford.

To terminate at Holt Junction at 11.25 p.m. Engine to marshal traffic at Holt Junction in readiness for 8.5 p.m. and 12.35 a.m. Paddington to pick up at one shunt.

New **RR.** trip, Holt Junction to Freshford and Freshford to Trowbridge (worked by engine of 11.0 p.m. Devizes).

	arr. a.m.	dep. a.m.
Holt Junction	RR	12†20
Freshford	12†38	RR
Freshford	RR	1 0
Trowbridge	1 15	RR

To run when Freshford requires clearance of traffic put off Through Trains to reduce same to a single load. Freshford to advise Holt when trip required.

Newport and Cardiff District traffic hitherto worked to Freshford for the 1.40 a.m. (5.30 a.m. **MO**) Salisbury to Cardiff to be conveyed to Trowbridge by the 7.30 p.m. Devizes to Westbury for the 1.40 a.m. (5.30 a.m. **MO**) Salisbury to Cardiff to attach there.

Commenced January 30th.

1937 –

BANKING AND SHUNTING POWER.

DEVIZES No. 1 Engine. Mondays to Fridays, 11.20a.m to 6.45 p.m. Works 10.30 a.m. Goods, Holt Junction to Devizes, shunts Devizes Yard and then works 6.52p.m. Goods Devizes to Westbury. When necessary will leave Devizes at 1.40p.m for Holt Junction, shunt as required and return not later than 3.0p.m.

Saturdays, 11.20a.m. to 2.45p.m., works 10.30a.m. Holt Junction to Devizes, shunts Yard and returns working 3.0p.m. Devizes to Westbury. Total hours per week, 40½.

Although the GWR ran its own road transport service they also put goods collection and delivery out to contract. This was known as a 'cartage agreement' and one such contract was entered into with F.B.Norris & Son of Trowbridge on 15th December 1916, appointing the firm as an agent to handle goods, for which the GWR would pay 1s.6d per ton. One of the conditions of the agreement was that:

The said agent, as and when required, shall and will provide a suitable and convenient Office or Receiving House and shall have painted in a bold and legible manner in some public and conspicuous part there of, the words 'Great Western Railway Company, F.B.Norris & Son Ltd., Agent', and shall have also the same words legibly painted on the sides of fixed covers of all vehicles used or kept under or in pursuance of this Agreement.

The agreement also allowed for 'Free Cartage' for the village of Holt from the station, for one mile in any direction.

The tannery of J. & T.Beaven provided their own transport between factory and station. This was a horse and cart which was still known to be in use at the time of the Second World War. Beaven's carter from the years of the First World War was William Denley whose wife kept the local grocery shop. By the late 1940s the horse and cart had made way for motorised transport, the wool being moved by the railway company's own lorry. Part of the tannery business dealt with the grading of wool and this would arrive in large bales at the station where it would be off-loaded, using the crane in the goods shed, onto the cart and later the lorry. After grading, the procedure was reversed with the wool leaving by rail to firms such as Patons & Baldwin of Halifax and Thomas Hardman & Sons in Bury.

The tannery, in the early days, by the very nature of its business, caused the air in Holt to be of a very unpleasant nature, the inwards traffic at the station accounting for most of the smells. Needless to say, the staff there did not enjoy having to work this traffic of which there would be truck-loads of skins, barrels of foul oils and dyes, plus trucks containing dog faeces used for softening the leather after curing. There were times when trucks of skins went astray and by the time they eventually arrived at Holt, they were trucks of maggots. On one occasion a shunter made himself most unpopular when on pulling the points, he split a truck in two, piling up several wagons of foul-smelling goods right outside the goods office door. It was a hot day and the office staff were sure the stench would never leave the area.

(left) Wool traffic for Beaven's at the goods shed in 1938. Goods checker Reg Clarke, with his son in the saddle, and A.Dove from Beaven's. (R.Clarke)
(right) Railway driver Harry Evans unloading wool for grading from a GWR Thornycroft 'Nippy' in 1948. (P.Gooding)

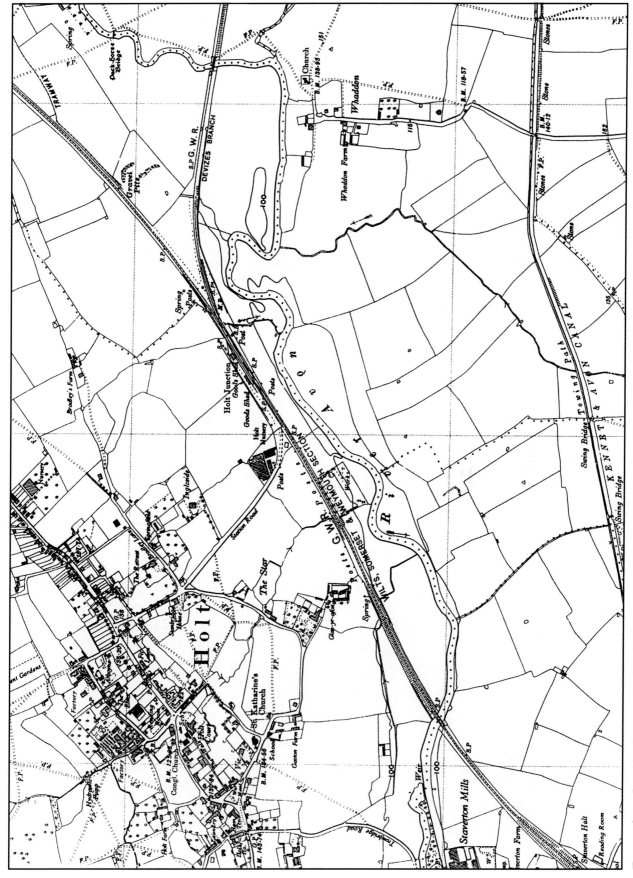

Extract from the 1922 O.S. map (revised 1936 and 1938) showing the junction of the Devizes Branch with the Wilts, Somerset & Weymouth section of the GWR.

Plaspower Hall, No.4955, heading a Reading train, via Devizes, stops at Holt Junction in 1945. The two smartly-dressed boys are Trevor Clelford and Bill Dowse. The coal bin in the goods yard can be seen beyond the locomotive. (P.Brown)

Pannier Tank No.5412 and auto-trailer approaching from Trowbridge, en route to Devizes, c.1950. This type of train was the mainstay of the stopping train traffic on the branch. The car on the approach road is a Series E Morris 8.

One of the more acceptable commodities arriving for the tannery, as far as the railway staff were concerned, was lime which came up from Cheddar in Somerset. The leather goods from the works would leave Holt by rail for the shops in London and other parts of the country. After the Second World War they left Holt for export as well.

Another major contributor to freight at Holt was the Nestlé milk factory at Staverton. By the turn of the century, with the canals in decline, the railway was used increasingly by this company, the products leaving the factory in a fleet of Sentinel steam and later Albion chain-driven lorries, for the stations at Holt and the Midland Railway at Bath (Green Park). From these stations the products, primarily condensed milk, would be sent to all parts of the country and to various docks for export.

During the First World War, production had increased with the Ministry of Munitions contracts for supplying the Forces. In 1916 plans were drawn up to install a private siding to the factory works. Sufficient land was brought in 1917 for £1,160 and talks to discuss the project were held between the company and the GWR. However the austerity of the war years and the serious recession experienced afterwards by the company brought the proposal to a temporary halt. By 1926 a full recovery had been made and expansion was

taking place. Milk was being sent from Holt station daily to the wholesale milk market in London and at a later date in smaller shipments, to various parts of South Wales. The factory brought in raw material including tin plate from South Wales for can production, box board for making the cases, sugar for the condensed milk, and coal for the factory boilers. Fresh milk arrived at Trowbridge station in 17-gallon churns where a special siding was installed. From there it was taken by road to the Staverton factory.

On 7th May 1934, an agreement was signed with the GWR 'to construct and lay down the siding accommodation' and 'to form the junction'. Conditions imposed were that Nestlé had to pay the GWR on 1st January each year by way of rent for easement over the GWR's land and also the current rate per hour for the period an engine was in use. The maintenance of the siding was to be shared between Nestlé and the railway company, although in practice it seems the railway did all of it. Nestlé and their staff, when on railway property, were under the control of the Holt Station Master and had to conform with all necessary railway regulations. When an accident occurred at 9.30am on 2nd November 1955, with a lorry crossing the private siding, Edwin Russell, the Holt Station Master, attended the subsequent enquiry as the representative of the railway.

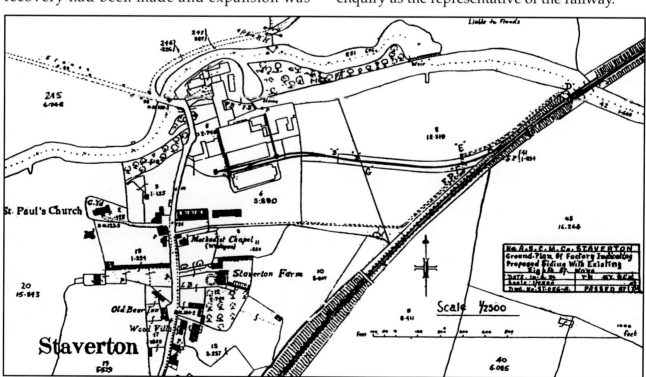

Map of the siding to the Nestlé factory at Staverton.

The siding formed the junction with the main line between Holt and Staverton station. The original 1916 proposal had been for the siding to sweep in from the Staverton station direction but this was reversed when installed in 1934. Entry was by means of a ground frame operated by a Holt shunter. When the siding came into use in September 1934 it eliminated considerable freight handling at Holt where leading porter Frank Webb had been responsible for this traffic which had been 'tripped' morning and evening. The new siding facility allowed milk supplies to be delivered directly into the condensary where provision had been made for handling milk tankers. The diagram shows the layout of the sidings which incorporated a turntable for directing the coal wagons to the boiler house. In the early days a horse was used for shunting but this went lame after two days and was not replaced.

Probably the busiest time for the workings was during the Second World War when supplies of surplus milk from all over the country were shunted into the factory to be turned into products which included 'iron rations' destined for prisoners of war and, later in the war, food parcels to be sent to Australia. As in the First World War, Ministry contracts were given priority, some of these continuing for many years after the war, with the Royal Navy being one of the main customers.

The private sidings ceased to be used in 1966 and were removed in June 1967 to make way for further factory development. In the period leading up to closure, Stan Tout was the shunter on duty at Holt on a day when the milk train from St Erth arrived at the ground frame of the Nestlé Factory siding with a King Class engine in charge. This had probably replaced a failed engine at Plymouth. The normal procedure on arrival at Staverton was for the engine to leave the wagons on the line from Bradford Junction to Staverton, before pulling forward and running back into the private Nestlé sidings. The engine would then carry out any necessary shunting before taking the wagons out of the siding and reversing onto its train to continue its journey.

A King Class locomotive, because of its size, was prohibited from entering the siding and Stan informed the driver accordingly. The driver, who was based at Old Oak Common, left Stan in no doubt that he should operate the ground frame, as he was intending to enter the siding with or without his assistance. Nothing was going to stop him from getting back to London that night and he entered and departed the sidings without experiencing any problems.

(left) Aerial view of the Nestlé factory soon after the siding was opened, with the rail line to Holt Junction to the left and to Staverton off to the right. (right) Some idea of the traffic involved may be seen in this roadside photograph. The rail installation and sidings end can be seen on the right, with insulated vans waiting and road vehicles unloading. This replaced the milk shelter at Holt. (Nestlé Company)

A Hymek approaches Holt in 1966. The milk shelter has clearly become home to coal merchants and contractors, and is in need of maintenance. (J.Sawtell)

Other freight despatched from Holt included tinplate boxes and timber coffin boards from Henry John Harding of Broughton Gifford, being sent to South Wales. There was no facility at Broughton Gifford Halt for dealing with freight. Fresh produce was also moved by rail with tomatoes, vegetables and flowers leaving the nurseries for the markets of Birmingham and Bristol. Farmer Charlie Tucker brought his cheese to the station by horse and cart from where it was sent to South Lambeth for the firm of David Greig, the London grocers. Trains of domestic coal entered a siding on the village side of the station and were unloaded at the coal stage. At the beginning of the century two coal merchants had their businesses in the yard; A.Mortimer who had a private owner wagon, and A.H. & S.Bird. About 1926, George Arlett took over the business and after Nestlé opened their private siding, he kept his coal stocks in the covered loading bay at the station, previously in use for milk storage. The down sidings were an assembly point for empty coal wagons and when there was sufficient to form a train they would be taken away. From January 1948, the Bathampton Coal Service was trading from the station yard, paying a rent of £3 per annum.

During the 1930s, builders' merchant Percy Gay collected his materials from the station yard.

Newspapers arrived each day by train but not so the Royal Mail which came to the village by road. Other freight trains seen at Holt were circus trains and farm removal trains of sometimes as many as 40 wagons. Gravel trains from nearby workings passed through Holt as the stone trains from the Mendip Quarries still do today. Holt enjoyed the services of regular goods trains in both directions. Around 1870, there was a departure from Reading at 6.20am calling at numerous stations from Newbury to Devizes where it arrived at 10.25am. It left for Seend at 11.15am, crossing the 10.00am mixed from Trowbridge. After Seend the train went on to Holt where generally it terminated unless it was carrying freight for Trowbridge. The returning Holt to Reading goods left at 12.40pm and as with the down train had a stop-over at Devizes from 1.10pm to 2.00pm. Other scheduled goods at this time were a 9.10am and 3.50pm mixed from Devizes to Trowbridge and a 7.40am Trowbridge to Devizes. In 1922, a daily goods service was running in both directions between Holt and Didcot.

Reg Clarke, who served Holt as a shunter and goods checker during the period 1934-1948, recalls the 1.45am Bristol (East Depot) to Reading regular freight calling at Holt and Devizes. Immediately after the Second World War, a weekday down pick-up goods to Westbury left Devizes at 5.45pm, crossing the 5.40pm auto from Westbury at Seend station. The departure time for this goods from Devizes changed to 5.15pm in 1956 because the passing loop at Seend was removed and it was necessary for the freight train to pass the up passenger in Holt station instead. At this time a regular freight working was the 9.10am pick-up goods from Holt to Devizes which operated from Monday to Saturdays. Shunting duties were often carried out en route at Seend or Bromham and if these were not completed promptly a considerable time could be spent in the siding awaiting clearance of the line by the up and down passenger traffic. It was not unknown for this goods to arrive in Devizes after midday. Engines used for freight were generally the 57XX 0-6-0 Pannier or 45XX 2-6-2 Tank, as the weight was too great for the 22XX 0-6-0s which were prone to derail on the sharp curve in the up goods yard of Devizes station.

Products from Fry's chocolate factory at Keynsham were sent to London from Bristol Temple Meads on a 10.05pm working known as the 'Cocoa Train'. This timing altered over the years. There were occasions when this train ran via Bradford Junction and Holt, having been diverted at Bath from the main Bristol to Paddington line. Fry's had their own private siding which joined the main line at Keynsham station. The railway's train drivers and guards were regularly presented with bags of chocolate on leaving the factory with the wagons to form the Cocoa Train.

The table below shows freight handling figures for the years leading up to the 1939-45 war:

As was the case at many stations, Holt received its fair share of accidents. On 19th October 1940, a derailment occurred involving the 7.58am Reading to Weston-super-Mare passenger train, hauled by 5933 *Kingsway Hall*, arriving at Holt at 10.52am. At the rear was a milk van siphon that on arrival had to be detached into the down siding. When the passengers had got on and off at the platform the train moved forward to clear the down siding points. Signalman Charles Millard then set the road for the siding, lowering the appropriate disc for the shunt. He then set the road points for the 10.30am Holt to Devizes goods and left his signalbox with the token, to hand to the driver of 0-6-0 PT engine 3780. Meanwhile passenger guard Hunt riding in Van Third of the passenger, seeing the points set for the siding and disc lowered, hand signalled the driver to set back. During the course of the movement he became aware that something was amiss and applied the vacuum brake. Whilst the siphon and leading wheels of the Brake Third had passed over the points, the rear wheels of the latter had become derailed. All the railway personnel at the scene, including Class 4 goods shunter C. Palmer who was nearest to the points, gave evidence that all the correct procedures had been followed and that there was no other person in the signalbox at the time. Following consideration of the evidence at the joint examination by the Locomotive, Traffic and Engineering Departments, a report was sent to the office of Superintendent of the line at Paddington, concluding that it was 'difficult to fix responsibility for this derailment, but from

STATION.	YEAR.	Forwarded.			Received.			Coal and Coke "Not Charged" (Forwarded and Received).	Total Goods Tonnage.	Total Receipts (excluding "Not Charged" Coal and Coke).	Livestock (Forwarded and Received).	Total Carted Tonnage (Included in Total Goods Tonnage).
		Coal and Coke "Charged."	Other Minerals.	General Merchandise.	Coal and Coke "Charged."	Other Minerals.	General Merchandise.					
		Tons.	Tons.	Tons.	Tons.	Tons.	Tons.	Tons.	Tons.	£	Wagons.	Tons.
Holt Jct. ..	1903	7	5,387	2,765	3,912	1,221	2,943	781	17,016	5,920	—	3,304
	1913	43	450	2,712	5,668	2,338	5,213	493	16,917	7,090	—	3,415
	1923	—	329	6,116	5,576	1,128	3,980	1,291	18,420	14,462	—	5,644
	1929	—	200	7,557	2,590	1,694	4,393	5,015	21,449	12,253	—	4,302
	1930	—	209	7,630	1,550	1,147	4,723	7,073	22,332	12,113	—	4,838
	1931	—	233	7,927	2,834	307	5,069	4,770	21,140	12,445	1	4,857
	1932	—	236	10,238	3,000	867	6,505	7,684	28,080	15,768	1	5,911
	1933	—	291	10,012	4,426	104	5,084	4,592	25,499	14,522	1	5,457
	1934	8	362	11,520	5,551	380	6,291	3,991	28,103	17,130	—	6,248
	1935	9	326	10,168	1,529	496	6,401	6,531	25,460	15,615	—	7,021
	1936	9	309	12,581	1,357	536	6,270	8,971	30,033	17,001	—	8,142
	1937	—	382	11,621	654	85	6,001	8,239	27,882	15,847	—	6,632
	1938	—	311	12,120	569	125	7,572	6,728	27,431	16,214	—	5,618

marks on the track it was evident that the points must have been moved in front of the trailing bogie of Van Third 3496'. A reply was received agreeing that 'the points must have been interfered with during the shunting operation. In the circumstances however, it is considered that the matter can not usefully be pursued further'. As a result of the accident the train was terminated at Holt and the passengers were sent to Trowbridge by the next train. The damage was to 12 chairs and sleepers, GW Brake Third 3496 had four wheels derailed and GW Brake Composite 7645 was buffer-locked. The delays caused were: 24 minutes to the 9.50am Reading, 40 minutes to the 10.20am Chippenham, 9 minutes to the 10.30am Weymouth and 14 minutes to the 12 noon Chippenham.

Another accident occurred in 1953 involving the fixed hand crane (FM 246) which was damaged when, with the goods shed doors closed, a shunt damaged both the crane and the shed. This resulted in the crane being declared unsafe. It was then demolished with the one ton of scrap being sold for the nett sum of £6.

If the method of producing electricity had not started to change at the time, it is possible that Holt Junction would still have been the site for considerable freight movement. Ian Hibbard recalls an occasion when in 1955, Station Master Reg Hopkins had a meeting at one end of Holt platform with representatives of the Electricity Generating Board at which they discussed a proposed coal-fired power station being built on the triangle of land between the branch and the Trowbridge to Melksham line. Plans left with the Station Master indicated railway lines entering and leaving the power station site, for the delivery of coal. Reg Hopkins recalls asking which coalfield the coal would be supplied from, as if it came from the East Midlands, South Wales or Radstock in Somerset, it could have posed operational problems. He was also asked to take water temperature readings daily from the nearby River Avon which he did and passed them on to the Board officials. Reg left Holt in 1955, leaving his successor Edwin Russell to continue the readings. The power station was never built, presumably because the coal-fired type were overtaken by nuclear power.

Holt Junction finally closed to goods traffic on 7th October 1963.

Dean Goods No. 2426 from the branch in the early 1950s. (Trevor J.Saunders)

The down sidings, extended in 1913 to accommodate 25 wagons, were at the north-east end on the approach from the branch, and were for storage of wagons awaiting collection. The main yard and traffic may be seen in the 1908 photograph on page 11. At times a locomotive was despatched from Trowbridge specifically to shunt the yard. Pannier 9615, seen below outside the signalbox, in about 1955, is doing that job. (I.Hibbard)

No.2208 Collet goods locomotive is seen here shunting in the yard, c.1955. (Trevor J.Saunders)

Wartime/Military

The First World War brought a considerable increase in both freight and passenger traffic with troop trains passing through Holt en route to and from the camps at Warminster, Devizes and the Plains near Patney & Chirton. The increased output of the milk commodities and the corresponding intake of raw materials at the Staverton Nestlé milk factory also made Holt station an active place.

Throughout the Second World War the station was again extremely busy, with 43 stopping trains each day as well as numerous goods, troop, government stores and ambulance trains passing through. In addition, all the building materials used in constructing the underground stores depots for the Ministry at Corsham, were brought in through Holt station and some 15 to 20 lorries hauled it away continuously, seven days a week. Throughout the war, Beaven's tannery had the Air Ministry contract for producing the standard glove used by R.A.F. aircrew. Vast numbers were made and despatched by rail.

Production of tinned milk was again stepped up for service and civilian use, and all three of Wiltshire's Nestlé factories, Salisbury, Chippenham and Staverton, were sending milk to London.

War-weary troops on their way to the camps at Warminster would on occasions alight prematurely from the 'Midnight Rocker' when it stopped by request only at Holt. Wearing full kit they would be assisted back on to the train to complete the last few miles.

As were most stations in the area, Holt was patrolled at night by members of the Home Guard who used the relatively comfortable facilities for relaxation purposes.

During the hostilities, a number of enemy bombs were dropped in the village, all in close proximity to the railway. Probably the junction was the intended target. One of the raids occurred on 15th May 1944 with the bombs coming down between the station and the Remand Home which lost its roof in the blast, as did the three cottages in Station Road owned by the railway.

Staff

The first members at Holt were two local men, Robert Thorn and Edward Pyle. They were known as section policemen who were sworn in like regular constables and even issued with truncheons, one of which, Edward Pyle's, survives today. He went on to become the very first Station Master, followed by Samuel Chalke in 1881. Station Master Goldsworth Beer was the third appointment with his service embracing the years of the First World War. He was a bearded gentleman, wore a frock coat with two brass buttons at the back and a braid pill box cap with a small peak. He was noted as being solemn, severe and quite terrifying. S.E.Hewett, who started work in the goods office in 1919, was thankful that he was seldom visited by Beer. Those seen crossing the tracks instead of using the footbridge would be sure to incur his wrath. Walter Bull was his eventual replacement, remaining in post until 1935, when Station Master R.Cowman took over. He served through the busy war years, finishing at Holt in 1952 when Reg Hopkins became the sixth appointment to the post. Reg took another appointment on the railway in 1955 and was succeeded by Edwin Russell, the last permanent appointment. When he left in 1964, the Calne Station Master, Jack Hurley, became responsible and in 1965, until closure in the following year, Wilf Clovier, the Melksham Station Master had jurisdiction at Holt Junction.

The complement at Holt in 1938 was:

1	Station Master	Class 3
1	Goods Clerk	Class 4
1	Goods Clerk	Junior
1	Porter	Grade 1
2	Porters	Grade 2
1	Goods Checker	
3	Shunters	Class 4
3	Signalmen	Class 3

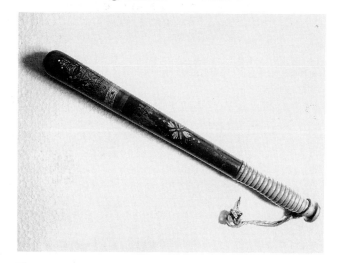

The truncheon issued to the first Station Master at Holt, Edward Pyle. (S.Kennedy)

Station Master Reg Hopkins watching over the next branch departure in 1955. (I.Hibbard)

junction with the branch. It was a Type 2 box, considered as a Principal Main Line type and continuously manned by signalmen Class 1. It was opened by 1884 with a brick-built base and timber top. The base originally had timber framing which was replaced with brick at a later stage. Its size was 19' 1" x 10' 1" x 7' and its first frame was a double twist 37-lever type. In August 1957 this was replaced with a 49-lever, 5-bar vertical tappet frame with 1 pull added to line the Up and Down Advanced Starting signals. Levers 34 and 35 were the Down Advanced and Down Starting, 37 and 36 were Down Branch Home and Inner Home signals, 40 and 39 were Down Main Home and Inner Home, 38 was a spare in case Down Branch Distant was made a working signal and 41 was a Down Distant. Levers 42 to 49 were all spares from the time of the new installation; possibly these were fitted for the sidings supplying the proposed power station which as it turned out, was not built.

During the subsequent war years there was little change in the staffing levels except that the position of junior goods clerk had been changed to a woman goods clerk, but in 1946, with the war ended and goods traffic reduced, it was considered insufficient to justify a Class 4 goods checker. The post was changed to Class 5 with a junior clerk replacing the woman and also doing some of the booking office work. The goods checker at this time was George Tucker, and Len Wilkins a goods porter.

Three signalmen from the early years at Holt were Bill Cornish, George Merrett and a Mr Cousins who on retirement, c.1923, was replaced by Tom Yeomans. Tom, on his own retirement in the 1950s, is recalled by latter day staff as returning weekly to the station to collect his pension. The signalmen in the early years worked shifts of 6am-2pm, 2pm-10pm and 10pm-6am. The changeover was made on Sundays when the box was closed in the late afternoon.

Signalling

The signalbox was positioned opposite the end of the platform on the down side and near the

The branch starter signal is on the right. (J.Sawtell)

33

Records for 1923 indicate that the box, now Class 3, at that time averaged 111 movements per hour, somewhat less than during the preceding war years. During 1913, track circuiting and the Outer Home signals were installed at a cost of £345.

The next box along the branch was at Seend and during the hours when it was in use, the Holt to Seend section was worked by tablets which were staffs approximately two feet in length with a spring-loaded loop at one end. At times when the Seend box was not in use, the Holt to Devizes section was worked by electric token which was introduced after 1914. The token had been patented by two GWR signal engineers, Mr Blackall and Mr Jacobs, and following successful trials on the Marlow branch in that year, the instrument became standard on the GWR and later British Railways.

The tablet at Holt was lost temporarily one night when it was dropped in the snow by the fireman during the handover. This delayed the train for a time and the reason was recorded on the standard form 1533, used for explaining such circumstances.

(left) Signalman Clarence (Bill) Bishop taking the token from the branch 'catcher' outside the signalbox on 2nd May 1965.
(right) Bill Bishop receiving the token in 1966. (J.Sawtell)

The speed of trains through junctions was always restricted, and at Holt all trains to and from the branch were subject to a maximum 15mph.

Depending on the tonnage of trains, a class of engine had to be used that was capable of hauling the load over any particular section of the line. The extract from the GWR *Working Timetable* for 1933, shows that that a 22XX County Class could only haul 220 tons up the 1 in 60 and 1 in 52 gradient of Caen Hill on the Holt to Devizes up section, but when used in the opposite direction, 308 tons could be handled.

Maintenance on the main line between Patney and Westbury took place on Sundays with diversions via Swindon or Devizes. On such occasions in the 1950s, Britannia Class locomotives could often be seen running unaided up the branch in the early evening. It required some skill on the part of the driver to slow the big engines sufficiently at Holt to allow the fireman to collect the single-line staff, not an easy task on an engine fitted with doors between the locomotive and tender, while maintaining momentum for the climb up the branch.

SECTION.		CLASS OF ENGINE.									
FROM	TO	4001-4072 (except 4000, 4016, 4032, 4037) "Halls" 49XX 59XX	29XX 31XX 43XX 51XX 56XX 61XX 64XX	"County." 22XX 101	"Bull Dog." 44XX&45XX 66XX 0-6-2 T. B & O Groups (New Boilers) 4-4-0 Cam. 57XX 77XX 87XX	2251.	"City," "Atbara," "Duke," 30XX & 39XX 0-6-2 T. "B" Group 0-6-0 M. & S.W. (G.W. Boilers)	3521 Type 0-0-0 & 0-6-0 T. (Stand. Gds.) 0-6-2 T. "A" Group	3200 to 3225 3521 Type (Small Boiler) T. 2-4-2 T. 4-4-0 (New Boilers)	2-4-0 T. Metro 4-4-0 M. & S.W. Old Boilers. 0-4-2 T. 58XX 898 Cam.	0-4-2 T. (517 Type) 2-4-0 (M. & S.W.)
		Tons	Tons	Tons	Tons	Tons.	Tons	Tons	Tons	Tons	Tons
Bathampton .. .. .. Trowbridge or Holt J. ..	Holt J. or Trowbridge.. .. Bathampton	360 420	330 420	312 420	283 420	— —	288 392	264 364	250 350	216 330	192 308
Holt Junction .. .. .. Devizes .. .. .. Patney	Devizes .. .. .. Patney .. .. .. Holt Junction	286a 352 352	264 330 330	220 308 308	198 264 264	— — —	176 242 242	170 242 242	162 228 228	132 198 198	110 176 176

(above left) Full frontal view of the signalbox in 1960, showing repairs and alterations. (I.Hibbard)

(above right) The signalbox viewed from the platform on 16th April 1966. (R.J.Coles)

Jack Eymes, the relief signalman from Frome, closing down the box after the last train had departed Holt on 16th April 1966. (J.Sawtell)

Approaching Holt Junction in the winter of 1963. (J.Sawtell)

A 'pick-up' goods label of 1940. (D.Lovelock)

Great Western Railway

NEWBURY RACES

Wednesday & Thursday, Jan. 27 & 28

EXCURSIONS TO

NEWBURY

(RACECOURSE STATION)

NOTE.—*If the Races are postponed or abandoned the special Excursion announced on this bill will not run.*

First Race, 1.30 p.m.   Last Race, 4.0 p.m.

FROM	AT	Day-Trip, Return Fares.		FROM	AT	Day-Trip, Return Fares.	
		First Class.	Third Class.			First Class.	Third Class.
	a.m.	s. d.	s. d.		a.m.	s. d.	s. d.
Weston-s.-Mare	9 45	17 0	10 0	Bath	10 55	12 0	7 3
Yatton	9 55	16 9	10 0	Bradford-on-			
Clevedon	9 35	17 0	10 0	Avon	11 12	10 0	6 0
Bristol—				Chippenham	10e 5	10 9	6 6
Bedminster	10 19	14 9	8 9	Melksham	10e25	9 6	5 9
Temple Meads	10 28	14 6	8 9	Trowbridge	11e 5	9 6	5 9
Clifton Down	9a52	15 0	9 0	Holt Junction	11 20	8 9	5 3
Redland	9a54	15 0	9 0	Devizes	11 44	7 0	4 3
Montpelier	9a56	15 0	9 0				
Stapleton Road	10 17	14 9	9 0				
Lawrence Hill	10 20	14 9	8 9				

Arrive Newbury Racecourse Station 12.30 p.m.

a Change at **Stapleton Road**
e Change at **Holt Junction.**

RETURN ARRANGEMENTS ON DAY OF ISSUE ONLY.

THE RETURN TRAIN WILL LEAVE NEWBURY RACECOURSE STATION AT **4.35** p.m. THE SAME DAY.

On the Return Journey passengers for Bristol (Temple Meads), Bedminster, Yatton, Clevedon, and Weston-super-Mare change at Lawrence Hill.

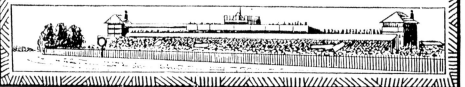

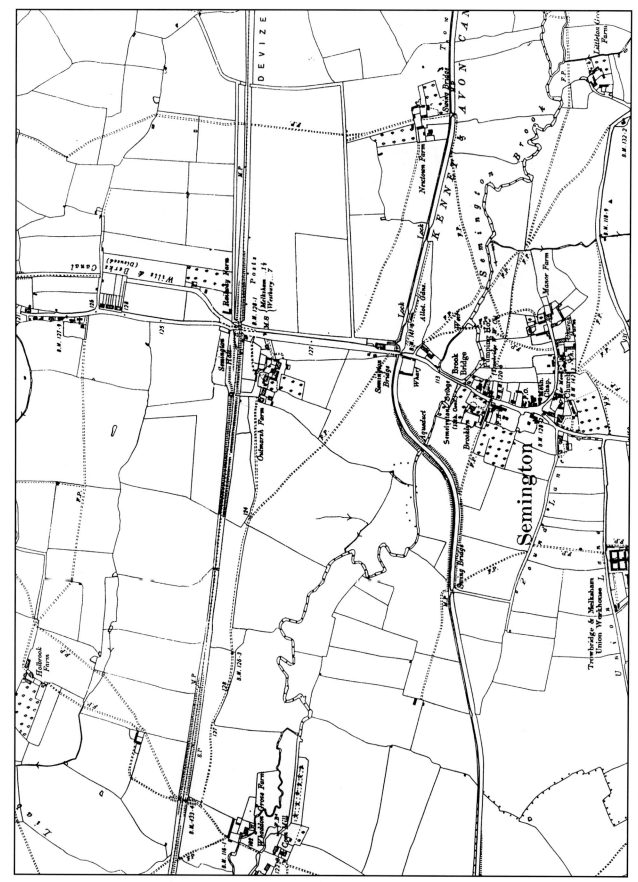

Extract from the 1926 O.S. map showing Semington village and halt.

2. Semington Halt

Semington is a small village on the A350 situated between Melksham and Westbury. It was the site of a workhouse which was later converted into St George's Hospital. At the time the railway station was opened in 1906, the population of the village was in the region of 450. The Kennet & Avon Canal passes through the village, and in the past was the site of the junction with the Wilts & Berks Canal.

The Station

The opening of Semington Halt coincided exactly with the introduction of the rail motor services between Trowbridge, Devizes and Patney & Chirton on Monday 1st October 1906. This type of train had been in use on other parts of the GWR since 1903. The station, 1 mile and 61 chains from Holt Junction, was unmanned and came under the jurisdiction of the Station Master of the former station. The halt was fairly basic in construction, the platform being short and below standard height. Because of the low platform, it was the passenger guard's duty on the rail motor services to lower a set of steps by the operation of a lever in the carriage, so allowing the passengers to get on and off with ease. There were occasions reported when it was forgotten to raise the steps before the train pulled out. This resulted in them being ripped off en route or on arrival at the next station platform of standard height.

Rail motor services had proved a success on the other local lines in Wiltshire and it was this that decided the railway company to open halts on the Devizes Branch. Semington station, on the up side of the line, stood high on an exposed embankment above the main road over which the railway crossed by way of Outmarsh Bridge, a three-span, box-girder type on brick pillars. One of the spans crossed over the disused Wilts & Berks Canal. In 1939, the bridge was strengthened to take heavier engines, as a result of the outbreak of war. The line was also slewed at the same time, with the cost of these works totalling £361. The original bridge, prior to the alterations, had been of the brick arch type.

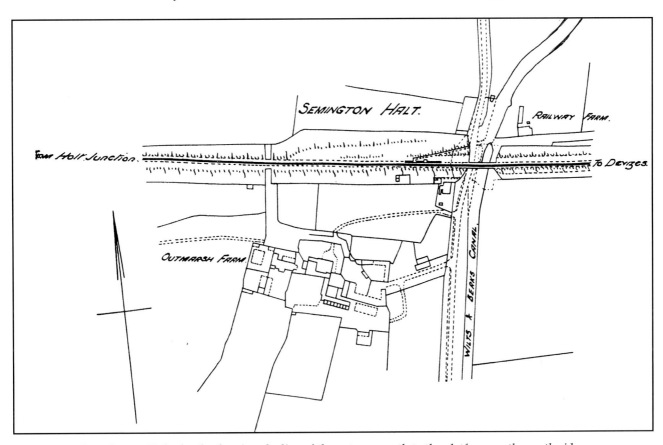

GWR plan of Semington Halt clearly showing the line of the entrance path to the platform on the north side.

The nameboard in 1963. Lighting for the platform was carried on the electricity pole. (C.L.Caddy)

The only access to the platform was via a footpath cut into the bank. A much needed wooden shelter with a sloping roof was added in July 1907 for the protection of waiting passengers. A replacement platform was provided on 22nd February 1909, built of railway sleepers with a surface of cinders. There were two station lamps, one on the platform, and one on the footpath. These were lit by oil until just before the Second World War, when they were converted to electricity on 5th March 1938.

Passenger Services

As in the case of Pans Lane Halt on the east side of Devizes, Semington handled primarily passenger traffic, there being no vehicular access.

Because the station was unstaffed, passengers were required to buy their tickets on the train or on arrival at their destination. The majority of trains stopping at this station were the local Devizes, Trowbridge and Westbury services.

With the opening of the station and the use of railmotor cars, six up and six down trains called daily, on weekdays only. The first Trowbridge to Devizes train of the day called at Semington at 6.46am and the last at 9.33pm. In the down direction the first train of the day from Devizes called at 7.49am and the last at 10.14pm. The timetable of the day did not list Semington but displayed a note to the effect that up trains called at Semington 4 minutes after leaving Holt and down trains 5 minutes after leaving Seend.

Military Traffic

Semington Halt was a convenient stop for RAF Melksham, which was approximately a mile away. Seend station was closer and had more stopping trains but the RAF personnel found it a more direct route, when on foot, to cross the fields between the back of the camp and the station at Semington. One of the more infamous people to have spent part of his RAF service at Melksham was Ronnie Biggs of 'The Great Train Robbery' notoriety. When travelling from his home in London to Melksham in the summer of 1947, little did he probably realise the significant part the railway would play in his later life.

Semington Halt platform looking towards Devizes with bridge rails and girder in the background. (D.J.Hyde)

40

A path led up to the platform from road level, through a swing gate, with the usual trespass notice. (D.J.Hyde)

From the opposite, south side, looking towards Melksham, the whole bridge can be seen, including the span over the Wilts & Berks Canal. (J.Sawtell)

As a stopping train leaves the halt under the eye of the guard, the permanent way hut on the Holt Junction side can be seen, above the railings to the approach path. (J.Sawtell)

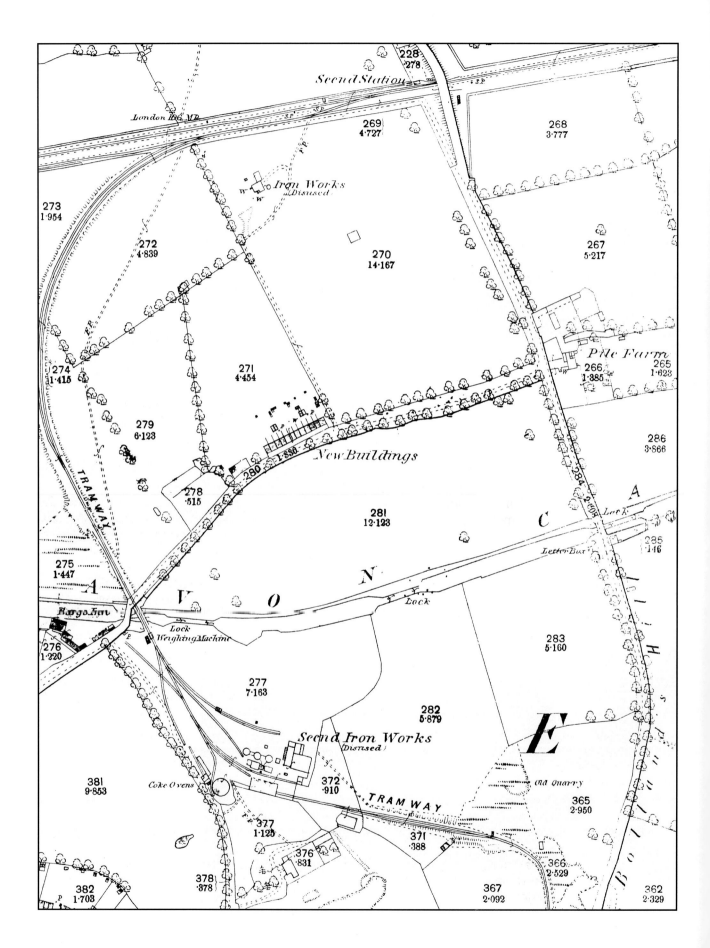

Secnd Station

London 106 MP

228
278

269
4·727

268
3·777

Iron Works
(Disused)

273
1·954

272
4·839

270
14·167

267
5·217

Pile Farm

266
1·385

265
1·628

274
1·415

271
4·454

286
3·866

279
6·123

New Buildings

280 1·886

278
·515

281
12·123

284 2·608

Lock

A

C

N

235
·146

Letter Box

275
1·447

A

V   O

Lock

283
5·160

TRAMWAY

Hargrave

Lock
Weighing Machine

276
1·220

277
7·163

282
5·879

E

Secnd Iron Works
(Disused)

381
9·853

Coke Ovens

372
·910

(Old Quarry)

365
2·950

377
1·125

TRAMWAY

371
·388

376
·831

366
2·529

382
1·703

378
·378

367
2·092

362
2·329

3. Seend Station

The village of Seend lies on a hog's back ridge formed by the larger towns of Trowbridge, Melksham and Devizes. On the south side it looks out over the flat country towards Bratton Downs on which stands the famous White Horse of Westbury. On the north side it looks down on the now revitalised Kennet and Avon Canal. Seend is built on a sand hill from which it derives it's name, old English for sand being 'send'. Running parallel with the canal is the track of the former branch line with its two station platforms and goods yard still in use today by a builders' merchant.

The Station

Exactly 14 months after the single broad-gauge line to Devizes was opened, Seend station came into use on 1st September 1858. Thought had been given to a station at Sells Green, a mile nearer to Devizes, but the site at the bottom of Bolland's Hill in Seend was favoured because of the Iron Works that had recently developed there. The population at this time was a little over 1,000; this remained fairly constant throughout the years of the railway.

The station mile post in 1858, indicating 106 miles from London, was measured via Holt and Chippenham. This, of course, was before the opening in 1862 of the Berks & Hants Extension from Hungerford to Devizes, when Seend station became 90 miles from the capital.

When built, the station comprised one platform with a station building on the up side of the line. A brick-built signalbox, 15' x 9'6", was added on to the east end of the platform in 1875 and, in a photograph of 1908, a corrugated cabin is seen between the station building and the box. This cabin was the station lock-up and tool cupboard. Considerable station improvements took place in 1908, with the building of a 400-foot long downside platform with waiting shed, plus the reconstruction of the station buildings and platform on the up side. This included removing and refixing the cast-iron Gentlemen's urinal and

moving the lock-up to the site of the signalbox, which was demolished. A new roadway to the station up side was provided and alterations carried out to a wing wall of the road bridge. A loop line was added to allow for passing trains, and, at the rear of the downside platform, new sidings were installed. The cost of these alterations amounted to £4,749.2s.10d. The signalbox was also replaced in 1908 with a larger one in a new position at the west end of the down platform. This provision, together with signals and telegraphs, cost £820.11s.8d. The station buildings were of the standard GWR design of the period, with the waiting shelter on the down side being of red brick, slate roof and with a wooden canopy. A picture of the station in 1911 shows the addition of another slightly taller metal cabin next to the corrugated lock-up. This housed a tap and elevated tank for domestic water. A further corrugated cabin, the lamp hut, where the signal and platform lamps were kept and maintained, was in position beneath the road bridge embankment at the end of the downside platform. The platform lamps, of which the up side had seven and the down side had five, were lit by oil.

Passenger Services

With the provision of their station, the residents of Seend could travel to Trowbridge and Devizes. A notice appearing in the *Devizes & Wiltshire Gazette* on 26th August 1858 stated:

> Notice is hereby given that the SEEND STATION will be open for passenger traffic on the 1st September next and that in consequence all the trains will leave Devizes five minutes earlier than at present.

Following the station opening, the usual Devizes to Trowbridge, Trowbridge to Devizes timetable was published in the paper, and an additional note was added saying that the down trains would stop at Seend at 7.35am, 10am, 12 noon, 2.20pm and 6.35pm; trains to Devizes at 8.35am, 10.35am, 12.40pm, 3.35pm and 8.20pm; there would be no trains to or from Devizes on Sundays.

(left) The 1886 O.S. map shows the original Seend station and the tramway to the Iron Works although the latter had been closed and possibly dismantled 10 years previously. The line is shown as narrow gauge passing over a wagon weighbridge before fanning out to sidings serving furnaces, coke oven, boiler house and transfer area from the small tramway which ran downhill from the quarries. The remains of the coal wharf by the north side of the canal road bridge can be seen. The 'New Buildings' marked were cottages for the use of the Iron Works employees.

The original signalbox at the Devizes end of the up platform in 1908, together with the corrugated station lock-up. (Seend W.I.)

The proud workmen, seen in this photograph and the one above with a wide variety of hats, are installing new sidings and rebuilding the station in 1908. (J.Burbidge)

This 1965 view shows the fine example of a Victorian Gentlemen's urinal, resited in 1908 on the up platform. (D.J.Hyde)

Seend station in a postcard of about 1911 as rebuilt with up and down platforms. The sidings have been rearranged after the final closure of iron traffic.

Seend Railway Station.

Looking east towards Devizes soon after rebuilding in 1908. The new signalbox has a coal bunker and the token apparatus net close by.

A later view in the opposite direction, probably in the thirties, showing the site of the former iron sidings, now the yard. Note the water tank and the corrugated-iron platform lock-up, in its new position on the site of the original signalbox. The original platform oil lamps are also still in place. The milk churns would have been a common feature on the platform. (LGRP)

The Station Master and a porter on the up platform on a quiet afternoon in the 1950s. The 1900-style design of standard station building in deep red brick with blue engineering brick base and blue slates, and deeply-inset doors and windows, can be clearly seen. There was a magnificent hanging lamp in the booking hall. (Trevor J.Saunders)

At the turn of the century, trade was brisk with 13,912 tickets issued in 1903 at an income of £801. Parcels dealt with numbered 10,208 at a total charge of £616. During the summer of 1908, whilst the major alterations were taking place to enlarge the station, passengers prepared to accept the disruption of the building work could buy a Saturday to Monday ticket and travel to Paddington by any train starting at or after 12.00noon on the Saturday. From Seend there were three choices of journey route available: 1) via Holt, Chippenham and Swindon; 2) via Devizes, Theale and Reading; 3) via Holt, Westbury, Lavington and Reading.

The return fares were:

	1st Class	2nd Class	3rd Class
1)	20s 0d	12s 6d	10s 0d
2)	18s 9d	12s 0d	9s 6d
3)	21s 3d	13s 6d	10s 9d

The return to Seend was by any train on the following Sunday (train services permitting) or on the Monday. If a trip to the seaside with the children was preferable, an excursion to Weston-super-Mare from Seend would cost, return, 10s.0d (1st Class), 6s.3d (2nd Class) and 5s.0d (3rd Class). Children under the age of three travelled free and between three and twelve at half price.

There were conditions in respect of luggage that had to be adhered to when buying an excursion ticket:

- No luggage allowed to passengers taking Day Trip Excursion Tickets.
- One package of luggage only allowed to passengers taking Excursion Tickets for a longer period than one day and this to be conveyed at their own risk.

Market tickets on a Saturday were available to Trowbridge on the 8.38am and 10.14am at 9d for 3rd Class and to Devizes on Thursdays on the 9.15am and 12.08pm at 6d.

Passengers at Seend around this time had the availability of a service that must have been very welcome on return from their journeys. The climb up the hill from the station to the village was considerable so local man Mr Cook's broughhams and wagonettes were in steady demand, as was the hand truck worked by George and Jonah Rawlings, both local residents, up until their deaths in 1908.

In 1909 the July/August timetable showed 15 down stopping trains on Mondays to Saturdays and two on Sundays.

From the mid-1920s to the mid-1930s there was a steady decline in passenger traffic from Seend but in 1935 an increase began that continued, as it did elsewhere on the branch, until falling away again following the end of the Second World War. During those war years a day return to London from Seend was 17s 6d and the short journey to Devizes could be made on one of ten trains. In a 1946 station report it was recorded that passenger bookings averaged about 250 per week of which approximately 150 were booked on Fridays and Saturdays.

In the early 1950s, a total of 21 trains a day, including goods, passed through the station but within the decade the services had been reduced to below that of pre-war.

In a copy of the *Western Region (Bristol Traffic District) Rules & Regulations Book* for 1960 it was indicated that 'Station Staff will not be employed at Seend Station between 7.20pm and 7.15am on weekdays'. It was necessary, therefore, for guards of trains calling there, when staff were not on duty, to collect the tickets of passengers getting off and then to hand these in at the next stopping station. The tickets were then to be cancelled and returned to Seend the next day on the first train. The unstaffed station was a contributory factor when, in 1963, eight railway carriages in the siding were wrecked in what the police described as the worst act of vandalism they had experienced in the county.

Devizes to Seend (Single) ticket. (D.H.Morris)

Freight Services

The industrial activity at Seend was not vast. At the end of the 15th century the woollen industry brought a fleeting prosperity, and, in the mid-19th century, commercial exploitation of iron ore began. This business never really took off, although several companies tried, with the railway,

Occasionally a Prairie Tank was used on the trailer coach, as here approaching from Holt. The yard crossover can be seen on the left. (Trevor J.Saunders)

Two signals outside the box (the one on the up platform side being of the concrete post type) indicate that either way working was possible when the box was switched out. Castle Class 4-6-0 No.4085, Berkeley Castle, a regular on the branch, passes with the down 3.31pm Saturday Bristol train in the fifties. It waited at Seend to cross with the up 2.20pm Bristol arrival for Newbury which may just be seen in the up platform. (Trevor J.Saunders)

Hall Class 4-6-0 No.4959, Purley Hall, pulling away from Seend station, on the far side of the road bridge with an up train in the 1950s. (Trevor J.Saunders)

to set up a number of agreements whereby they would transport ore from the local station. In 1857 the Great Western Iron Ore Smelting & Coal Company was formed and planned to erect two blast furnaces on the side of the hill just above the Kennet & Avon Canal. Narrow-gauge tramways would bring the ore down to the furnaces from the quarries at the top of the hill, and the finished product would be taken by a railway line over a bridge built beside the canal bridge to a wharf, where it would leave on barges for the markets. In 1858 the railway line was extended into a siding of the now opened Seend station, and a contract was negotiated with the GWR for the transportation of coal, coke, lime and ore in the iron company's own trucks. In the following year, however, the company went bankrupt, probably because the cost of transporting the fuel to the furnaces and finished ore to the markets absorbed too much of the profits.

A Mr Sarl, from the failed company, finished building the incomplete furnaces by 1861 but, by 1864, he experienced financial difficulties and went into liquidation. In December that year the Seend Iron Company Ltd was formed, taking over the assets of the previous company. They entered into an undertaking with the GWR for the use of the canal wharf or 'landing place' and

> to pay the sum of 3d for every ton of coal minerals, iron and other goods and merchandise, materials and things of every kind which shall from time to time be so landed or loaded in addition to the ordinary tolls and payments for traffic on the Seend Canal, and the navigation therewith connected, and also on the express condition that, on the expiration or determination of the agreement, the Seend Landing Place shall not be considered as an established Private Wharf.

Two years later, on 17th November 1866, this company also ceased trading. During the next 23 years the workings had a succession of owners, none of whom fared any better than their predecessors. In 1873 Richard Berridge, a partner from a London brewery, took over and operated the works, prospering initially; but, in 1875, the railway line over the Kennet & Avon Canal was closed and the furnaces and coke ovens were recorded as 'not used' by 1876. In 1899, owing to rising costs and competition from companies in

the North Country, the firm was closed and the works demolished the following year. The O.S. Map of 1886 actually indicates the works being disused.

In the meantime the railway company continued to allow use of the sidings previously provided for the iron works by entering into an undertaking, dated 28th March 1887, with Messrs Robbins, Lane & Pinniger of Honey Street Wharf near Marlborough, who at the time had a coal merchant's business. Another undertaking, dated 24th September 1889, was signed between the GWR and a Thomas Ward of Fitzalan Chambers, Sheffield, but use of the sidings did not last long and because of this, coupled with their becoming 'out of repair', both undertakings were terminated by the General Manager's Office at Paddington Station at the end of November 1894. Instructions were also given at the time to the Engineer 'to take up the junctions and so much of the sidings leading to the iron works as is on our land'.

While no iron was smelted at Seend after the 1880s, ore was extracted from 1905 by the Seend Iron Mines Company and sent by rail to Baldwins Ltd at their Swansea Hematite Iron & Steel Works, Landore, where it was smelted. At this time the ore was taken to the railway by horse and cart. The mine owners were quoted for providing a private siding on the east side of the road bridge. The siding was to hold 30 trucks near the 90-mile post for the traffic of the iron company, with a necessary roadway and loading bank, the cost being £1,024. In addition, the GWR would provide a 60-ton wagon weighbridge, 32' x 6'2", and an office costing £280, together with a two-lever ground frame, signals and telegraphs at £259. Towards the outlay of £1,560 the GWR were prepared to make an allowance of 3d per ton from the conveyance rate until the cost was defrayed. The mine owners, however, were not in a position to find the capital sum. The GWR, therefore, agreed to do so with an allowance being applied by them in reduction of the capital outlay. Baldwins, who were keen to receive the good quality ore from Seend, undertook, in the event of the traffic ceasing before the allowance reached the capital sum, to pay the balance to the GWR, with the sidings then being used privately by them. In addition the GWR could use the sidings and could charge companies other than Messrs Baldwins 3d per ton on the tonnage, with these charges going towards off-setting the balance being guaranteed by Baldwins. The sidings were

Seend Iron Works c.1879. The stone arch carrying the road over the Kennet & Avon Canal and the bow girder bridge beyond taking the rails over the canal which then fan out to the furnace and works. The rails in the foreground ran from a junction with the tramway, either by a sharp curve or by wagon turntable to the canal wharf where Somerset coal was transferred for use in the works' boiler house and coke ovens, seen in the background on the right and left, respectively. (Seend W.I.)

Seend Iron works c.1873. The open truck with a tiled roof structure could be a small locomotive or a brake vehicle; the hand lever seems to be on the end. Several broad-gauge tilt wagons can be seen in this and the photograph above. A low platform is piled with pig iron, possibly waiting to be moved north to Staffordshire. The nearest furnace is still under construction. (Seend W.I.)

Seend Iron Works c.1868. This shows the furnace under construction. The platform seen in the previous photograph has yet to be built. The narrow-gauge trams used from the quarries may be seen in front of the nearest furnace. The six-wheel and four-wheel iron-sided GWR broad-gauge wagons are loaded with over 20 tons of ore, hence the four horses waiting to move. The coke oven is in the background. (Seend W.I.)

From the up platform, through the bridge to Devizes, can just be seen the 60-ton wagon weighbridge that formed part of the new Iron Works siding. Ore was transported here by pony and cart and unloaded onto a ramp. Later in 1919 an aerial ropeway unloaded at a shute arrangement in the same siding. The lamp hut, hard by the bridge, has survived and is in use at Didcot with the Great Western Society. (A.Alexander)

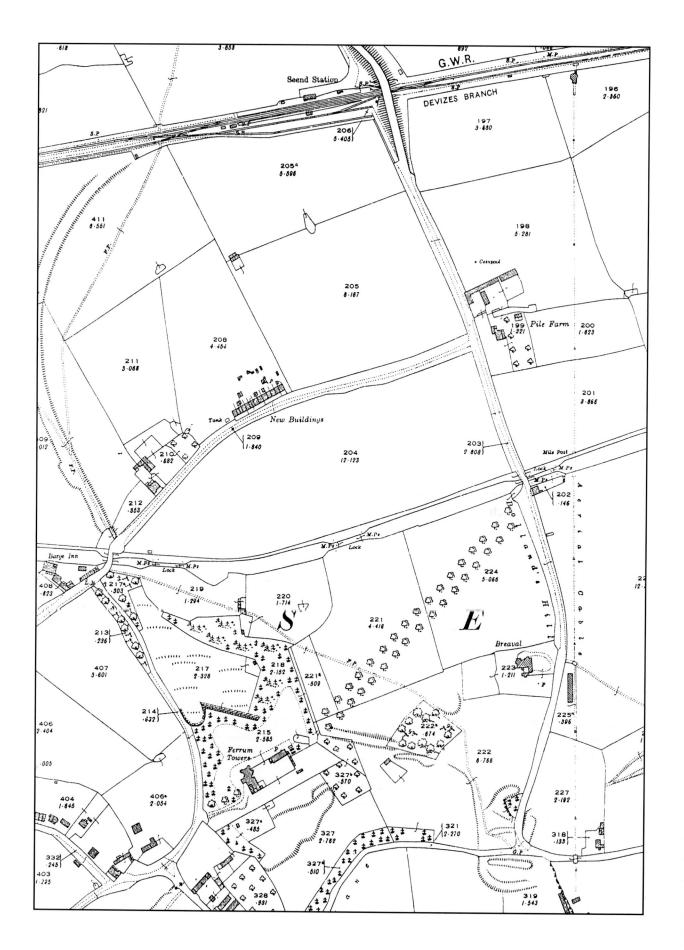

to come into use on 5th February 1906 under a Private Siding agreement dated 17th February 1906. By 1910, ore production at Seend had once again ceased, which presumably led the GWR General Manager to terminate on 31st March 1911 the *Private Siding Agreement (28574)* with the Seend Iron Mines Company and the additional agreement with Baldwins. Still this was not the end of the railway's involvement in shipping ore on the Devizes Branch. With the outbreak of war in 1914, production again took off and by 1917 had reached a total of 24,470 tons. After the war, production was much reduced although the GWR had an agreement with Avon Valley Iron Company, dated 31st August 1919, whereby an aerial cable delivered ore in suspended buckets from the quarry on top of the hill to the railway siding by the 90-mile post (see the 1924 O.S. map on the previous page, which also shows no sign of the former Iron Works other than the splendidly-named ironmaster's house, *Ferrum Towers*). The boys of the village were known to take advantage of riding the empty buckets back up to the top of the hill in order to save the climb by foot.

In 1922, an old Scottish firm of iron-masters, Merry & Cunningham, installed new machinery and sent ore to Westbury for treatment, but, shortly after commencing production, the works were completely destroyed by fire. In 1925, the Parish Council became concerned about possible danger from the overhead buckets, and in 1928 the system was dismantled and sold for scrap.

The quarries came to life again and for the last time during the Second World War when Pete Weston, a junior clerk on the station at that time, recalls the ore leaving the sidings at Seend for various gas works in different parts of the country.

Iron ore was not the only commodity dealt with at the station. There were many years when it was kept busy dealing with the more usual type of freight associated with a country branch line. From the opening of the milk factory at Staverton just prior to the turn of the century, churns were sent there daily from Seend and in the opposite direction to London. Considerable importance was placed on this traffic during the General Strike of 1926, with 28,833 churns being forwarded and a slight increase on this the following year. The capacity peaked in 1928 at 30,264 churns, earning receipts for the railway of £1,922, but from then on it declined to such an extent that in 1934 only 36 churns were handled at a total income of £3.

There was, however, a slight increase again during the years of the Second World War, when the milk was sent to West Ealing by passenger train. Coal shipments came into Seend for a number of local coal merchants and also to supply the nearby RAF Melksham depot.

In 1859, J.Moore had a coal business in Seend Cleeve, as did Adam Wragg in adjoining Martinslade. In the early days their coal came on the canal by barge, from which it was unloaded at both the Seend and Devizes Wharves, and also at Wragg's Wharf in Sells Green. In a local advertisement at the time Adam Wragg was 'Sole Vendor for Timsbury Coals, Forest of Dean, Staffordshire & Other Coals'.

This business ceased trading around the turn of the century. In 1867 coal merchant George Taylor Sainsbury was receiving his supplies at the Devizes Wharf and stations at Seend, Devizes and Woodborough. By 1889, George Holden was established as a coal merchant in Seend Cleeve and traded there until about 1915. At the beginning of the century the firm of Manly & Dowty (Coal Merchant & General Haulier) was receiving coal by rail at Seend, but by 1911 the firm was in the name of W.J.Dowty only. This business was closed down by the end of the 1920s. Other latter-day coal merchants using the railway facilities at Seend station were the three firms of Parsons, Deverill and J.Crook & Son. The last coal business using the station yard was that of Cecil Edward Hillier & Sons, who traded there from 1937 until 1990, some 24 years after the closure of the line.

Because of the considerable gradient between Holt Junction and Devizes, there was a restriction on the number of Class 1 coal wagons that could be hauled on this stretch of the line which included Seend. Joe Burbidge, who started his railway career as a lad porter at Seend in 1942, recalls in later years the stone trains from Somerset quarries passing daily through the station on the up line around 4.30am. They would be double-headed to Devizes, whereupon the leading engine would come off and run back light to Trowbridge.

Unloading of coal took place from the coal siding that ran parallel with the refuge siding at the rear of the down platform. From June 1956, entry and exit was by way of ground frames. The movement was executed by the freight trains running to the east end of the up platform and reversing over the down main into the refuge siding, which was formed on the original tramway line from the ironworks. At the Devizes end of the station, entry

CHRISTMAS FURLOUGH—FORWARD TRAINS

Starting	Thursday, Dec. 19th.	Thursday, Dec. 19th.	Thursday, Dec. 19th.		Thursday, Dec. 19th.
Train No.	19.F.9.	19.F.11.	19.F.13.		19.F.15.
From	Seend	Seend	Seend		Melksham
To	Paddington	Paddington	Paddington		Bristol (T.M.)
Personnel	900	900	900		800
Formation	Brake Compo 11 Thirds Brake Compo	Brake Compo 11 Thirds Brake Compo	Brake Compo 11 Thirds Brake Compo		Brake Compo 10 Thirds Brake Compo
Approximate Load ..	390 Tons	390 Tons	390 Tons		360 Tons

	arr. p.m.	dep. p.m.	arr. p.m.	dep. p.m.	arr. p.m.	dep. p.m.		arr. p.m.	dep. p.m.
Seend		2 10	—	2 43	—	3 35	Melksham	—	2 25
Devizes	C2 25S		C2 58S		C3 50S		Holt Jct.		2 32
Patney and Chirton ..	2 35 D	2 40	3 8 D	3 13	4 0 D	4 5	Bradford Jcts.		2 36
Bedwyn	3 0		3 33		4 25		Bathampton		2 52
Newbury	3 16		3 49		4 42		Bath	2 56 a	2 59
Reading	3 37		4 9		5 5		Bristol (T.M.)	3 20	—
Slough	3 57		4 29		5 27				
Southall	4 7		4 33		5 37				
Paddington	4 20	—	4 54	—	5 50	—			

a—Personnel for South Wales change Bath and proceed by 11.0 a.m. Brighton to Cardiff.

D—Detach Assistant Engine.

RETURN CHRISTMAS FURLOUGH TRAINS

Starting	Sunday, Dec. 29th.		Sunday, Dec. 29th.		Sunday, Dec. 29th.
Train No.	29.F.19.		29.F.21.		29.F.22.
From	Paddington.		Paddington.		Paddington.
To	Cardiff (General).		Pershore.		Seend.
Personnel	1,100		1,000		1,000
Formation ..	Brake Compo 12 Thirds Brake Compo		Brake Compo 10 Thirds Brake Compo		Brake Compo 12 Thirds Brake Compo
Approx. Load ..	420 Tons.		360 Tons.		420 Tons.

	arr. p.m.	dep. p.m.		arr. p.m.	dep. p.m.		arr. p.m.	dep. p.m.
Paddington	ML	8 50	Paddington	ML	9 10	Paddington	ML	10 15
Southall	9 4		Southall	9 23		Southall	10 29	
Slough.. ..	9 15		Slough	9 34		Slough	10 40	
Reading	9 37	9 41	Reading	9 55		Reading	11 0	
Didcot		10 4	Didcot East Jct. ..	10 17		Newbury	11 24	
Steventon		10 9	Oxford	10 34	10 45	Bedwyn	11 40	
Swindon Junction ..	10 36 Q	10 42	Yarnton	10 52				a.m.
Loco. Yard		10 44	Charlbury	11 4	11 12	Patney & Chirton ..	11 59 P	12 1
Kemble	11 0	K 11 7	Kingham	11 24	11 33			a.m.
Chalford	11 21	11 26	Moreton-in-Marsh ..	11 44	11 52	Devizes	12 10	12 16
Stroud	11 35	11 40		a.m.	a.m.	Seend	12 25 a.m. Dec. 30th.	
	a.m.	a.m.	Honeybourne	12 6	12 14			
Gloucester	12 0	12 10	Evesham		12 21			
Beachley Junction ..		12 45	Pershore	12 30 a.m. Dec. 30th.				
Severn Tunnel Jct. ..		12 59						
Newport	1 13	1 17						
St. Brides		1 22						
Cardiff (General) ..	1 34 a.m. Dec. 30th.							

K—Special connection.

Kemble .. dep. 11.17
Cirencester Town arr. 11.25

Q—Personnel for Chiseldon, Ogbourne and Marlborough change at Swindon Jct. and proceed by 10.50 p.m. Swindon to Marlborough recreational Special.

The forward and return timetables for the Christmas 1946 furlough trains

to come into use on 5th February 1906 under a Private Siding agreement dated 17th February 1906. By 1910, ore production at Seend had once again ceased, which presumably led the GWR General Manager to terminate on 31st March 1911 the *Private Siding Agreement (28574)* with the Seend Iron Mines Company and the additional agreement with Baldwins. Still this was not the end of the railway's involvement in shipping ore on the Devizes Branch. With the outbreak of war in 1914, production again took off and by 1917 had reached a total of 24,470 tons. After the war, production was much reduced although the GWR had an agreement with Avon Valley Iron Company, dated 31st August 1919, whereby an aerial cable delivered ore in suspended buckets from the quarry on top of the hill to the railway siding by the 90-mile post (see the 1924 O.S. map on the previous page, which also shows no sign of the former Iron Works other than the splendidly-named ironmaster's house, *Ferrum Towers*). The boys of the village were known to take advantage of riding the empty buckets back up to the top of the hill in order to save the climb by foot.

In 1922, an old Scottish firm of iron-masters, Merry & Cunningham, installed new machinery and sent ore to Westbury for treatment, but, shortly after commencing production, the works were completely destroyed by fire. In 1925, the Parish Council became concerned about possible danger from the overhead buckets, and in 1928 the system was dismantled and sold for scrap.

The quarries came to life again and for the last time during the Second World War when Pete Weston, a junior clerk on the station at that time, recalls the ore leaving the sidings at Seend for various gas works in different parts of the country.

Iron ore was not the only commodity dealt with at the station. There were many years when it was kept busy dealing with the more usual type of freight associated with a country branch line. From the opening of the milk factory at Staverton just prior to the turn of the century, churns were sent there daily from Seend and in the opposite direction to London. Considerable importance was placed on this traffic during the General Strike of 1926, with 28,833 churns being forwarded and a slight increase on this the following year. The capacity peaked in 1928 at 30,264 churns, earning receipts for the railway of £1,922, but from then on it declined to such an extent that in 1934 only 36 churns were handled at a total income of £3.

There was, however, a slight increase again during the years of the Second World War, when the milk was sent to West Ealing by passenger train. Coal shipments came into Seend for a number of local coal merchants and also to supply the nearby RAF Melksham depot.

In 1859, J.Moore had a coal business in Seend Cleeve, as did Adam Wragg in adjoining Martinslade. In the early days their coal came on the canal by barge, from which it was unloaded at both the Seend and Devizes Wharves, and also at Wragg's Wharf in Sells Green. In a local advertisement at the time Adam Wragg was 'Sole Vendor for Timsbury Coals, Forest of Dean, Staffordshire & Other Coals'.

This business ceased trading around the turn of the century. In 1867 coal merchant George Taylor Sainsbury was receiving his supplies at the Devizes Wharf and stations at Seend, Devizes and Woodborough. By 1889, George Holden was established as a coal merchant in Seend Cleeve and traded there until about 1915. At the beginning of the century the firm of Manly & Dowty (Coal Merchant & General Haulier) was receiving coal by rail at Seend, but by 1911 the firm was in the name of W.J.Dowty only. This business was closed down by the end of the 1920s. Other latter-day coal merchants using the railway facilities at Seend station were the three firms of Parsons, Deverill and J.Crook & Son. The last coal business using the station yard was that of Cecil Edward Hillier & Sons, who traded there from 1937 until 1990, some 24 years after the closure of the line.

Because of the considerable gradient between Holt Junction and Devizes, there was a restriction on the number of Class 1 coal wagons that could be hauled on this stretch of the line which included Seend. Joe Burbidge, who started his railway career as a lad porter at Seend in 1942, recalls in later years the stone trains from Somerset quarries passing daily through the station on the up line around 4.30am. They would be double-headed to Devizes, whereupon the leading engine would come off and run back light to Trowbridge.

Unloading of coal took place from the coal siding that ran parallel with the refuge siding at the rear of the down platform. From June 1956, entry and exit was by way of ground frames. The movement was executed by the freight trains running to the east end of the up platform and reversing over the down main into the refuge siding, which was formed on the original tramway line from the ironworks. At the Devizes end of the station, entry

CHRISTMAS FURLOUGH—FORWARD TRAINS

	Thursday, Dec. 19th.	Thursday, Dec. 19th.	Thursday, Dec. 19th.		Thursday, Dec. 19th.
Train No.	19.F.9.	19.F.11.	19.F.13.		19.F.15.
From	Seend	Seend	Seend		Melksham
To	Paddington	Paddington	Paddington		Bristol (T.M.)
Personnel	900	900	900		800
Formation	Brake Compo 11 Thirds Brake Compo	Brake Compo 11 Thirds Brake Compo	Brake Compo 11 Thirds Brake Compo		Brake Compo 10 Thirds Brake Compo
Approximate Load	390 Tons	390 Tons	390 Tons		360 Tons

	arr. p.m.	dep. p.m.	arr. p.m.	dep. p.m.	arr. p.m.	dep. p.m.		arr. p.m.	dep. p.m.
Seend	—	2 10	—	2 43	—	3 35	Melksham	—	2 25
Devizes	C 2 25 S		C 2 58 S		C 3 50 S		Holt Jct.	2 32	
Patney and Chirton	2 35 D	2 40	3 8 D	3 13	4 0 D	4 5	Bradford Jcts.	2 36	
Bedwyn		3 0		3 33		4 25	Bathampton	2 52	
Newbury		3 16		3 49		4 42	Bath	2 56 a	2 59
Reading		3 37		4 9		5 5	Bristol (T.M.)	3 20	—
Slough		3 57		4 29		5 27			
Southall		4 7		4 39		5 37			
Paddington		4 20	—	4 54	—	5 50			

a—Personnel for South Wales change Bath and proceed by 11.0 a.m. Brighton to Cardiff.

D—Detach Assistant Engine.

RETURN CHRISTMAS FURLOUGH TRAINS

	Sunday, Dec. 29th.		Sunday, Dec. 29th.	Sunday, Dec. 29th.
Train No.	29.F.19.		29.F.21.	29.F.22.
From	Paddington.		Paddington.	Paddington.
To	Cardiff (General).		Pershore.	Seend.
Personnel	1,100		1,000	1,000
Formation	Brake Compo 12 Thirds Brake Compo		Brake Compo 10 Thirds Brake Compo	Brake Compo 12 Thirds Brake Compo
Approx. Load	420 Tons.		360 Tons.	420 Tons.

	arr. p.m.	dep. p.m.		arr. p.m.	dep. p.m.		arr. p.m.	dep. p.m.
Paddington	ML	8 50	Paddington	ML	9 10	Paddington	ML	10 15
Southall	9 4		Southall	9 23		Southall		10 29
Slough	9 15		Slough	9 34		Slough		10 40
Reading	9 37	9 41	Reading	9 55		Reading		11 0
Didcot	10 4		Didcot East Jct.	10 17		Newbury		11 24
Steventon	10 9		Oxford	10 34	10 45	Bedwyn		11 40
Swindon Junction	10 36 Q	10 42	Yarnton	10 52				a.m.
Loco. Yard	10 44		Charlbury	11 4	11 12	Patney & Chirton	11 59 P	12 1
Kemble	11 0	K 11 7	Kingham	11 24	11 33			a.m.
Chalford	11 21	11 26	Moreton-in-Marsh	11 44	11 52	Devizes	12 10	12 16
Stroud	11 35	11 40			a.m.	Seend	12 25 a.m.	Dec. 30th.
	a.m.	a.m.	Honeybourne	12 6	12 14			
Gloucester	12 0	12 10	Evesham		12 21			
Beachley Junction		12 45	Pershore	12 30 a.m.	Dec. 30th.			
Severn Tunnel Jct.		12 59						
Newport	1 13	1 17						
St. Brides		1 22						
Cardiff (General)	1 34 a.m.	Dec. 30th.						

K—Special connection. p.m. Kemble .. dep. 11.17 Cirencester Town arr. 11.25

Q—Personnel for Chiseldon, Ogbourne and Marlborough change at Swindon Jct. and proceed by 10.50 p.m. Swindon to Marlborough recreational Special.

The forward and return timetables for the Christmas 1946 furlough trains

to come into use on 5th February 1906 under a Private Siding agreement dated 17th February 1906. By 1910, ore production at Seend had once again ceased, which presumably led the GWR General Manager to terminate on 31st March 1911 the *Private Siding Agreement (28574)* with the Seend Iron Mines Company and the additional agreement with Baldwins. Still this was not the end of the railway's involvement in shipping ore on the Devizes Branch. With the outbreak of war in 1914, production again took off and by 1917 had reached a total of 24,470 tons. After the war, production was much reduced although the GWR had an agreement with Avon Valley Iron Company, dated 31st August 1919, whereby an aerial cable delivered ore in suspended buckets from the quarry on top of the hill to the railway siding by the 90-mile post (see the 1924 O.S. map on the previous page, which also shows no sign of the former Iron Works other than the splendidly-named ironmaster's house, *Ferrum Towers*). The boys of the village were known to take advantage of riding the empty buckets back up to the top of the hill in order to save the climb by foot.

In 1922, an old Scottish firm of iron-masters, Merry & Cunningham, installed new machinery and sent ore to Westbury for treatment, but, shortly after commencing production, the works were completely destroyed by fire. In 1925, the Parish Council became concerned about possible danger from the overhead buckets, and in 1928 the system was dismantled and sold for scrap.

The quarries came to life again and for the last time during the Second World War when Pete Weston, a junior clerk on the station at that time, recalls the ore leaving the sidings at Seend for various gas works in different parts of the country.

Iron ore was not the only commodity dealt with at the station. There were many years when it was kept busy dealing with the more usual type of freight associated with a country branch line. From the opening of the milk factory at Staverton just prior to the turn of the century, churns were sent there daily from Seend and in the opposite direction to London. Considerable importance was placed on this traffic during the General Strike of 1926, with 28,833 churns being forwarded and a slight increase on this the following year. The capacity peaked in 1928 at 30,264 churns, earning receipts for the railway of £1,922, but from then on it declined to such an extent that in 1934 only 36 churns were handled at a total income of £3.

There was, however, a slight increase again during the years of the Second World War, when the milk was sent to West Ealing by passenger train. Coal shipments came into Seend for a number of local coal merchants and also to supply the nearby RAF Melksham depot.

In 1859, J.Moore had a coal business in Seend Cleeve, as did Adam Wragg in adjoining Martinslade. In the early days their coal came on the canal by barge, from which it was unloaded at both the Seend and Devizes Wharves, and also at Wragg's Wharf in Sells Green. In a local advertisement at the time Adam Wragg was 'Sole Vendor for Timsbury Coals, Forest of Dean, Staffordshire & Other Coals'.

This business ceased trading around the turn of the century. In 1867 coal merchant George Taylor Sainsbury was receiving his supplies at the Devizes Wharf and stations at Seend, Devizes and Woodborough. By 1889, George Holden was established as a coal merchant in Seend Cleeve and traded there until about 1915. At the beginning of the century the firm of Manly & Dowty (Coal Merchant & General Haulier) was receiving coal by rail at Seend, but by 1911 the firm was in the name of W.J.Dowty only. This business was closed down by the end of the 1920s. Other latter-day coal merchants using the railway facilities at Seend station were the three firms of Parsons, Deverill and J.Crook & Son. The last coal business using the station yard was that of Cecil Edward Hillier & Sons, who traded there from 1937 until 1990, some 24 years after the closure of the line.

Because of the considerable gradient between Holt Junction and Devizes, there was a restriction on the number of Class 1 coal wagons that could be hauled on this stretch of the line which included Seend. Joe Burbidge, who started his railway career as a lad porter at Seend in 1942, recalls in later years the stone trains from Somerset quarries passing daily through the station on the up line around 4.30am. They would be double-headed to Devizes, whereupon the leading engine would come off and run back light to Trowbridge.

Unloading of coal took place from the coal siding that ran parallel with the refuge siding at the rear of the down platform. From June 1956, entry and exit was by way of ground frames. The movement was executed by the freight trains running to the east end of the up platform and reversing over the down main into the refuge siding, which was formed on the original tramway line from the ironworks. At the Devizes end of the station, entry

The coal merchant's Fordson truck is loaded in the yard direct from the coal wagons in the early fifties. (Rokeby collection, National Monuments Record Centre)

to the down sidings was by way of a single-line facing junction with a 10mph speed restriction. The sidings were prohibited to all 'red' engines.

In addition to the Bristol (East Depot) to Reading and Reading to East Depot slow freight which used the branch until the mid 1950s, an 8.05pm express freight from Paddington to Bristol (Kingsland Road) could be seen stopping for water at Devizes and again at Seend to have the wagon brakes pinned down.

Freight trains of potatoes arriving in the sidings during the First World War are recalled by local man Percy Hiscocks. These were for use as animal feed on the farms and came with blue treated skins to prevent them being attractive for human consumption. They were off-loaded into horse-drawn carts. When nearing the summit of the hill from the station, Percy would find some reason to step out in front of the horse so that it came to an abrupt stop, the consequence of which was that some of the potatoes would fall from the back of the cart. These would later be picked up and taken to the Hiscocks' home where, after peeling away the blue skins and being cooked, they tasted no different from any other potato.

Freight weighing at Seend was not possible after the removal of the large wagon weighbridge

installed for the iron ore trade. Wagons were therefore generally double-labelled with the weighing station on one side and the eventual destination on the other.

Freight handling at Seend ended on 10th June 1963, some three years before closure for passengers. Parcels however were still carried but any arriving at periods when the station was unmanned had to travel on, to be put off at Holt Junction in one direction and Devizes at the other. They would be returned to Seend by first means the following day.

(2829)   (W. 62) 250,060—1-06.
GREAT WESTERN RAILWAY.
MARKET GOODS.
PERISHABLE.
From _Seend_
To _Bristol_
Route via _____
Date _7/9/06_ Train _____
Wagon No. _5409_ Sheet No. _____
Consignee _Adamson & Cooper_

Market goods to Bristol (Redcliffe Wharf) was a frequent traffic. The label is dated 7th September 1906.

54

War Time/Military

The two world wars, as on the branch generally, added to the station business. The Second World War saw the introduction of signalwomen to cover for the shortage created by those railway men who had joined the armed forces; this tended to be the policy in the smaller type of signalbox. At Seend, porter Robert Weston was joined on the staff by his wife Winifred and she was one of two women in the signalbox at that time. Their son Peter also served there as a junior clerk from 1943.

The two military camps of RAF Melksham and the airfield at Keevil generated heavy movements in freight and personnel. Both establishments received provisions through Seend station and locally-grown vegetables were despatched from there to supply the N.A.A.F.I. Porter Joe Burbidge recalls the considerable number of U.S. troop trains arriving, many of them during the blackout. The white lines on the platform edges were frequently repainted at this time as an aid to prevent passengers from falling over the edge in the dark. There was a higher demand than normal for return tickets by troops going on leave on Fridays and returning on Sundays. To meet the demand, Seend staff were allowed to issue over-stamped single tickets. Special leave trains were put on at times for the benefit of the personnel at RAF Melksham. Known as furlough trains, they would run westerly from Melksham station to Bristol Temple Meads and in the opposite direction, from Seend to Paddington. The forward and return timetables for Christmas 1946 furlough trains are shown on the next page.

The 2.40pm Trowbridge to Patney auto-train and the 3.05pm Bristol Temple Meads to Paddington were used extensively by personnel of the U.S. Air Force based at Keevil Airfield and those from RAF Melksham. These trains on a Saturday were crowded with men and women from the camps travelling to dances and the public houses in Devizes. The 'market' trains to Devizes on Thursdays were popular with the people of Seend; these departed at 9.44am and 12.16pm.

One of the branch engine drivers living in Seend during WW2 regularly made an unscheduled stop at the station, where his wife waited to provide him with sandwiches for his lunch. This provided an extra service utilised by the military, who would swarm aboard during the brief stop.

One of the failings of RAF Melksham was the lack of fuel for the stoves in the accommodation huts. On occasions, such as the extreme weather conditions during the winter of 1947/48, when the fuel was exhausted, personnel were released from the course which they were attending at the camp and sent to their homes until conditions improved a few weeks later. They were marched from the camp the 1½ miles to Seend station, where trains were waiting to take them away. This was also the arrangement at Bank Holiday times.

Staff

In 1867, the Station Master at Seend was Charles Jackson. By 1875 he had been succeeded by William Boughton. With the position of Station Master came acceptance as an official of the village, and a notable one was John Hodder, who was in post in 1880 and held it for longer than most. In 1895 he stood for election to the Parish Council, but was unsuccessful. On his retirement, however, he was presented with a cheque for £100 by the village in appreciation of the valued service he had provided. He enjoyed his retirement in Seend until his death there in 1915. James Hancock held the post after John Hodder, but only for a short period of time, as by 1908 Fred Arnold was in charge. He, like John Hodder, was to be another long-serving and respected member of the community. Fred was a member of the Seend Parish Council for a number of years, holding the position of chairman for part of the time. At the station he was remembered as being something of a martinet and was insistent that the porters wore their boots well polished. He was probably very pleased with his porter G.Reeves, who, in 1917, was awarded 10s.6d. for his alertness in detecting a hot axle box on a passing goods wagon. Not long after this, another porter joined the station staff, this being Bert Clack, who was returning from army service, and who had had previous GWR service.

Fred Arnold, on retirement just before the Second World War, was succeeded by Harold Fred Ludgate. He was to be the last officially appointed Station Master, as from January 1952 Seend lost the post, which was then covered by the Devizes Station Master, Sidney Bray. Other posts at the station also went at this time, leaving Robert Weston as a bit of a 'one-man-band' as he combined the roles of 'Station Master', porter, ticket collector, booking clerk, and, in between, answered the telephone on Seend 203. Harold Ludgate went on to be Station Master at Corsham and at Pill.

CHRISTMAS FURLOUGH—FORWARD TRAINS

	Thursday, Dec. 19th.	Thursday, Dec. 19th.	Thursday, Dec. 19th.		Thursday, Dec. 19th.
Starting					
Train No.	19.F.9.	19.F.11.	19.F.13.		19.F.15.
From	Seend	Seend	Seend		Melksham
To	Paddington	Paddington	Paddington		Bristol (T.M.)
Personnel	900	900	900		800
Formation	Brake Compo 11 Thirds Brake Compo	Brake Compo 11 Thirds Brake Compo	Brake Compo 11 Thirds Brake Compo		Brake Compo 10 Thirds Brake Compo
Approximate Load ..	390 Tons	390 Tons	390 Tons		360 Tons

	arr. p.m.	dep. p.m.	arr. p.m.	dep. p.m.	arr. p.m.	dep. p.m.		arr. p.m.	dep. p.m.
Seend	—	2 10	—	2 43	—	3 35	Melksham	—	2 25
Devizes	C2 25S		C2 58S		C3 50S		Holt Jct.		2 32
Patney and Chirton ..	2 35 D	2 40	3 8 D	3 13	4 0 D	4 5	Bradford Jcts.		2 36
Bedwyn	3 0		3 33		4 25		Bathampton		2 52
Newbury	3 16		3 49		4 42		Bath	2 56 a	2 59
Reading	3 37		4 9		5 5		Bristol (T.M.)	3 20	—
Slough	3 57		4 29		5 27				
Southall	4 7		4 39		5 37				
Paddington	4 20	—	4 54	—	5 50	—			

a—Personnel for South Wales change Bath and proceed by 11.0 a.m. Brighton to Cardiff.

D—Detach Assistant Engine.

RETURN CHRISTMAS FURLOUGH TRAINS

	Sunday, Dec. 29th.		Sunday, Dec. 29th.	Sunday, Dec. 29th.
Starting				
Train No. ..	29.F.19.		29.F.21.	29.F.22.
From	Paddington.		Paddington.	Paddington.
To	Cardiff (General).		Pershore.	Seend.
Personnel ..	1,100		1,000	1,000
Formation ..	Brake Compo 12 Thirds Brake Compo		Brake Compo 10 Thirds Brake Compo	Brake Compo 12 Thirds Brake Compo
Approx. Load ..	420 Tons.		360 Tons.	420 Tons.

	arr. p.m.	dep. p.m.			arr. p.m.	dep. p.m.		arr. p.m.	dep. p.m.
Paddington	ML	8 50		Paddington	ML	9 10	Paddington	ML	10 15
Southall	9 4			Southall	9 23		Southall		10 29
Slough	9 15			Slough	9 34		Slough		10 40
Reading	9 37	9 41		Reading	9 55		Reading		11 0
Didcot	10 4			Didcot East Jct. ..	10 17		Newbury		11 24
Steventon	10 9			Oxford	10 34	10 45	Bedwyn		11 40
Swindon Junction ..	10 36 Q	10 42	K—Special connection.	Yarnton		10 52			a.m.
Loco. Yard ..	10 44		p.m.	Charlbury	11 4	11 12	Patney & Chirton ..	11 59 P	12 1
Kemble	11 0	K 11 7	Kemble .. dep. 11.17	Kingham	11 24	11 33			a.m.
Chalford	11 21	11 26	Cirencester Town arr. 11.25	Moreton-in-Marsh ..	11 44	11 52	Devizes	12 10	12 16
Stroud	11 35	11 40		Honeybourne	12 6	12 14	Seend	12 25 a.m.	Dec. 30th.
	a.m.	a.m.	Q—Personnel for Chisel-	Evesham		12 21			
Gloucester ..	12 0	12 10	don, Ogbourne and Marl-	Pershore	12 30 a.m. Dec. 30th.				
Beachley Junction ..		12 45	borough change at Swin-						
Severn Tunnel Jct. ..		12 59	don Jct. and proceed by						
Newport	1 13	1 17	10.50 p.m. Swindon to						
St. Brides		1 22	Marlborough recreational						
Cardiff (General) ..	1 34 a.m. Dec. 30th.		Special.						

The forward and return timetables for the Christmas 1946 furlough trains

Florence Sainsbury, having completed her shift in Seend signalbox on a summer's day in 1941, is seen outside the Brewery Inn at Seend Cleeve wearing her GWR uniform. The inn was a regular calling place on her way home. (Greta Buckland)

Records for 1925 show the station strength as seven, comprising one Station Master Class 4, three porters (one Grade 1, and two Grade 2), one goods checker and two signalmen Grade 5. By 1938 the porters were only two of Grade 1, but the war years brought an increase in establishment with there being two lad porters and two clerks, making a total of ten. In addition to Robert Weston, the other porters were Alfred (Pop) Stapleton, Lawrence Buckley (lad) and Joe Burbidge (lad). The signal staff were, in the early stages, Don Chilcott and Jack Gregory, who tragically was to be killed in a road accident on his way home to Bath from working the box. Later the posts were filled by Winifred Weston and Florence (Duck) Sainsbury and later still, in 1945, by Dave Nash, son of Seend ganger George Nash. Miss Bowles was the Class 5 clerk with Pete Weston the junior clerk. The goods checker on the station payroll did in fact work at Bromham & Rowde Halt which was manned from 8.00am to 5.00pm and at this time Fred Dollimore carried out the duties.

Following a visit by the District Inspector in 1946, he recommended that, although the traffic had increased to some extent compared with 1938, it did not appear to be at a level which justified anything in excess of pre-war staff. He therefore proposed that the services of the clerk and the Grade 2 porter (who was a woman at that time) be dispensed with and that the Station Master should be able to perform all the clerical work quite well without assistance. The report went on to advise that with the removal of the woman porter, the post be dispensed with and not filled by a lad as previously proposed. All the requirements were met by two Grade 1 porters overlapping in the middle of the day. The early turn porter incurred a small amount of overtime on Fridays to provide the requisite platform strength for the 5.30pm furlough train. With the signalbox closed on Sundays, the two operators could share in the Sunday duty on the platform to avoid undue frequency of Sunday work for the porters. It appears the Station Master was far from happy

Seend station staff in 1927:
(rear, from the left) porter Ernie Arnold, goods checker Fred Dollimore, unknown, signalman Bill Brooks.
(front, from the left) signalman Harry Lodge, Station Master Fred Arnold, porter G.Reeves. (Paul Strong collection)

with the proposed reductions but could advance no satisfactory reason against them.

With the 1952 economy measures leaving Robert Weston as the porter in charge, he had to ensure before going off duty at 7.20pm, that the platform and approach yard oil lamps were lit and the yard gates closed. The signalman was responsible for extinguishing the lamps after this. For trains stopping after 9.20pm, the guard of the last train was required to do it.

From September 1962, Seend became an unstaffed halt when the morning London train stopped calling. Robert Weston was then moved to Devizes station to carry out level crossing keeper's duties until his subsequent retirement.

An interesting story involving the two lad porters, Lawrence Buckley and Joe Burbidge, relates to an occasion when using the four-wheeled platform trolley, they made a delivery from the station to a property in Seend village at the top of the hill. They decided on the return journey to ride the trolley down the hill. It appears that they passed the local policeman who was not

too impressed with the mode of transport and the speed at which it was travelling.

Signalling

Seend station was provided with two signal-boxes during its period in operation. The original one was of 10 levers, later upgraded to a stud frame containing 17 levers in c.1906. With the enlarging of the station in 1908, a new 28-lever, brick-built, GWR pattern box was built, measuring 25' x 12' x 8'. This had a horizontal tappet frame and became operational from 30th August.

The tablet catcher previously outside the original box on the east end of the up platform was removed as part of the alterations at that time. The new signalbox on the west end of the down platform had the catchers immediately outside for both up and down movements. The fireman of an up train would sling the Holt to Seend tablet onto the tablet catcher whilst grabbing the Seend to Devizes token from the machine. The exchange of tokens with down stopping trains would be

*The first signalbox at the east
end of the up platform in 1908.
(J.Burbidge)*

*(left) Two of the signalbox staff stand proudly outside the
second box in this postcard view taken in the early years
of the century. The oil lamp for the board crossing to the
token catcher is clearly visible as are the siding rails behind.
(Duncan Harper collection)
(below) Signalman Harry Lodge, on the right, and colleague
stand equally proudly by their box in the thirties. (B.Brooks)*

Porter Robert Weston on the left and relief signalman Harry Roxbee stand with a young boy at the far end of the signalbox in the late 1940s. The back of the box had a window for a view of the yard and sidings and the lower windows belonged to the locking frame room. (Trevor J.Saunders)

made when the engine came to a halt near the box. During 1919 the electric token instrument, by then about 20 years old, was renewed at a cost of £235. Switching-out apparatus, enabling the box to be closed for eight hours nightly, was authorised in March 1922 at a cost of £1,300. The box was switched out on Sundays and normally also at night time. Signals 15 and 16 were locked out while the box was open, operating only when it was closed in conjunction with switch lever 14. When the box was in circuit, the ETS sections were Devizes to Seend and Seend to Holt Junction. The box was classified as Light Cross Country with signalmen Class 3.

From 1923 Seend Box was Class 5 and manned on a two-shift basis from 6am-2pm and 2pm-10pm. The Class 5 boxes were re-graded in c.1950 and shift times reduced. Signalman Graham Darby remembers in 1952 helping the Trowbridge station staff to load fish boxes onto the 6.10am which stopped only on request at Seend. After alighting on arrival at Seend and with the train off into the Devizes section, Graham would commence his duty by opening the box at 6.40am. His shift would last until 2pm when he would be relieved by the on-coming signalman, who would man the box until it was closed for the night at 9.20pm. Graham remembers an occasion at this time when he was manning the box and a land slip had occurred at Lavington on the main line, resulting in all trains being re-routed via the branch. He left the box to hand the token

to the fireman of an express, the driver of which was presumably unfamiliar with the line. Graham on the down platform could hear the engine roaring down the incline from Devizes and as it came into view he knew there was no way it was going to stop. The train fairly rattled through the station, rocking considerably, and signalman Darby feared the possibility of a derailment. Fortunately this did not happen and eventually the train was brought to a stop further along the line, with the fireman being sent back along the track to collect the token from the signalbox.

During the periods when Seend Box was switched out, the Holt to Devizes and Devizes to Patney sections were worked by electric token. This differing system was implemented to prevent confusion which may have been caused by having two separate sets of tokens.

With the closure of Seend box on 10th June 1956, plus the station loop, the siding connections with the Devizes to Holt Junction single line were worked from three ground frames released by the electric token, used for the Devizes to Holt Junction section. The sidings were only to be used as a crossing place for light engines, freight trains, engineer's trains and empty stock trains. In no circumstances was a passenger train to be placed in the sidings whilst another train passed. The token sections were now Patney & Chirton to Devizes and Devizes to Holt Junction.

An Intermediate Token Instrument, with shut-in facilities for the receipt and issue of tokens

Former lad porter at Devizes, Bill Brooks, was one of the signalmen at Seend in the 1930s. (B.Brooks)

in accordance with standard instructions, was provided in a hut on the up side of the line next to the 90¼-mile post and during the time trains or engines were locked in the sidings, trains could pass over the single line in the ordinary way. Telegraph communications on a separate circuit were provided between this hut and the Devizes signalbox.

When an engine or train was ready to leave the sidings, the person in charge, after withdrawing the token, needed to turn the points to enable the train to be drawn onto the single line, after which the points had to be restored to normal and locked. The token was then removed from the ground frame and the train allowed to proceed to Devizes Home Signal or Holt Junction Home Signal with the driver carrying the token in the ordinary way. When the token was handed to the driver, the chargeman had to instruct him verbally that the section was clear to Devizes Home or Holt Junction Home Signal as appropriate. In all cases the signalman at Devizes or Holt Junction, before despatching a train or engine to the sidings at Seend, had to ascertain there was room to accommodate it.

Down trains calling to do work at the sidings had to come to a stand with a portion on the falling gradient and the guard or chargeman was to ensure the necessary precautions were taken to secure the train before the engine was despatched.

Entry to the Intermediate Token Instrument hut was by way of the electric token, and instructions were issued to ensure the door was locked again after use.

The names of some of Seend's signalmen and women have already been mentioned; others who worked the box included Bill Brooks in the 1930s, who was a good servant to the branch over a period of 49 years. He started his life on the railway in 1917 as a lad porter at the age of 17. Jack Perrett was also a signalman there for a few years. He joined the railway as a porter at Devizes after service in the army during the Second World War. Jack worked the box until its closure in 1956. Harry Lodge lived close by in Seend Cleeve and worked the box for some years. In the 1950s, leading up to closure, other regular signalmen were Sid Perrett from Bromham, Jim Gunthorpe from Patney, and William Wakeham from Marden, a village close to Patney & Chirton station.

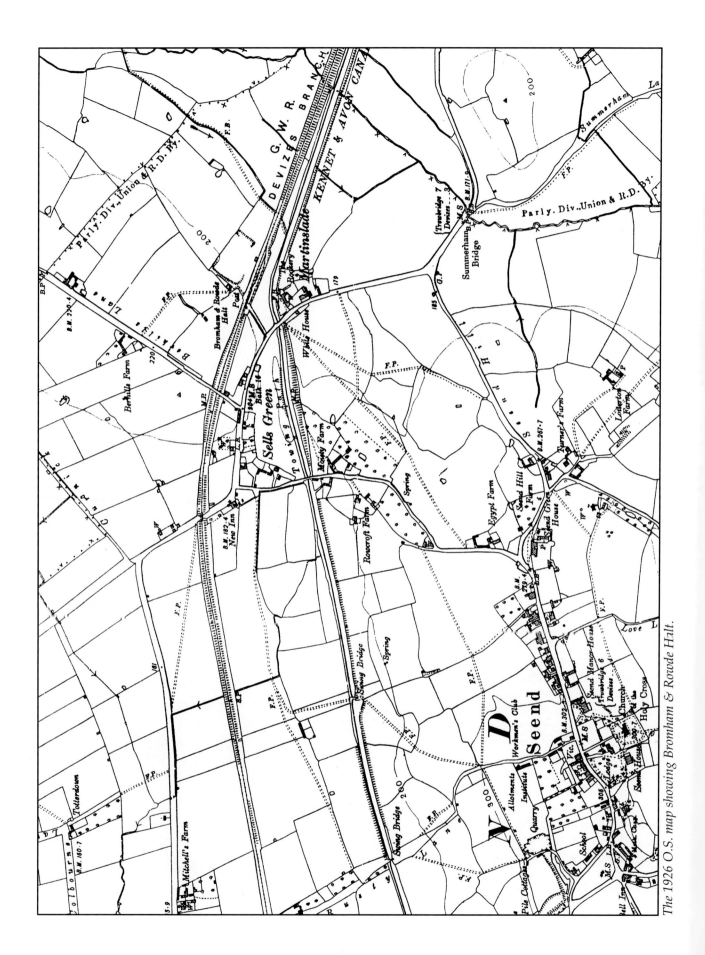

The 1926 O.S. map showing Bromham & Rowde Halt.

4. Bromham & Rowde Halt

Bromham & Rowde Halt was sited in the Parish of Seend at Sells Green and close to Martinslade and Seend. Both villages of Bromham and Rowde, whose population at the time of opening was slightly in excess of 1,000 people, were three miles from the station but it was from these places that the railway company assessed their business would be generated, as it was a thriving vegetable produce growing area.

Station Buildings

The building of the station was authorised on 6th May 1908, and it opened on 22nd February 1909. It was built on the level and comprised one 150-foot platform near the $88\frac{3}{4}$-mile post on the down side of the line, 5 miles 22 chains east of Holt. Initially it was provided with a metal pagoda waiting shelter, a lampman's hut and a milk stage. Later plans show a wooden booking office east of the milk stage, now covered by a canopy. The initial specification included a goods (loop) siding to hold 15 trucks and a corrugated iron office. A loading gauge straddled the centre of the loop. At the proposal stage the station was to have been known as 'Wragg's Wharf'. Oil lamps to include lighting for the approach road and goods yard were installed and the entire cost of the station construction, including the wooden corral-type fencing, siding and gates, was £1,113.8s. At the Devizes end of the platform, a level crossing served the Seend Brickyard Works and Hill View Farm.

In 1938 a scheme was produced to electrify the lighting on the station and in the approach road but it is thought with the start of the war a year later, this was not introduced. A paraffin vapour lamp was issued to Bromham for emergency use. The lighting was operated by the Seend porter and put out by the guard of the last train.

The Devizes omnibus, en route to Melksham, stops at the New Inn in Sells Green (now The Three Magpies) before passing under the railway bridge between Seend station and Bromham & Rowde Halt. (A.Alexander)

Most of the available facilities can be seen here. The oil lamps, to be extinguished by the guard of the last train; the pagoda waiting shelter; the shelter for milk traffic; and the office for tickets and paperwork, with the timber siding beyond, are all visible in this photograph from the 1950s. (Lens of Sutton)

The halt from the road crossing, looking to the west. The original pagoda waiting shelter can be seen beyond the canopied milk stage and the booking office in the foreground. (Trevor J.Saunders)

The deeper valance on the road side of the platform shelter can be seen in this 1964 view. It faced south and therefore had to give protection from both sun and rain. The gate to the platform for milk movement is visible at the far end, with the office entry from the road side. (D.J.Hyde)

A down train for Bristol, hauled by No.7908, leaving Bromham & Rowde Halt on 31st June 1954. The whistle board was the warning for the approach of the level crossing. The cranes of the sawmill can be seen on the right. (D.Lovelock)

The level crossing at Bromham & Rowde was to be the site of a couple of notable accidents over the years. In 1861, shortly after the line opened, a Mr Newman was killed when he was taking tiles from the brickyard with his horse and cart; he was struck by the 3.00pm train from Devizes. He had gone back to shut the gate while the horse continued over the crossing. Seeing the 'iron horse' approaching, Mr Newman ran with his whip to hurry his horse on but he was not quick enough and was crushed between the cart and the engine tender. An 11-year-old boy who was riding on the cart was flung onto the engine but escaped unhurt, as did the horse. At that time it was the practice for all local trains from Devizes to Holt to run tender first. At the inquest this was not considered to be a contributory factor, the main cause being that the 75-year-old Mr Newman had his watch 15 minutes slow.

A similar occurrence took place on the crossing on 25th March 1963, just three years before the branch closed, when Bert Sheppard, a farmworker, was caught by the train on his way to work at Hill View Farm. He had nosed his 1946 Austin 10 onto the unmanned crossing as the early morning Trowbridge to Paddington diesel went through. It caught the front of the car, buffeting it between the lineside fencing and the length of the train while dragging it down the line. The car, which was unrecognisable after the accident, was finally deposited beside the track. Ernest McDonald, a permanent way man, who was on the station, was amazed to see the driver emerge from the wreckage with just cuts and bruising. Bert Sheppard was in the habit of crossing the line every day at the same time and as with the earlier accident, on this occasion he was late. He was very thankful, however, that he had not been a second earlier.

Passenger Services

Railmotor cars provided the backbone of the passenger services to and from Holt and Devizes in the early timetables with the up trains calling four minutes after departure from Seend Station and the down trains six minutes after leaving Devizes. Passengers were left to work out the exact times for themselves as the station name was not shown in the timetable. The first railcar of the day was the up 7.17am Trowbridge to Devizes, calling at Bromham & Rowde at 7.38am. The first down service was the Devizes to Trowbridge calling at 8.06am.

A further six local trains called at the station through the weekdays, three in either direction. The final train of the day to Devizes could be taken at 9.58pm and to Trowbridge at 10.46pm. There were no Sunday trains at this time.

By the summer of 1930, services to the station had improved considerably with there now being six up trains during the week, the first being at 8.28am and the last at 10.14pm. One of these six trains, however, only called 'to pick up passengers' for the market in Devizes on a Thursday and this was at 11.36am. Down trains were also plentiful, there now being seven, the first calling at 8.14am and the last of the day at 10.40pm. Passengers wishing to alight at 8.40pm from the earlier 7.18pm Newbury to Bristol Temple Meads, were required to notify the guard at Devizes. There was still not a Sunday service but anyone wishing to return to London could of course use the alternative Seend station where the 5.42pm from Trowbridge departed at 5.58pm. This was a stopping train which reached Paddington at 9.12pm, a journey of 3 hours and 14 minutes. A faster alternative was the later mainline running of the 7.11pm Westbury, 7.23pm Lavington train, calling at Savernake, Newbury and Reading, arriving in London at 9.20pm in a time of just 2 hours 9 minutes.

The timetable for the summer of 1933 showed just three up trains from Bromham & Rowde could be caught, at 8.23am, 9.47am and 6.14pm, with three down at 8.12am, 1.04pm and 6.51pm. These were of course, all Monday to Saturday services.

With the hostilities of the Second World War drawing to an end, the services to the station remained unaltered, only the times having changed. This was soon to be altered and with the end of the GWR came a loss of services under the newly-formed British Railways.

At closure in April 1966, the 8.00am and 11.47am Devizes to Westbury and the 6.31pm Patney to Westbury were still stopping at the halt together with the 9.36am and the 5.45pm Westbury to Devizes. These were weekday services with some different timings on Saturdays.

Freight Services

As indicated earlier, from the time the station opened it received considerable business from the market gardens of Bromham with the produce arriving by lorry. Other outgoing freight included hay and milk from the local farms. Throughout the 1920s and up until the mid-1930s the milk traffic was considerable. More milk was handled at this station than in neighbouring Seend. In 1926, the year of the General Strike, 62,760 filled churns went out, much of this to the capital. The revenue this earned was £4,684. The milk was delivered by road to the station where the churns were placed in a milk pound at the rear of the canopied milk stage from where it was loaded onto the trains.

Sugar beet was a crop grown in the area and sent out in open wagons, much of it to sugar factories in Bury St Edmunds, Netherfield near Nottingham and, following the Second World War, to Kidderminster.

A market goods label of 1918 to Bristol (Redcliffe Wharf). (R.Packham)

GREAT WESTERN RAILWAY.
MARKET GOODS.
PERISHABLE.

(2829)
W 34 250,000 8/14.

From Bromham & Rowde
To Bristol Redcliffe wharf
Route via
Date 8·10·18 Train
Wagon No. 1938 Sheet No.
Consignee England

Send proper figures.   *Supervised by Send*
page 119

24 Rts – Est 341 1 26

GREAT WESTERN RAILWAY. Bromham & Rowde

(481 A)

STATION _Bromham & Rowde_

Joint with _the ( ) Railway._

DIVISION _____

Names of other Stations, etc., Receipts from which are included below

Names of Stations, Halts, Marshalling Yards, etc., supervised

	YEAR	1925		1926		1927		1928		1929	
		NUMBER	RECEIPTS	NUMBER	RECEIPTS	NUMBER	RECEIPTS	NUMBER	RECEIPTS	NUMBER	RECEIPTS
NUMBER OF AUTHORISED STAFF	Clerical and Supervisory							1		1	
	Wages		£		£		£		£		£
	Total Traffic Paybill Expenses		£		£		£		£		£
TRAFFIC											
Passenger	By Rail		£		£		£		£		£
	By Road Motor Cars		£		£		£		£		£
	Season Tickets		£		£		£		£		£
	Excess Fares Collected		£		£		£		£		£
	Total Passenger Receipts		£		£		£		£		£
Various	Platform Tickets		£		£		£		£		£
	Seat Registration		£		£		£		£		£
	Cab Rents		£		£		£		£		£
	Lavatories		£		£		£		£		£
	Other Receipts		£		£		£		£		£
	Total Various Receipts		£		£		£		£		£
	Total Passenger and Various Receipts		£		£		£		£		£
Misc. Parcels	Parcels Forwarded	763	£ 86	647	£ 76	554	£ 71	393	£ 54	391	£ 50
	Parcels Received	563	£ 25	509	£ 14	236	£ 17	414	£ 10	432	£ 13
	Miscellaneous Forwarded	51281	£ 4098	62872	£ 4695	62006	£ 4627	46391	£ 2906	51066	£ 2986
	Miscellaneous Received	123	£ 1	148	£ 4	128	£ 1	93	£	120	£ 2
	Total Parcels and Misc. Traffic and Receipts	52730	£ 4210	64175	£ 4789	63224	£ 4716	46301	£ 2970	51949	£ 3051
TOTAL COACHING RECEIPTS			£ 4210		£ 4789		£ 4716		£ 2970		£ 3051
	Forwarded Milk Traffic (included in Miscellaneous)	CANS 51279	RECEIPTS £ 4083	CANS 62716	RECEIPTS £ 4684	CANS 61966	RECEIPTS £ 4620	CANS 46364	RECEIPTS £ 2901	CANS 51044	RECEIPTS £ 2981
Goods		FORWARDED TONS	RECEIVED TONS	FORWARDED TONS	RECEIVED TONS	FORWARDED TONS	RECEIVED TONS	FORWARDED TONS	RECEIVED TONS	FORWARDED TONS	RECEIVED TONS
	Coal and Coke, Not Charged		894		553		840		794		789
	Coal and Coke, Charged		944	18	836		1034	10	896	7	910
	Other Minerals	6	3154	572	5001	578	6402	136	2964	659	2400
	General Merchandise, Carted	31	27	125	19	30	29	342	24	304	86
	General Merchandise, Not Carted	2801	1411	1855	1493	1924	1369	1409	1001	1443	837
	Total Tonnage	2838	6436	2460	10802	2532	9674	1897	5674	2823	4972
	Total Receipts	£ 1928	£ 2056	£ 1594	£ 3869	£ 1793	£ 2915	£ 1408	£ 1763	£ 1739	£ 1681
		TONNAGE	RECEIPTS	TONNAGE	RECEIPTS	TONNAGE	RECEIPTS	TONNAGE	RECEIPTS	TONNAGE	RECEIPTS
	Total Forwarded and Received	9274	£ 3984	13156	£ 5463	12206	£ 4708	7576	£ 3171	7295	£ 3420
	Tonnage of Free, Permitted, etc., Traffic (Not included above)							282		109	
	Other Receipts i.e., Domestic, Point to Point, Tolls, etc. (Not included above)		£		£		£		£		£
		WAGONS	RECEIPTS	WAGONS	RECEIPTS	WAGONS	RECEIPTS	WAGONS	RECEIPTS	WAGONS	RECEIPTS
	Live Stock Forwarded and Received	2	£ 6	4	£ 10	4	£ 6	2	£ 4	2	£ 8
	Total all Goods Tonnage and Goods and Live Stock Receipts	TONNAGE 9274	RECEIPTS £ 3990	TONNAGE 13156	RECEIPTS £ 5473	TONNAGE 12206	RECEIPTS £ 4714	TONNAGE 7858	RECEIPTS £ 3175	TONNAGE 7404	RECEIPTS £ 3428
TOTAL RECEIPTS (i.e., Coaching, Goods and Live Stock)			£ 8200		£ 10262		£ 9430		£ 6145		£ 6479

Freight traffic handled at Bromham & Rowde Halt in the second half of the 1920s.

In 1922, the sawmill of Percy Thomas Gregory was operating on the east side of the station approach road. He entered into an agreement with the GWR, dated 20th June 1922, whereby for the annual rental of £3.1s he had the use of a gateway in the boundary fencing providing access to his factory from the roadway. This rental was reduced to one guinea on 1st June 1936, following re-siting of the gateway. Sometime during 1922/23, the railway company installed an additional mileage siding which branched off the existing goods loop in a westerly direction from a point near the east ground frame. The timber mill was totally destroyed by fire, at a cost of £5,000, in the early hours of 3rd August 1939.

Following this, the site and business was taken over by the firm of Partridge Cox & Company Ltd whose offices were in Cumberland Road, Bristol,

close to the City Docks. The company wanted to use the railway for their business and so entered into an agreement with the GWR dated 3rd December 1941 to extend the existing siding by 100 feet, so allowing traffic to and from their sawmill to be loaded and unloaded by means of a crane they themselves erected. The extension to the siding necessitated the removal and re-erection of the buffer-stop, repositioning of the lamp hut near to the west end of the station platform, and removal of the goods yard lamp post and some fencing. In addition to this a carriage body had to be disposed of by the sawmill company and they had to cut down a tree. The entire provision cost Partridge Cox & Co £220. Timber deliveries came into the private siding in 'Macaw' bogie bolster wagons, with capacities of up to 30 tons each.

In 1946 the sawmills came under the ownership of Seend Electric Saw Mill Ltd and a transfer agreement was arranged with the GWR dated 14th November of that year.

At some stage the private siding was enclosed to form a compound from the point at which the extension was started. Rail entry to the compound was by way of a single 15-foot gate over the line. The Seend Electric Saw Mill Ltd had built a sleeper level crossing over their siding immediately inside this gateway and two additional 10-foot gates replaced the fencing next to the existing gate. This work formed an agreement with the new British Transport Commission made on 11th February 1949. The mill owners had some 10 years' use from the siding but this then tailed off, presumably in favour of road transport. The Divisional Manager of the Western Region of British Railways (Bristol Division) wrote to Seend Electric Saw Mill Ltd on 10th July 1963, notifying them that with the rationalisation of railway operations, freight services had been withdrawn from Bromham & Rowde station. No traffic had been dealt with from the private siding for some years and as British Railways wished to remove their siding they asked the company to accept their letter of 10th July 1963 as formal termination of the 1941 private siding agreement.

The Seend Electric Saw Mill Ltd confirmed their agreement to the termination, notified their intention to remove the sleeper crossing and thanked British Railways for the courtesy and assistance given to them by their staff over the many years when they consigned all their output by rail.

The station was not provided with cattle pens, carriage shoots, crane or weighbridge, so traffic requiring any of these facilities could not be accepted without making prior arrangements. There were in fact occasional shipments of livestock but if four wagon loads were moved in a year, then it was a busy one. To give an example two wagons were loaded in 1929 and that was the last despatched until 1934 when one wagon was used.

Coal came into Bromham & Rowde for the coal business of W.J.Dowty but not in such regular deliveries as at Seend where the merchant preferred to off-load his stock. Coal also arrived in smaller quantities for use by the local market gardeners to heat their greenhouses.

Wartime/Military

In keeping with other stations on the branch, the halt was that much busier in times of war. Probably the incident that gained most notoriety

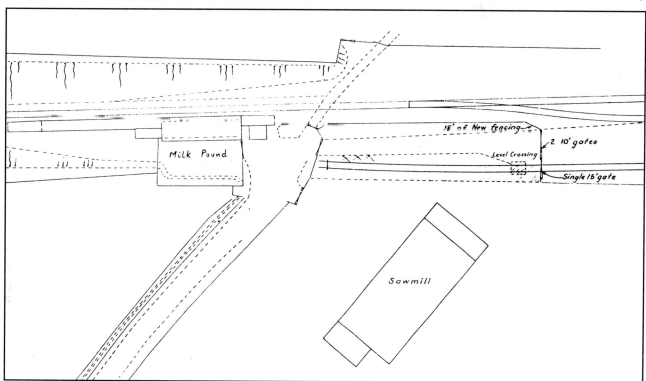

1949 plan showing the final arrangements for the private sidings.

68

occurred in August 1942, when a German aircraft, following a raid on Bristol, machine gunned the station when trying to hit the nearby sawmill. Two motorcyclists, who were spending the night in the waiting shelter, received serious injuries when bullets pierced the sides of the shelter on the platform.

The land army girls were billeted at Sells Green, not far from the station and they would use the railway for their nights out in Devizes, taking the last train back at the end of the day, this being the 10.35pm Devizes to Trowbridge. This was how Devizes porter, Trevor (Ginger) Brothers, was to meet his future wife. She was one of the land-army girls taking the last train before he went off duty at the station.

Staff

As previously mentioned, the halt was manned by one man, who was a goods checker. He appeared on the staff strength of Seend station. He worked the station during weekdays from 8.00am to 5.00pm and Fred Dollimore was the man who held this position for many years. It was probably following his retirement that the halt ceased to be

regularly manned. After 1st November 1951, it was manned by a relief from Devizes. All the freight administration was carried out at Seend station, where the cash and documentation would be sent in the afternoon.

There was an instruction in respect of this station whereby the Tilley lamp at the halt had to be collected by the guard of the first up train each morning and taken to Devizes for servicing. It would then be returned to the halt and lit by the Devizes shunter. The guard of the last down train was charged with extinguishing it.

Signalling

The station was not known to have any signals at any stage of its operation. The points at each end of the loop were worked from ground frames released by the electric token for the Devizes to Holt Junction section of the single line. Guards of freight trains calling at the siding were responsible for working the points, and when the train was ready to leave, had to ensure that everything was in order for the train to proceed, before handing the token to the driver. As at Seend station the siding at Bromham & Rowde was barred to 'red' engines.

GREAT WESTERN RAILWAY.
HALF-DAY EXCURSION
TO
READING,
NEWBURY, HUNGERFORD, SAVERNAKE,
MARLBOROUGH,
DEVIZES
&c.
On MONDAYS in AUGUST and SEPTEMBER,
COMMENCING MONDAY, AUGUST 11th, 1902,
AN EXPRESS EXCURSION
Will leave PADDINGTON STATION at 12.45 noon.

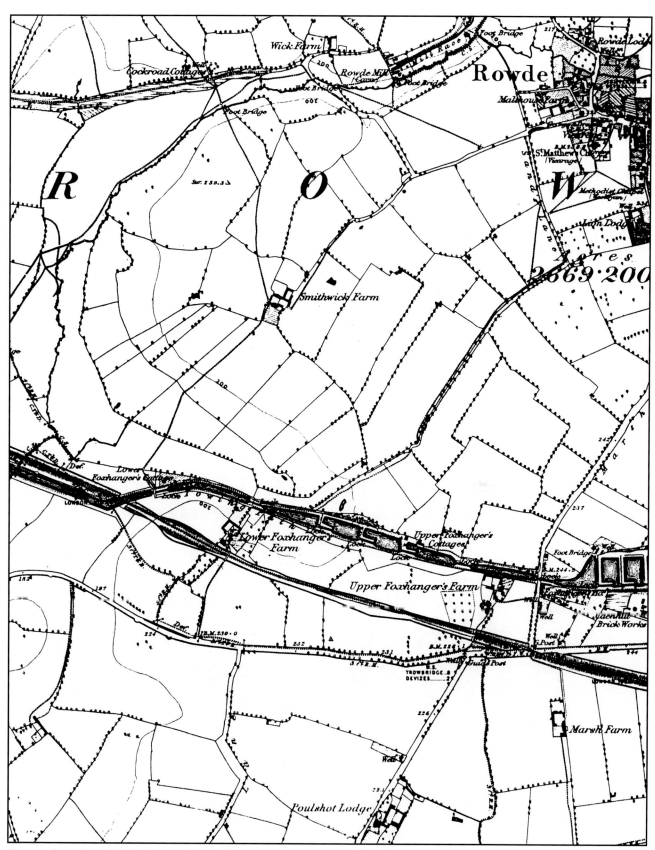

Extract from the 1886 O.S. map showing Foxhanger Bridge crossing the Kennet & Avon Canal shortly before the latter reaches the bottom of the Caen Hill flight of locks.

70

5. The Devizes Bridges

There were two bridges on the line between Bromham & Rowde and Devizes.

Foxhanger Bridge

After leaving Bromham & Rowde Halt the line ran for half a mile on an embankment parallel to the Kennet & Avon Canal before crossing it by way of Foxhanger Bridge. From here into Devizes the gradient of the line rose considerably at 1 in 93, 60 and 52 successively.

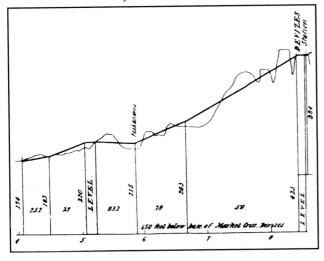

The bridge at Foxhanger's, 88 miles 17 chains from London, was a three-span girder construction with stone and brick abutments on each embankment and, as with Whaddon Bridge near Holt, was supported by cylindrical cast-iron piers infilled with concrete. The bridge abutments, as with the tunnel at Devizes and some other bridges on the line, were initially constructed to allow for future doubling of the track which was considered a possibility. The 1845 Act had required that this bridge should be good and substantial and that a clear water way should be kept of at least 30 feet under one arch. The railway and canal companies between them had to agree suitable building materials and after construction, should the railway company, following seven days notice from the canal company, fail to make any necessary repairs, then the latter could arrange them at the former's expense.

Foxhanger Bridge, frequently suffered degrees of movement resulting in corrective measures. The problems tended to be caused by water seepage into the embankment. In 1906 there was movement of one pair of cylinders supporting the timber decking and Barlow rail, which was used as running rail on the bridge only. The bedstones had to be raised and the decking replaced with one of 6-inch timber. The estimated cost of this work was £67. Even after completion of the work, the Divisional Engineer at Bristol was unhappy with the stability of a pair of cylinders on the tow-path side of the canal as they moved when trains passed over. Consequently these were strengthened, probably the following year, when the permanent way between Seend and Devizes was re-railed with a heavier type. It appears that at this time consideration was being given to using heavier engines on the section. More strengthening took place in 1926, this time to the piers on the Seend side of the canal.

Late in its life a considerable amount of work was needed to raise and re-align the bridge as it had moved at the Devizes end. The work was authorised in 1954 for lifting to a gradient of 1 in 84, replacing timber decking with steel, providing new girders, bracing and stiffeners, and an additional supporting pier on the tow-path. The existing cast-iron columns were also encased in concrete block. The estimated cost for this was £8,250 with the improvements completed in 1956.

Under normal circumstances a mandatory speed limit of 40mph on the bridge was in force for all 'red' group engines but this was reduced to 5mph for all engines from the time the bridge problem was diagnosed. Obviously this was not a very satisfactory situation for trains embarking on the steep climb up the Caen Hill embankment.

After crossing the canal, the line went through a deep cutting and passed Lower Foxhanger's Farm and its occupation crossing, where the railway cutting opened up into a large expanse on either side of the line before narrowing again prior to climbing the embankment and crossing the A361 by way of the Fish Bridge at the bottom of Caen Hill. Locally the reason expressed for this expanse of railway land, having been passed down from previous generations, is that it was originally purchased by the railway company for possible future development as a station site to serve Poulshot and Rowde. No firm evidence however, has yet been found to substantiate this.

Foxhanger Bridge over the Kennet & Avon Canal in 1954 before the cast-iron support columns were encased in concrete for strengthening purposes. (British Rail)

Foxhanger Bridge following the encasement of the columns. (C.Fletcher)

An 0-6-0 Pannier Tank crossing Foxhanger Bridge on its climb to Devizes in April 1954. (Michael Wheeler)

With strengthening work completed in 1956, a four-coach train hurries down Caen Hill embankment before crossing Foxhanger Bridge. (Trevor J.Saunders)

0-6-0 Pannier Tank No.7764 crosses Foxhanger Bridge with a mixed goods train for Devizes in c.1950. (Trevor J.Saunders)

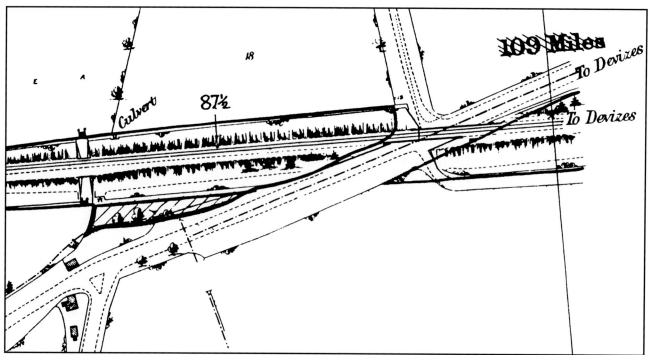

The position of Fish Bridge shown on the GWR Engineers' two-chain survey. Note that the original mileage measurements from Paddington via Chippenham and Holt Junction have been superseded by those via Newbury and Patney & Chirton.

Fish Bridge

The line crossed over the Bath Road on the Fish Bridge at 87 miles and 35 chains from London, arguably the most well-known and discussed structure on the 13 miles of the branch. There have been different views on why it became known by its name. One suggestion was that an advertisement hoarding displayed a picture of a fish as part of an advertisement for MacFisheries. This is possible as a picture of the bridge in the June 1958 copy of *The Railway Magazine*, shows a hoarding board on the right side abutment viewed from the Seend side of the bridge. During the period from 1928-35, an eye-witness also testifies to there being hoardings on both sides of the road and to seeing bill-posters with brush and paste changing the advertisements.

The most probable reason for the name, however, is the shape of the first of the two bridges that spanned the A361 at this point. Costing over £10,000 when originally built, it was of tubular construction, having wrought-iron flange-type main girders with a timber deck. It was the line's longest bridge at 160 feet and was supported by brick and stone abutments. As with Foxhanger Bridge there was a 40mph speed restriction for 'red' group engines. At the planning stage another type of structure had been considered built of timber with wrought-iron tie rods.

In 1901 the original bridge was replaced by one of lattice girders and three steel braces with a trough floor. Its square spar was 35 feet and its skew span 110 feet. While the second bridge was being installed and the original removed, local permanent way man, Ted Rossiter, was appointed to the site as night watchman, presumably to ensure that no one who may have been walking the line came to grief. This was not the last time that the Fish Bridge was to receive such service as during the war years of 1939/45 the duty of guarding the bridge at night time fell to the Home Guard.

Fish Bridge was the site of a tragedy in June 1889 when Emily Lister, the Headmistress of Devizes British School was shot and pushed out of the 11.10am Reading to Trowbridge train by her former boyfriend Gus Keeling. The two had been seen arguing at Devizes station prior to the arrival of the train. Miss Lister, on the way to her parents' home in Birmingham, had bought a ticket for Bristol and at the last moment Gus Keeling bought one to Seend. It seems they sat in an empty 3rd Class compartment and passengers later indicated that 'loud quarrelling' had been heard. When the train was passing over Fish Bridge, two shots were fired followed by the schoolmistress falling from the train and down the embankment. Inspector Upchurch of Reading, having become aware of a problem, stopped the train near Seend Brickyard.

A permanent way man named Burgess had, meanwhile, found the lady bleeding heavily and together with George Williams, a plasterer working on a cottage near the line, transported her to Devizes Hospital. Gus Keeling, it is thought, tried to make his escape by using the footboard on the outside of the carriage but he must have fallen from it as his mutilated body was found beside the track from where it was taken to the Devizes Workhouse.

Lister and Keeling had been teachers in Brighton and he had wanted to marry her, but she wanted no more to do with him on finding out he had spent time in an asylum. A letter from the schoolmistress was found on Keeling telling him the relationship was at an end. He had very little money when taking the train and asked her for some. On refusal, he shot her and pushed her out of the window with the fall resulting in the loss of an eye. She recovered sufficiently to return to teaching. Gus Keeling was disowned by his relations and had a pauper's funeral.

Previously there had been another death at the Fish Bridge when a tramp took his life by jumping from it. He was buried in the local churchyard at Rowde and his headstone read simply:

To Some Mother's Son.

The original Fish Bridge, the shape of which is thought to have given rise to its name. It was to be replaced in 1901. (Devizes Town Council)

A Woodward's postcard showing the replacement bridge from the same spot, looking up Caen Hill towards Devizes.

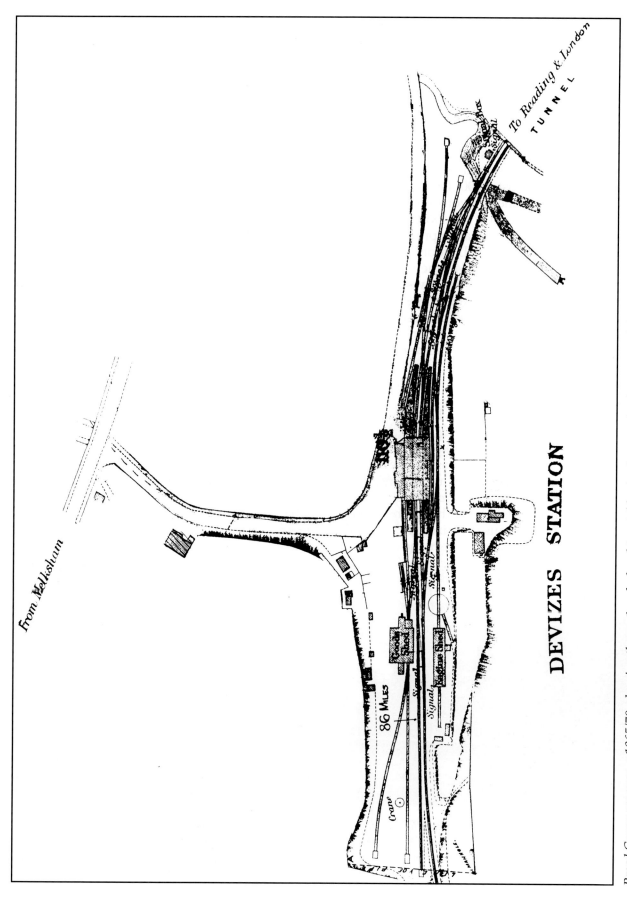

Broad Gauge era map, c.1865/70, showing the engine shed and turntable. Again, note the change in mileage calculation introduced with the opening of the BHER extension in 1862.

A permanent way man named Burgess had, meanwhile, found the lady bleeding heavily and together with George Williams, a plasterer working on a cottage near the line, transported her to Devizes Hospital. Gus Keeling, it is thought, tried to make his escape by using the footboard on the outside of the carriage but he must have fallen from it as his mutilated body was found beside the track from where it was taken to the Devizes Workhouse.

Lister and Keeling had been teachers in Brighton and he had wanted to marry her, but she wanted no more to do with him on finding out he had spent time in an asylum. A letter from the schoolmistress was found on Keeling telling him the relationship was at an end. He had very little money when taking the train and asked her for some. On refusal, he shot her and pushed her out of the window with the fall resulting in the loss of an eye. She recovered sufficiently to return to teaching. Gus Keeling was disowned by his relations and had a pauper's funeral.

Previously there had been another death at the Fish Bridge when a tramp took his life by jumping from it. He was buried in the local churchyard at Rowde and his headstone read simply:

To Some Mother's Son.

The original Fish Bridge, the shape of which is thought to have given rise to its name. It was to be replaced in 1901. (Devizes Town Council)

A Woodward's postcard showing the replacement bridge from the same spot, looking up Caen Hill towards Devizes.

(above left) The view up Caen Hill towards Devizes, with the turning to Rowde on the left, showing the advertisement hoarding on the abutment which became the subject of much comment in recent years. (Trevor J.Saunders)

(above right) Looking down the hill towards Melksham, one can see how close to the bridge was the turning to Rowde.

(left) The rail level view towards Devizes showing the girder and rib work. (Trevor J.Saunders)

(below left) A view of the permanent way hut at lineside, just west of the bridge. (C.L.Caddy)

(below right) A carriage window view of the permanent way hut. (J.Sawtell)

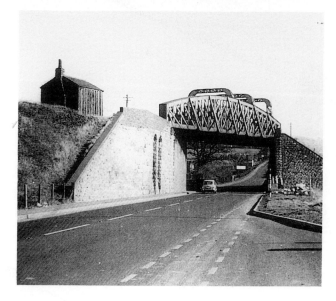

Lower Park Farm Bridge between Caen Hill and Devizes. The occupation bridge to Lower Park Farm had become unsafe in 1952 and was replaced with a concrete span. The bridge remains in use as part of a public footpath. (both British Rail)

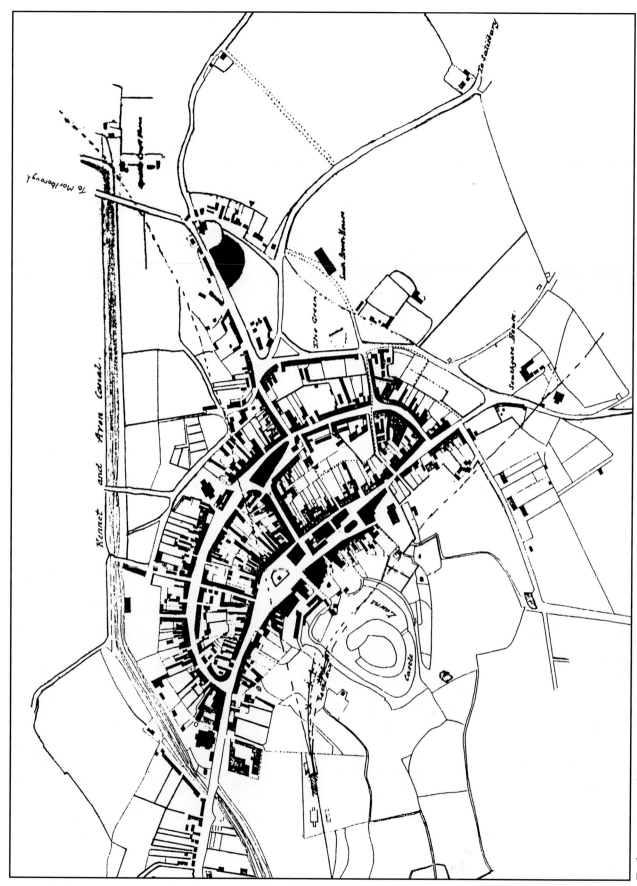

Early town map of Devizes showing proposals for the railway's route eastwards towards Hungerford, as sketched in by a railway draughtsman, c.1860.

6. Devizes Station

The town of Devizes is situated some 400 feet above sea level in the centre of Wiltshire on a spur of greensand overlooking the Avon Vale to the north-west and the Vale of Pewsey to the south.

In the 1830s Devizes was a flourishing market town in the centre of a considerable agricultural area with a population of just 5,000. Local businesses using barges on the Kennet & Avon Canal were dissatisfied with this slow form of transport and looked to attract the railway to provide an improved service, hoping to be on a line between London and Bristol. Hopes faded, however, in 1834 when the GWR decided against a line through the Pewsey Vale in favour of a route via Swindon. At the time the editor of the *Devizes & Wiltshire Gazette* had described the GWR proposals as 'simply a device for the transportation of pigs from Bristol to Brompton'. Such endearing remarks surely did not help the town's aspirations. Despite their disappointment a number of townsfolk arranged for Brunel to survey the area between Devizes and Melksham where a line could meet the intended branch from Chippenham to Westbury. This was completed and plans drawn up in 1836 with the line to be known as the 'Devizes & Melksham Great Western Branch Railway'. The launch for this took place at the *Bear Hotel* on 2nd July 1836 with shares alloted, but the scheme made no progress, maybe because Devizes citizens still saw themselves on a through route to the capital.

The Bear Hotel, c.1910, in Devizes Market Place, is next to the Corn Exchange, which is on the corner of Station Road, and was a calling place for the horse bus from the station, and earlier, a stopping place for London to Bath stagecoaches.

The GWR at this time was anxious to curry favour with the townspeople in case they were persuaded to support other companies' schemes. In 1844 the GWR adopted the Wilts, Somerset & Weymouth Railway Company, with Brunel proposing plans for a connection from Thingley on the GWR main line near Chippenham, together with a Melksham to Devizes branch. This would still only leave Devizes as a branch line terminus, however. A chance of being on a direct line came when the Kennet & Avon Canal company, seeing its business losing trade, gave consideration to converting the canal to a railway. They later changed this idea to building a line to run alongside the canal and so was launched the 'London, Newbury & Bath Direct Railway'.

In 1845 the WSWR received parliamentary approval but the Devizes Branch aspect still did not take off because of delays caused by the Supplementary Bills to alter the junction and the difficulty in purchasing land and property and settling compensation. Other railway schemes continued to be proposed, one of which was the GWR's Hungerford to Westbury line, avoiding Devizes. Because of the various schemes afloat and because the town was still without an agreed rail connection, the Mayor of Devizes, Joseph Crockett, called a meeting to consider the proposals. The feeling of this meeting, later supported by the Borough Council, was that Devizes, being in the centre of the county, a town with a large weekly market, an Assize Court and the largest prison in the area, was entitled to an appropriate railway service. These opinions were made known to the GWR who replied indicating that they wished to provide routes from Devizes to Bath and also from Hungerford to Exeter. This would be accomplished by uniting the new line from Hungerford with the Wilts & Somerset line at Devizes and the line to Exeter diverging towards Westbury at a point south-east of Devizes (Stert).

The WSWR arrived in Westbury, opening in 1848, but the Devizes line was not progressing because of the continuing land purchase difficulties. The company had run out of finance by 1850 and was taken over by the GWR who planned to open the line but themselves found difficulties in completing the scheme. However, following lawsuits against them and to keep faith with the local communities, the GWR was empowered to raise an additional £1 million for completion within three years. It had taken a long time and many obstacles had needed to be overcome but at long last the railway was coming to Devizes.

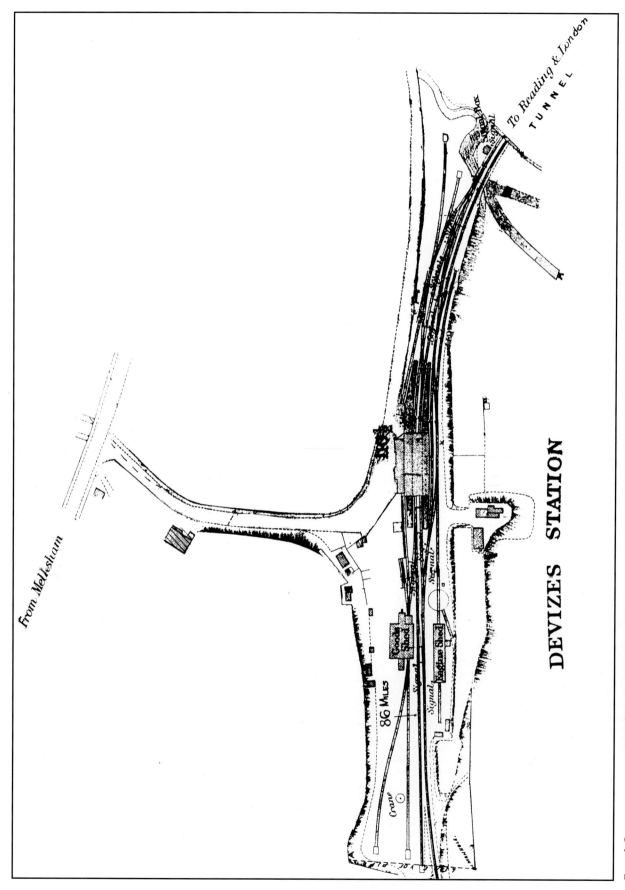

From Melksham

86 Miles

Crane

Goods Shed

Signal

Engine Shed

Signal

Signal

To Reading & London

TUNNEL

DEVIZES STATION

Broad Gauge era map, c.1865/70, showing the engine shed and turntable. Again, note the change in mileage calculation introduced with the opening of the BHER extension in 1862.

Station Buildings/Opening

At a meeting in Devizes Town Hall in August 1844, the then company agreed that the site for Devizes station should be near the Market Place and the *Bear Hotel*. This was finally realised with its construction in 1856 just below the Market Place, with Station Road leading up the hill to Northgate Street at the west end of the station and to the Market Place and the *Bear Hotel* from the eastern end of the station. The terminus station with an overall roof had the station building on the north side with the roof supported by a high wall on the opposite side of the line. The platform at that time was 121 feet long with two tracks passing it to buffer stops by the high ground at the east end. A local newspaper report of the time described the station as 'a very pretty building affording every accommodation that can be desired in a place of that description'. The building was of Gothic character with walls of rubble masonry. On the roadside elevation was a verandah roof, 30' x 7', along part of the front. The shed over the double line of track measured 121' x 42'. The building comprised, from east to west, a First Class Waiting Room and Ladies' W.C., the Booking Office, the Superintendent's Office, the Parcels Office, the Second Class Waiting Rooms and Ladies' W.C., the Lamp Room, the Porter's Room, an exit passage from the platform and the Gentlemen's W.C. The area covered by the building was 2,098 square feet and its total building cost came to £2,243. Outside the main entrance, a stone path crossed the unmade-up road at right angles; similar paths were also provided to cross other dirt roads in the town.

A goods yard on the upside west end of the station was provided with a large goods shed, measuring 67' x 45', of grey Bath stone with black timber ends. It had a roadway and single track either side of the internal loading platform on which stood a wooden 30cwt crane. Leading from the platform at one end was an office and at the opposite end a small warehouse. At the east end the signalbox was built on columns overlooking the track. Access to the box was by a series of stairs and landings with entry at the rear. This is indicated on the 1886 O.S. map. On the opposite, down side, a small engine shed was erected with a single line running through. The building measured 50' x 20' with an inspection pit of 40' x 6' x 6'6" depth. A turntable was sited on the line into the shed which had one short line off

it suitable for the stabling of one engine. The first occupant of the shed was the Fury Class locomotive *Dreadnought*.

The 8½ miles of track between Holt and Devizes opened for passengers on 1st July 1857, eleven years after construction work was first planned. The town had waited a long time for its railway and with the construction completed it was to be rushed into service a week early. There was very little time to organise the customary celebrations but the Mayor of Devizes held a meeting on 29th June to discuss the celebration arrangements. As a result, shops were closed and a general holiday was declared. Consequently several hundred people assembled at the station on the opening morning to see the first train leave at 7.45am. Throughout the day the station remained crowded with cheering people as each train left in turn. Some people spent much of the day travelling to and fro on the trains for the sheer joy of it. At Holt, the passengers were welcomed by a band playing 'Hail the Conquering Hero Comes'.

Little was to change at the town's station site until an Act which received Royal Assent on 13th August 1859 enabled the Berks & Hants Extension Railway, under the Chairmanship of the Marquis of Ailesbury to construct a line from Hungerford to Devizes. 30,000 shares of £10 each were made available in August 1858 producing a capital of £300,000. Work began in 1861 and was to provide Devizes with its original concept of being on a direct line to London. The original 1866 venture by the Company for an extension from Stert to Westbury had not materialised and was finally abandoned in 1870. This of course was just as well for Devizes, which undoubtedly would have been deprived of many services it was later to receive.

Consideration was given to two routes by which the course of the railway could be brought from the Pewsey Vale to the terminus station in Devizes. One proposal was to go through Stert, Hillworth and by tunnel under the lower east grounds of Devizes Castle. Another was to bring the line in from a north, north-easterly direction by tunnel under the London Road close to the town side of the canal bridge. The line would then run to the rear of the properties facing on to Estcourt Street before passing under Commercial Road, Northgate Street, the Market Place and emerging at the station site. The former of these options was chosen.

WILTS SOMERSET & WEYMOUTH RAILWAY.

A building of Gothic character, with walls
of rubble masonry: quoins &c. of Ashlar, with
a shed over double line of rails 111 feet long and
43 feet wide, and verandah roof 30 feet long &
7 feet wide along part of Front of Station

Total Cost of Station £ 2243.0.0

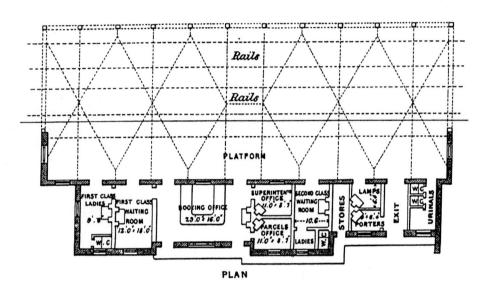

PLAN

Area of Building   2098 sq.re feet
D.º of Shed   5456 sq.re feet
Cube Content of Building 39862 cub feet

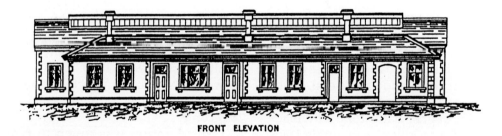

FRONT ELEVATION

THIS STATION CONTAINS
1.st Class Ladies Room & W.C.
1.st Class Waiting Room
Booking Office
Superintendents Room
Parcels Office
2.nd Class Waiting Room
Ladies D.º & W.C.
Stores
Lamps
Porters
Exit
Urinals & 2 W.Cs

Price per cubic foot of Building 9¼.d
D.º per square foot of shed 2.s 6⅝.d

Scale 20 F.t to an Inch.

(left) Devizes station plan and drawing from Railway Bridges, Culverts, and Stations by J.W.Grover (1870).

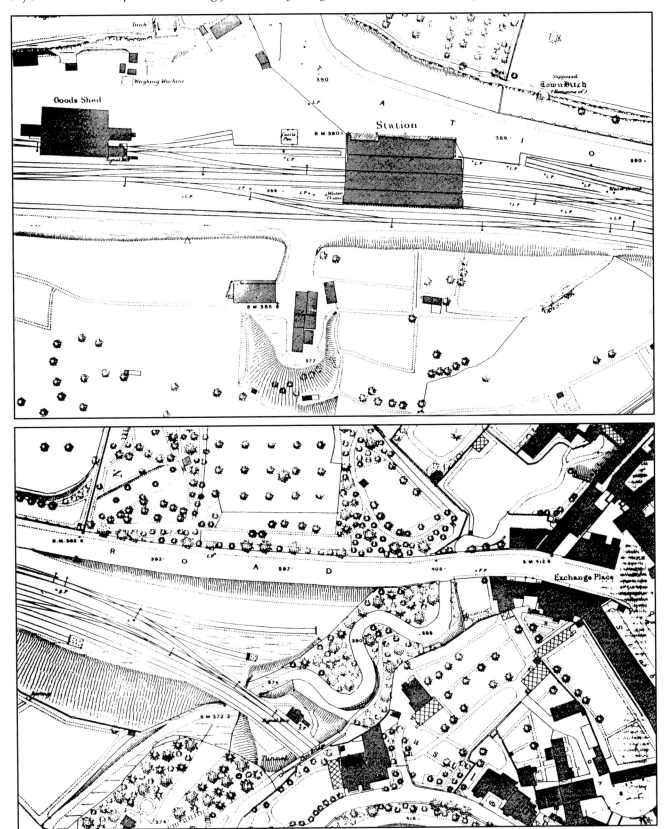

An extract from the 1886 O.S. 25" to 1 mile map showing the signalboxes and station buildings.

The exterior of Devizes station from the east end, with a saddle tank at rest on the up platform. The track plan is as in the broad-gauge plan but now narrowed to standard gauge though retaining broad-gauge bridge rail. The new signalbox was completed in 1897 and the footbridge in 1889.

With the construction completed at a cost of £250,000, the 24½ mile broad-gauge single track from Hungerford to Devizes was officially opened on 11th November 1862, making the line no longer a branch but a through route. The line later provided an alternative route from Bath to London and was used on occasions such as when there were rock falls in Box Tunnel. The directors of the BHER arranged a special train on 4th November. They were accompanied on the trip by dignitaries and shareholders who had paid 4 shillings each for a return ticket which included lunch at the Devizes Corn Exchange. The meal was attended by 300 people supplied 'with an abundance of game from Savernake' and 'stimulated by an illimitable supply of champagne, claret and choice wines'. At various points on the journey along its route, villagers waved flags and banners, and at Devizes several hundred people gathered in the rain to 'cheer lustily' as the train, bedecked with flags of all colours, and wreathed with evergreens and flowers, emerged from the tunnel into the station.

With the new line entering the station from the east, an additional signalbox was necessary and this was sited at the west end of the tunnel, on the up side, close to the wooden footbridge that crossed the tunnel mouth at that point (see the 1886 O.S. map).

The railway company held a meeting on 16th May 1871 where the need for extra carriage shed accommodation was considered. The Superintendents presented lists of places where it was desirable to have sheds for sheltering carriages not in use. Devizes station was one of the places indicated as having existing accommodation for 5 coaches with no further needs. No record of such a structure is known but possibly the station itself with overall roof was being referred to though it is difficult to see how stored coaches would not have interrupted the routine traffic.

During the weekend of 28th June 1874, the complete line from Hungerford to Holt Junction was converted to standard gauge and the first section of the General Instructions, issued by the Engineer's Office in Swindon is shown on the opposite page.

Great Western Railway

LOCOMOTIVE DEPARTMENT.

CONVERSION OF GAUGE
BETWEEN READING AND HOLT JUNCTION,

Including the Marlborough Branch.

NOTICE TO ENGINEMEN AND FIREMEN.

Every Engineman working over the above-mentioned Lines, during the Conversion of the Gauge, will be supplied with a copy of the printed TIME TABLE AND GENERAL INSTRUCTIONS issued for the use of the Company's Servants, for which his signature will be taken. No Engineman must on any account take charge of an Engine or Train on any part of these Lines after June 26th, or subsequently during the Conversion, who has not previously received and signed for, the Time Table and General Instructions.

The Enginemen are requested to make themselves thoroughly acquainted with the Time Bill and General Instructions, and they will be expected to read them through with great care as soon as they receive them, and if they meet with anything which they do not properly understand, or which they think requires explanation, they must at once apply to their Superintendent, or Foreman, or one of the Locomotive Inspectors on duty, in order that there may be no misunderstanding whatever on the part of the men engaged in this work.

The particular attention of the Enginemen is directed to clause 18 of the General Instructions on Page 6 as to stopping "dead" at the end of each Section; also to Clause 23 on the same page. ALL FACING POINTS MUST BE APPROACHED WITH VERY GREAT CAUTION, and at the Crossing Places the greatest care must be taken to have the Engine or Train so under control, as to prevent the possibility of overshooting the Points.

Enginemen and Firemen must keep a constant look out for any signal that may be given by the Permanent Way Men or others, whether by means of a Red Flag or other Hand-signal: They are to proceed with great caution, especially on approaching curves, when they must take care to sound their small whistles, so as to give timely warning of their approach to the men working on the Line.

Enginemen and Firemen are particularly requested to be with their Engines in good time, and to bestow the greatest care upon the oiling and examination of the working parts, Axle Boxes, &c. They must be particularly careful to have a good supply of coal before starting from each end, and to fill up their tanks at every watering place, so as to be fully prepared for any unexpected stoppage or delay. So much depends upon the Engines being in the best possible working order, that it is hoped very great attention will be paid to this matter, MORE ESPECIALLY WITH THE NEW NARROW GAUGE ENGINES.

Firemen are also required to make themselves well acquainted with the Time Table and General Instructions, and the Enginemen must afford them every opportunity of doing so. As far as possible the Enginemen and Firemen should read the Instructions TOGETHER, so as to obtain a perfect knowledge of them before commencing to work the single line.

J. ARMSTRONG.

Engineer's Office, Swindon.
22nd June, 1874.

These two photographs taken inside the overall roof of the original 1857 station make a remarkable record of the building, the staff and employees, and are a reflection on the social and class attitudes of the period. The first general view, looking across the station, more or less to the north-east, was taken at 11.40am on Friday 3rd June 1893. The 'baulk road', with the old broad-gauge bridge rails, narrowed to 4'8½", is still in position, nearly 20 years after conversion. The old footbridge with its steps facing eastwards away from the station building is visible through the open end arch. A new footbridge, reversing the staircase was built in 1910. A new signalbox, replacing the two existing boxes (one at the tunnel entrance and the other in an elevated position close to the goods shed) was built in 1897 just beyond the footbridge steps. By reference to the plans of the station buildings arrangements it can be seen that some change of use has occurred. From right to left: the end door, seen directly behind one of the newly-installed hanging gas lamps, was to the Ladies' Waiting Room – originally only for First Class Ladies! The next door was to the General Waiting Room, formerly the First Class Waiting Room. The kiosk and table was Wyman's Bookstall, moved in the rebuilding of 1910 against the end wall, but at this time right outside the Booking Hall door, to attract passengers' attention. Through the windows of the booking office may be seen the glazed screen above the ticket window. The door to the left now leads to the Parcel Office and Cloakroom, converted from the Superintendent's Office using the same window, directly below the advertisement for 'International Tea'. The Station Master's (lately Superintendent's) Office is next and has had a narrow window added on either side of the door. This was formerly the Second Class Waiting Room, with a separate Ladies' Room. It is thought that the Station Master, Mr. Abrahams, is standing fourth from the left. A small number of the other staff are identifiable, some of whom may be seen in the photograph of the shunting saddle tank locomotive No.1698 (see page 174), probably taken at about the same time or certainly within the year. George Warren, the ticket collector, is prominent in his frock coat, standing third from the right of the main group, directly beneath the english drop dial station clock on the rear wall, which shows the time as 11.40am. Signalman Alford, probably from the west signalbox, by the goods shed, is leaning on the platform edge, far right, and foreman Silk is standing between the rails. The shunter with his pole, which is often used as a badge of office in photographs, is the same man seen in the locomotive photo. The shunting horse, owned by Sainsbury's, coal merchants and GWR carter agent, is seen on the track at the extreme right, held by Samuel Stockham, grandfather of Mrs Willcox who kindly supplied these photographs. The horse was used to move wagons when a locomotive was not available. The photographs have been accurately dated by reference to the newspaper headlines on the billboards around the bookstall. The papers include: The Morning Post; The Times; Lloyds News; Financial Times; Truth; The Sporting Life; and the clearest example, The Daily Graphic. They variously refer to the following events: crime in Ireland; the occupation of Uganda; a statement in Parliament; The Liberator inquiry (a building society scandal); Ramsgate inquest; and the Queen's birthday celebrations (her birthday was on 24th May), with the Royal Wedding (George and Mary, later King George V and Queen Mary, married on 24th May 1893). Sports headlines include reference to the Surrey v. Gloucestershire cricket match; Epsom Races and The Oaks. GWR posters refer to Improved Banbury and Cheltenham services (these occurred in 1891); Improved West of England services; and the introduction of a new Plymouth to Paddington express in June 1893. The West of England services were timed at Exeter in 4½ hours and Plymouth in 5½ hours from Paddington. Also seen is the New Express Service from London, Trowbridge, Dorchester to Weymouth. Some of the enamel

signs and boards mention long-forgotten products such as: Horniman's Tea; Branson's Coffee; International Tea; and Garton's Ales & Stout. The second photograph of staff is taken in front of the gated covered way forming the parcels and mail entrance from the station approach road. Foreman Silk is seen on the track on the left, next to signalman Alford with his bushy beard, leaning against the platform. Ticket collector Warren in his coat is clearly seated in the centre. Samuel Stockham is on the far right. The bowler-hatted gentlemen will include the goods agent and Mr Abrahams, the Station Master, as well as other permanent staff. Were the buttonholes a regular part of the uniform? (M.Willcox)

With the conversion the opportunity was taken to make other changes. These included a second rail running into the station side of the tunnel, terminating with a buffer stop inside. The two signal boxes, on the upside west end of the tunnel and the other on the gantry near the goods shed entrance, were still in use at this time. The reduced width of track allowed for a platform to be installed on the downside and the up side was extended to match.

In September, while inspecting the conversion, James Grierson, the General Manager for the GWR, recommended transferring the engine shed from Devizes to Trowbridge. He was of the opinion that the position it occupied was going to be needed for freight traffic owing to the development of Devizes in population and trade. This transfer probably went ahead the following year. Together with Captain Tyler from the Board of Trade, the decision was taken at the same time to stop the construction of the water tank near the shed as this also could form an obstruction. The eventual site for this was on the side of the embankment at the back of the upside goods yard. The tank measured 20' x 9 'x 6' and had a capacity at 5'6" of 6,187 gallons, and 6,728 gallons in total. It was gravity fed by way of a 4-inch pipe which came down the incline at the western end of Station Road and water was extracted from the Kennet & Avon Canal via a catchment pit near the locks beside Town Bridge in Northgate Street. The tank initially fed two water cranes at the station. The GWR Locomotive Department paid the GWR Canal Company £100 per annum for the supply of water. On 6th September 1876, a reduction of this amount was applied for. The application was put before the Canal Committee on the 27th October together with one for Savernake station. The resolve was that 'the Committee does not regard the present payment as in any way excessive and that particulars and information as to the quantity of water consumed and as to the application to other purposes than the supply of locomotives especially at Devizes Station, be laid before the Committee'. The Engineer's Office at Swindon was, as a result of this, tasked with providing the information by the Company Accountant's Office at Paddington.

These findings were to highlight a problem insomuch as an excessive amount of water seemed to be used. The Locomotive and Carriage Department at Swindon were asked to provide details of water they used. Their reply of 6th November 1876 indicated that water was required by four engines stationed at Devizes, viz:

Passenger	Goods
No.483 Tender Class	No.1147 Tank Class
No.613 Tank Class	No.800 Tender Class

No doubt the engines working trains between Reading and Devizes (49½ miles) take water at Savernake and Newbury, the intermediate stations between Reading and Devizes. The Traffic Dept. is supplied at Devizes Station for 2 w.c.s and 1 urinal with 3 stalls and at the Savernake Station there is exactly the same supply and for which this Dept. has received credit (as agreed in 1868) as follows:

| Devizes | £10 per annum |
| Savernake | £ 6 per annum |

Mr Beasley proposed on 27th July last to reduce the amount for both stations from £16 to £12.10.0d.

As a result of this memo, a representative was sent to investigate why more water was being used at Devizes station than would be required by the four engines taking water. His initial discovery was that in one 24-hour period, 17,748 gallons of water was used of which it was worked out that 8,174 gallons were going to waste. With a search being made for the source of the waste, it was found that the ball was off the inlet valve of the cistern supplying the station urinals and that the water was running away full bore through a 2-inch waste pipe. When the fault was remedied, and with an estimated 4,000 gallons used weekly for the four boiler wash-outs, the station consumption was considered to be at an acceptable level.

In a letter from the Swindon Locomotive & Carriage Department dated 9th August 1877, it was proposed to 'do away with Devizes as a watering station as soon as the water cranes are fixed at Trowbridge, except on special occasions'.

In 1877 a visit from the Board of Trade had resulted in reminders to the GWR of certain outstanding provisions which, unless they were actioned, could result in the closure of the line. Some examples included gradient boards and work to the shelter on the Devizes station downside island platform. By 1878 considerable trackwork with sidings was in evidence.

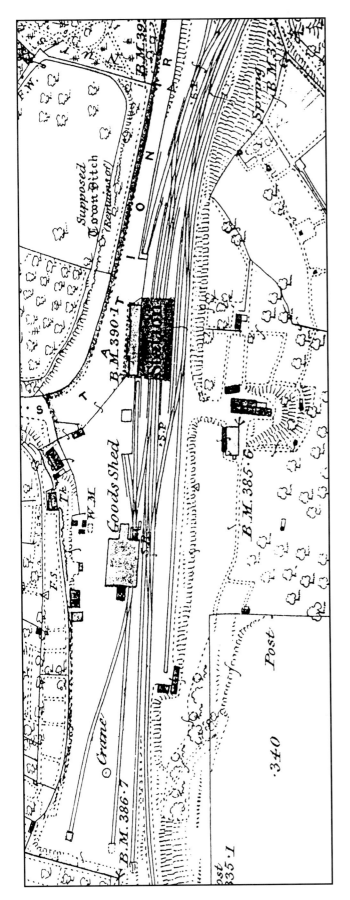

The Ordnance Survey 6" to 1 mile map for 1886 (left) shows a crane in the goods yard. The crane was a two-gear, 18-inch radius model with 6-ton capacity (FM No. 3270) and was additional to the 30-cwt one in the shed. The weighbridge and office at this time was situated opposite the goods shed office near the embankment at the back of the yard. The 7'6" x 5' office was of timber and the 10' x 6'11" weighbridge was of 7-ton capacity. Three years later in June 1889 an iron latticework footbridge with canopy had been completed between the two platforms with each staircase descending in the direction of train travel. In addition, the passenger waiting facilities on the down platform were improved.

On 31st July 1894 the GWR obtained an Act for a line from Stert to Westbury and the doubling of the line from Hungerford to Stert. This was to return Devizes to being practically a branch-line station again and steps to have the line doubled through the town came up against GWR financial restrictions. In 1897 the War Office and Devizes Borough Council opposed a line to Salisbury from east of Devizes but the GWR dropped the idea anyway.

Construction of the new line to Westbury commenced in 1897, but because of engineering difficulties, the intended junction at Stert was changed to Patney, 1½ miles further east. The new line became operational on 29th July 1900.

Devizes station in the meanwhile had been receiving improvements. Messrs A.Jackaman & Son, contractors from Slough, were awarded a GWR contract on 16th December 1895 to provide improved goods yard accommodation and other works for which they had tendered at £1,225. The contract allowed primarily for excavating from the cutting and formation of sidings, the construction of two replacement cattle pens with metalled access roadway, together with a wharf and carriage shoot and the taking down and re-erecting of a timber coal pen, in which coal for station use was stored. Ron Church, the foreman for Hinxman's the coal merchant, tells that fires in the station itself were only allowed between the Devizes Autumn Fair on 20th October and the Spring Fair on 20th April. If the coal allocation for the station was all used before April, he could expect a visit from the station staff. The December 1895 contract also made provision for water services, drainage and new fencing. The work was completed in the first half of 1896, following which some additional sidings were put in to accommodate 70 trucks. Existing sidings were altered and provision made to serve the cattle pens and wharf. This siding was also used as a headshunt when the up line was not available for shunting purposes. Work was completed later in the year at a cost of £2,160. At the same time as these works, a new signal cabin was erected at the east end up side of the main station building to replace the two existing ones. The box, measuring 30' x 12' and built of blue brick and timber, was operational in 1897 and was completed at a cost of £858.16s.1d.

From the up platform looking west, the yard line to the right with the goods shed and its office in the background, with its later additional upper storey.

The goods shed and offices from the end of the down platform, with the tall yard lamp shown fitted with a later top, c.1955. (I.D.Beale)

The young Bill Brooks as a lad porter in 1917, standing by the cart weighbridge near the embankment at the back of the yard. (B.Brooks)

The exterior of the station and road-side view seen in this c.1907 postcard. Note the steam railmotor and the replacement signalbox on the up platform. The smoking chimney suggests the date was between 20th October and 20th April.

The view from the east end of the platform following work to extend the station towards the tunnel, c.1908. (B.Keepence)

The signalbox entrance steps can be seen on the up platform underneath the 1910 footbridge. (Lens of Sutton)

Station improvements continued again in 1907, with the extension of the up and down platforms and the widening of the down platform. Outside the goods shed, provision was made for a new platform and verandah, and internal alterations were made as well. A lamp hut and other small buildings were removed and repositioned and parts of the permanent way were renewed and extended. The 1908 account for this work shows the cost to have been £3,994.19s. A new 8-inch water main from the hillside water tank was laid in December 1907, coming under the goods yard and sidings to a position opposite the cattle pen between the up and down main, where it ran east in line with the extended 170-yard curved up platform. In conjunction with this, the two existing water cranes which had previously been positioned just off the ends of the platforms were moved onto the platform extensions and provided with new jibs and 6-inch drains between the tracks to take away any excess water. The costs of this provision for the Locomotive Dept amounted to £300.18s. The crane was seldom used by drivers in the down direction, as a 4,000-gallon tender, as used on through train engines, when filled at Newbury, and with light steaming, could reach Bath, if not Bristol. The 1907 improvements required signalling renewals costing £719.17s., and telegraph works at £88.11s.3d.

Construction of a six-stall stable for the GWR Horse Department took place in 1908, the contract being let to Gilbert Brain of Bristol. The building was erected in the goods yard, just below the water tower on the site occupied by the offices and stores of F.Bird & Sons, coal merchants. These buildings were moved to a position between the new stable and the station approach road. The stable, measuring 52'3" x 19'6", was built of red brick with a pitched, slated roof. Inside the stables at the east end was a provender store and at the opposite end there was an external manure pit. The building's internal works were limewhited and the lighting points were fuelled by gas. At this time a contract was also placed with Gilbert Brain to provide the station with a newspaper kiosk.

September 1909 saw the authorisation of further station improvements which involved the construction of verandahs over each platform in place of the existing overall roof which by now required renewal. At the same time a new and larger footbridge, with a corrugated asbestos roof,

The water crane on the up platform, c.1964. (J.Gander)

was built in place of the existing one. The replacement had the staircase on the up platform reversed so that it now faced the station buildings. A general waiting room, lavatory accommodation for men and a separate ladies' room on the down side replaced the existing waiting shed. New fencing, gates, lighting and signalling work were also included. The contract was advertised in *The Railway Gazette* for 10th June 1910 and let to Mr W.J.Bloxham. These passenger station improvements were completed during the following year. The track layout had again also been altered by this time.

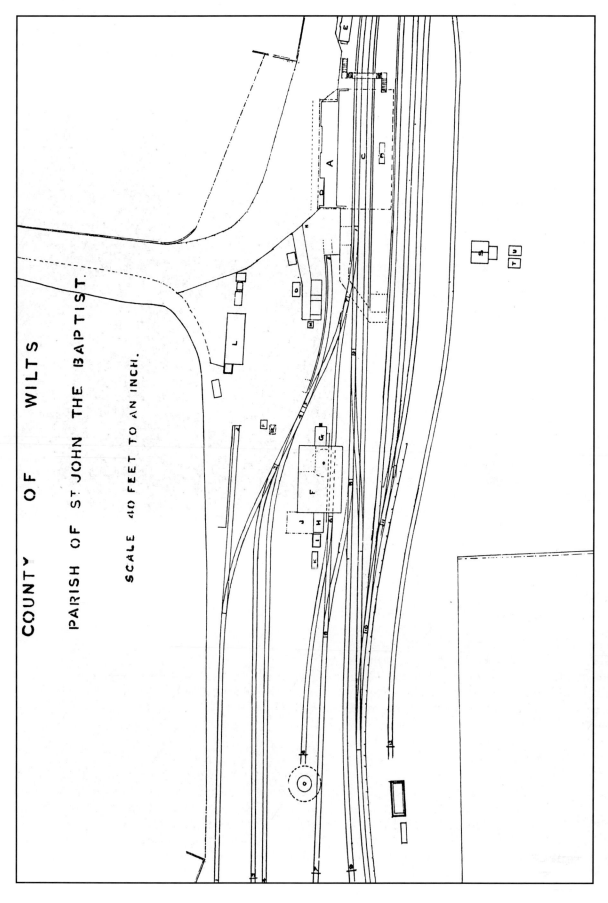

COUNTY OF WILTS

PARISH OF St JOHN THE BAPTIST.

SCALE 40 FEET TO AN INCH.

A GWR map showing the layout of the station at a date between 1897, when the replacement signalbox (marked E on the map) was built just east of the footbridge, and 1909, when the footbridge itself was replaced. The original bridge, with the steps on the up platform facing east, can be seen, as can the line of the overall roof. The 1908 stables are also clearly marked (L). The semi-detached building south of the domestic goods yard may have housed railway offices.

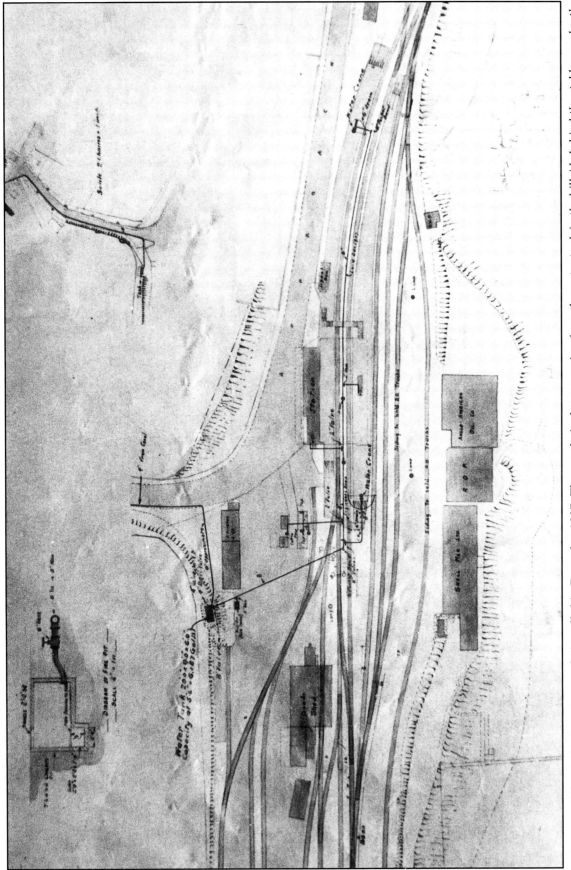

A diagram of the station's water supply installed in December 1907. The supply is shown coming from the water tank in the hillside behind the stables, under the goods yard and siding and then east between the up and down main lines. The position of the two water cranes is clearly shown. Various later additions have been made to the map: the inset at the top left of the fire pit, added in 1940 and sited just below the water tank; Silcock's 1933 warehouse, just west of the goods shed; the pre-1958 depot of coal merchant A.Hinxman at the east end of the stables; and the areas south of the downside goods yard which are shown as occupied by Shell Mex, Russian Oil Products and the Anglo American Oil Company, all of whom arrived at various dates from 1916 onwards.

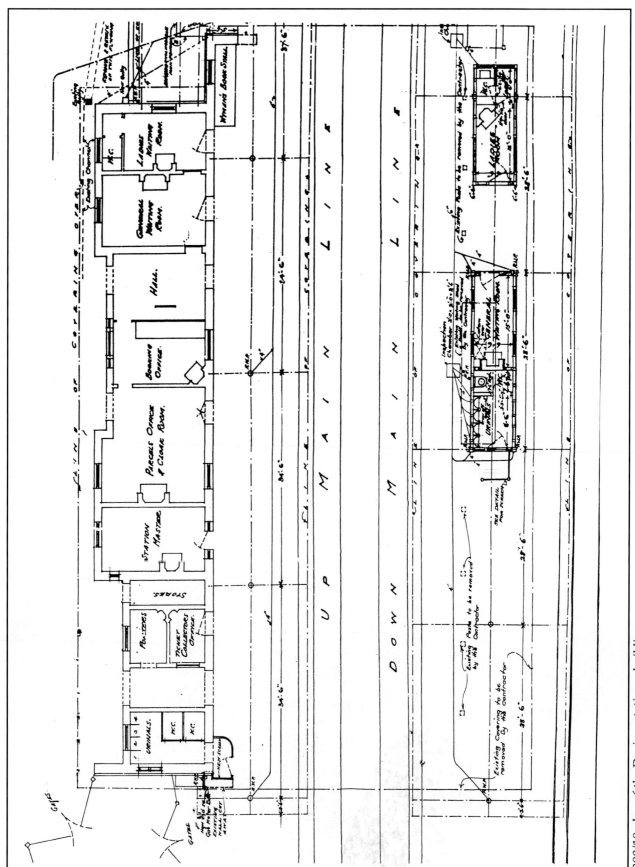

1909/10 plan of the Devizes station rebuilding.

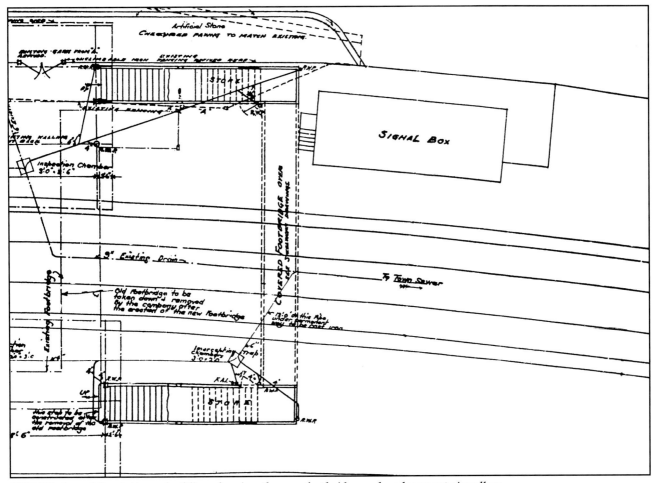

1909/10 plan of the station rebuilding showing the new footbridge and replacement signalbox.

A view of the up platform, looking east, with a lone staff member walking towards the signalbox, c.1964. (J.Gander)

The 1910 covered footbridge viewed from Station Road, c.1964. (J.Gander)

The footbridge approach to the island platform, with the replacement signalbox clearly visible, c.1964. (J.Gander)

Track level view looking east to the end of the station building, showing the nameboard and Gentlemen's W.C., with the island platform on the right.

A view of the island platform looking east. (J.Gander)

A Pannier Tank leaving Devizes for Patney & Chirton in the 1920s. Note the half-harp lamp on the right. (Rokeby collection, National Monuments Record Centre)

A postcard view of the island platform showing the new footbridge and a station lamp. The latter is at 45º to the platform face for easier identification from approaching trains. A number of people are awaiting a train on the up platform.

A 1920s view westward to the station, showing the station approach road, fully extended platforms and square post starter signals. (Mowat collection)

A lineside view of the station buildings showing the water crane on the west end of the island platform, c.1956. (I.D.Beale)

In this April 1966 view, the former oil company building in the downside yard can be seen to the left of the weighbridge in the cattle dock. The notice on the building indicates it had been used by Hinxman's, the coal merchants, who were taken over by F.J.Reeves in November 1962. (D.J.Hyde)

The brick office and 20-ton weighbridge which replaced the old wooden one in 1921. (J.Gander)

In 1931, a 1,000-gallon underground petrol tank was provided for refuelling the railway lorries. This was sited in the up yard, at the end of the sidings near the level crossing. During 1933 a new warehouse was erected near the existing goods shed. It was built for a cost of £283.16s.8d. and a rent of 15 guineas per annum was charged. The building was of pre-cast concrete, 42' x 17'6", with end walls and pitched roof of corrugated iron. It was used by the animal feed firm of Silcock. During 1934 the complete track between Patney and Holt was renewed. In 1938 the second weighbridge was replaced by another of 20-ton capacity, 16' x 8', GW No.5198. Next to this stood a standard 13' x 8' corrugated-iron lampman's hut. Garage accommodation, which was believed to be a corrugated-iron shelter in the downside yard, was provided in 1937 at a cost of £103.

The stables were no longer used for the railway horses which were now kept at the rear of *The Old Crown* in New Park Street and previously to that had been stabled at the *White Lion* in Northgate Street. The stables at the station were then used to store cement for J.Bibby & Sons and the adjoining galvanized sheds were occupied by Hinxman & Company, coal and builder's merchants.

With the onset of war again, the GWR thought it prudent to provide water for fire-fighting purposes and in 1940 built a fire pit in the upside goods yard. The pit measured 7' x 4' x 4', was made of concrete and fitted with a 6-inch valve which was connected to the existing 8-inch main by a T-junction just below the water tank at the west end of the former stables. An 8-inch fire hydrant was installed midway along the up and island platforms, between the two sets of rails.

The military were provided with a Railway Transport Office on the up platform during the war, built at the footbridge end of the station building. An exit way in the railings to the roadway was made at this point to allow military personnel and prisoners of war to leave the platform without passing through the station buildings. The railway needed extra office accommodation because of the increased traffic and this was overcome by using camp coaches which, during 1944, required repairs to the blackout curtains at the windows.

Track alterations were authorised on 1st November 1948 and relaying included the replacement of two single connections with one of three-way, together with slewing of the permanent way. The cost of this work was £903.

An office, 30'6" x 15'6", for the permanent way Inspector was completed in 1951 at the east end of the up platform. This was brick-built with a tiled, pitched roof. It had gas heating and was lit by Westminster lamps. The construction, furniture and telephone installation amounted to £839.7s.5d.

The cattle dock and goods yard had separate gated entrances from Station Road, as seen here beyond the Austin A30 outside the station building in the mid-1950s. The newer brick building beneath the canopy at the eastern end was the rail transport office (RTO) for services personnel. (Lens of Sutton)

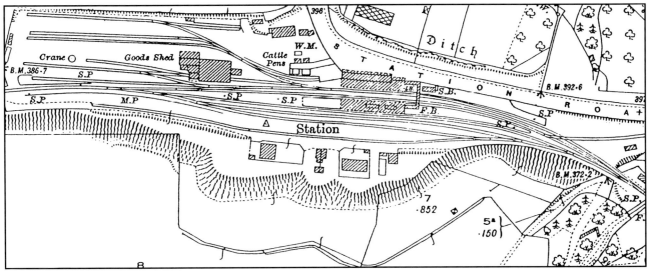

The O.S. map of 1923. Note the changes from earlier plans. The cattle dock and weighbridge area, the 'Bear' siding at the east end, signal and platform lengths are all in their final condition, remaining thus until closure.

A short siding ran past the front of this small office, leaving the down main and crossing the up main line just before the tunnel. It turned away sharply north-east and ended abruptly against an embankment above which Station Road led to the Market Place and the *Bear Hotel*, which had a stable yard and rear entrance just above. It was inevitably known as the 'Bear' siding. As may be noticed in early plans its curvature varied over the life of the station, and it may be conjectured that this was the original proposed route into a tunnel when connection to the B&H extension was planned. As well as the *Bear Hotel*, the Corn Exchange is also directly in line with this route, which may have caused the fresh proposal for an alternative route under the castle grounds. After use by the oil company, Russian Oil Products, the siding was later used by the permanent way department. Between this siding and the office, District Permanent Way Inspector Bill Noakes kept a tidy rose garden bordered with Snow in Summer (*Cerastium*). At the rear of the office was a small timber store outside which stood a frame support-ing three fire buckets. A series of other small sheds was located in this area of the station. On the east side of the Bear siding was what was possibly the top part of the original signalbox which stood at the mouth of the tunnel. It was made of wood, 19'2" x 11'8", with a slate roof, and was used as the permanent way Inspector's office until the replacement was built in 1951. Afterwards it was used by the signal lineman. Adjoining it was a further black wooden storage cabin in which the permanent way trolley was kept. On the base

of the former signalbox at the tunnel entrance stood a similar cabin, 23'6" x 10'6", which was used by the permanent way staff.

On the station during the 1950s, Devizes children crossing between the up and down platforms by way of the footbridge, recall kicking the green enamel advertisement plates on the risers of the stairs. The plates advertised Sloper's, the local furniture store. Other advertisements remembered on the station at this period were for 'Stephen's Ink - One Big Blot' and on the waiting room wall, 'Come to Sunny Torquay'.

Porter Jack Allen remembers that the station safe was broken into at this time and the contents stolen.

An additional trader's store in the up goods yard was completed in 1956. Like the adjoining Silcock's store of 1933, it was built of pre-cast concrete with a pitched, corrugated-asbestos roof. The store was elevated by a series of concrete octagonal piers presumably to assist in the prevention of entry by rodents as it was used by Bibby's for animal feed storage. The construction costs amounted to £1127.9s.3d. Also in 1956 it was necessary for the siding to be slewed with the provision of stop boards at a cost of £14 and £5 respectively. Prior to the provision of this store, but on the same site, Bibby's had been using six out-of-service iron mink vans, marked with white crosses, which were usable for storage needs. These later became redundant and were re-railed at a cost of £10.10s.1d. The station also suffered generally from a lack of storage facilities and the following are various orders issued from Swindon to help the situation:

107

19/9/45   Sundry Order No 4283
Prepare condemned covered goods vans
Nos. 8329, 58459, 58784 & 69285 for Goods
Dept. use as storage accommodation at Devizes.

24/3/48   Sundry Order No 4376
Prepare storage van 205492 from Llanidloes
and despatch to Devizes.

24/5/48   Sundry Order No 5038
Prepare condemned covered goods No. 8954
as storage van for use at Devizes.

July 1957 brought the centenary of the station
and to commemorate the event a flower bed was
formed on the Patney end of the up platform.
Flower beds were known to have been on the
platform since at least 1921 and they continued to
be an attractive feature of the station with goods
guard Sid Woolacott and both signalmen Rowley

Reeves and Bert Clack taking a pride in looking
after them up until their retirement in 1965. Bert
Clack specialised in growing roses.

The station lighting was by gas lamps throughout
its existence, although a scheme was considered in
the 1960s to convert to electricity. Lamp locations
altered over the years; at one time the down yard
was provided with two and the up yard had
two, one at each end of the goods shed. In its latter
years the island platform had five, the up platform
four, of which one was suspended beneath the
footbridge and one on the signalbox. Just off the
up platform at the west end, near a set of wooden
steps to the cattle dock, was another. There was
one on the cattle dock behind the weighbridge
office and one inside the yard gates leading
towards the cattle dock.

The original station telephone number was
Devizes 14 and when the goods office was connected
at a later date, its number was Devizes 508.

The Bear siding curves away to the left passed the recently-constructed permanent way office on the left where the Inspector is tending his flower beds, c.1955. The telegraph linesman's hut may be seen in the background, just before the tunnel entrance. It is highly likely that this is the top of the former east signalbox, replaced when the platform box was built. (I.D.Beale)

At around the same time as the previous photograph, this view from the up platform, when compared with the 1908 view from the same position (see page 92), shows the development and changes. Note the signal has a metal arm, although on a wooden square post, soon to be replaced (see page 185). (J.Spencer-Gilks)

On 31st March 1956 a Castle arrives with the 3.15pm Newbury train and passes the permanent way siding where a private owner coal wagon has been left by the telegraph lineman's hut. The black timber building housed the permanent way gangers' trolley and equipment. (D.Lovelock)

A similar view, this time taken from the tunnel mouth in February 1966. The up main is all that is left of the track with both the down main and 'Bear' siding having been lifted. (T.Gaylard)

The panorama from the western bracket signal looking east to the station. From left to right, note: the water tank on the cliff behind the yard 'back road'; the new warehouse with Iron Mink vans marked with white crosses indicating their restricted use (in this case as stores for the yard); the entire loop serving the goods shed; the two platform lines and the island platform; the down yard loops; the service road; and on the extreme right, the buildings now used for coal traffic but previously used by the oil companies. (I.D.Beale)

Passenger Services

As can be seen in the timetable produced for the opening services on 1st July 1857 (see the next page), the first up train of the day left Devizes for Trowbridge at 7.45am, its journey time being 25 minutes. The 9.40am departure however, seems to take 20 minutes and the 7.30pm, 22 minutes. The 7.30pm departure on Sunday on the other hand took 30 minutes to arrive at Trowbridge. Similar differences can be seen with the down trains but what is surprising is that their times are comparable with the up trains whereas with the climb up Caen Hill it would be expected that the journey would take slightly longer. Passengers wishing to travel to London from Devizes had to take the train to Trowbridge for a connecting service but it is interesting to note that the services from Paddington via Swindon, Chippenham and

Melksham were through trains to Devizes. This necessitated on arrival at Holt, which was without a station at that time, the engine running around its train to pull it up the branch tender first. Again a variance can be seen in the timings between Melksham and Devizes; whilst the norm seems to be 22 minutes, it is doubtful whether this was achieved very often.

With the timetable published in the *Devizes & Wiltshire Gazette* was a notice indicating:

The RAILWAY TO DEVIZES is now OPEN for the Conveyance of Passengers and Parcels. Full particulars as to fares, times, etc., can be obtained at any of the Stations on the Line.

Of course Devizes was the only station on the line at that time. Other notices indicated that the *Bear Inn*, 'by appointment, G.W.R.', was the

GREAT WESTERN RAILWAY.
OPENING TO DEVIZES.
TIME TABLE, July 1st, 1857   *London Time is kept at all the Stations.*

DOWN TRAINS.

STATIONS:			1st, 2d and 3d Cla.	1st, 2d and 3d Cla.	1st and 2d Class.	Exprs. 1st and 2d Cla.	1st and 2d Class.	1st and 2d Class.	1st and 2d Class.	Exprs. 1st 2d Cla.	1st, 2d and 3d Cla.	1st, 2d and 3d Cla.	1st, 2d and 3d Cla.	1st and 2d Class.
			A.M.	A.M.	A.M.	A.M.	A.M.	P.M.	P.M.	P.M.	A.M.	A.M.	A.M.	P.M.
PADDINGTON	...	Depart	...	6 0	...	9 40	11 0	1 0	...	4 50	...	...	8 0	2 0
Reading	...	"	...	7 10	...	10 27	12 0	2 20	...	5 37	...	...	9 50	3 21
Didcot	...	"	...	7 55	...	10 54	12 27	3 2	...	6 5	...	...	10 45	4 3
Swindon	...	"	...	8 53	...	11 40	1 25	4 10	...	6 48	...	...	12 30	5 10
Chippenham	...	"	...	9 35	...	12 10	2 0	4 45	...	7 22	...	...	5 45	5 45
Melksham	...	"	...	9 53	..	12 28	2 18	5 3	...	7 40	...	...	6 5	6 5
BRISTOL	...	Depart	6 45	...	10 0		1 20	3 30	...	6 10	7 0	...	5 10	5 10
Bath	...	"	7 15	...	10 40		1 50	4 0	...	6 40	7 30	...	5 40	5 40
Trowbridge	...	Arrive	7 50	...	11 15		2 25	...	...	...	8 5	...	6 15	6 15
WEYMOUTH	...	Depart	6 10	...	9 10		12 30	...	4 40	...	...	8 10	...	...
Salisbury	...	"	6 55	...	10 15		1 5	...	5 25	...	7 5	...	...	...
Trowbridge	...	Arrive	8 20	...	11 38		3 0	...	6 52	...	8 30	10 55	...	...
TROWBRIDGE	...	Depart	8 30	...	11 40		3 5	...	6 55	...	8 35	10 55	6 25	6 25
DEVIZES	...	Arrive	9 0	10 15	12 5	12 50	3 30	5 25	7 20	8 6	9 0	11 30	6 55	6 55

UP TRAINS.

STATIONS.			1st, 2d and 3d Cla.	1st, 2d and 3d Cla.	1st and 2d Class.	1st and 2d Class.	Exprs. 1st and 2d Cla.	1st and 2d Class.	1st and 2d Class.	1st and 2d Class.	1st, 2d and 3d Cla.	1st, 2d and 3d Cla.	1st, 2d and 3d Cla.
			A.M.	A.M.	A.M.	P.M.	P.M.	P.M.	P.M.	P.M.	A.M.	A.M.	P.M.
DEVIZES	...	Depart	7 45	9 40	10 45	12 15	1 55	4 45	6 20	7 30	7 30	10 40	5 45
Trowbridge	...	Arrive	8 10	10 5	11 10	12 40	2 20	5 10	6 45	7 52	8 0		6 10
TROWBRIDGE	...	Depart	...	10 5	11 15	12 40	2 25	5 13	...	7 52	8 5	...	6 15
Salisbury	...	"	...	...	12 45	2 0	4 0	...	...	9 15	...	...	7 50
Weymouth	...	Arrive	...	12 40		3 5	4 50	7 45	...	10 5	10 30	...	9 5
TROWBRIDGE	...	Depart	8 20	...	11 38		3 0	...	6 52		8 30	...	8 30
Bath	...	"	8 55	...	12 10		3 35	...	7 30		9 6	...	9 6
Bristol	...	Arrive	9 35	...	12 45		4 10	...	7 55		9 40	...	9 40
TROWBRIDGE	...	Depart	8 13	...	11 45		2 51	...	6 47		10 55		
Melksham	...	"	8 36	...	11 58		3 7	...	7 0		11 8		
Chippenham	...	"	8 50	...	12 30		3 30	...	7 10		11 30		
Swindon	...	"	9 15	...	1 8		4 5	...	7 50		12 15		
Didcot	...	"	9 55	...	2 15		4 45	...	8 45		1 55		
Reading	...	"	10 30	...	2 52			...	9 18		2 50		
PADDINGTON	...	Arrive	11 10	...	3 50		6 0	...	10 15		5 0		

GREAT WESTERN RAILWAY.
OPENING TO DEVIZES.

NOTICE is hereby given, that the RAILWAY to DEVIZES is now OPEN for the Conveyance of Passengers and Parcels.

Full particulars as to fares, times, &c., can be obtained at any of the Stations on the Line.

July 1st, 1857.

BEAR INN, DEVIZES.

BY APPOINTMENT. G. W. R.—Office for receiving and delivering of Parcels from this date.

No charge for Booking.

2nd July, 1857.

THE STAR COACH continues to leave the BEAR INN Devizes, daily at 11.

	Inside.	Outside.
Fares to Marlborough	5s.	3s.
„ to Hungerford	6s.	4s.

2nd July, 1857.

The timetable of 1st July 1857 published in the Devizes and Wiltshire Gazette.

Luggage from Devizes station was conveyed by the GWR horse and cart to the Bear Hotel in the Market Place. (D.H.Morris)

office for receiving and delivering of parcels and the *Star* coach continued to leave the *Bear Inn* daily at 11.00am. Fares to Marlborough and Hungerford were, inside 5s. and 6s. respectively and outside 3s. and 4s.

Excursion trains from Devizes were to prove popular over the years especially those to the seaside town of Weymouth. The very first of these took place on Wednesday 15th July at 6s. for 1st Class and 4s. for others. The Mayor of Devizes decreed it a public holiday and requested that shops be closed for the day. Over 1,000 people travelled in 23 coaches and were accompanied by the band of the Royal Wiltshire Militia who played on Weymouth station platform as the day trippers left the train. For many Devizes people, this was not just their first experience of train travel but also the first time they had seen the sea. The train was seen off by crowds of people who packed the station, the adjoining yards and the embankments for a mile along the line. The train left the station with considerable difficulty at 7.45am, the time of

the scheduled service to Trowbridge. The arrival time in Weymouth was slightly after 11.00am. A memorable day in glorious sunshine was had by the party who were made welcome by their Weymouth hosts. The return journey started at 7.15pm and, hauled by three engines, eventually arrived safely at Devizes, where once again crowds of people welcomed home the travellers.

As previously indicated in the Holt chapter, after the initial euphoria and when the GWR found the Devizes service was not receiving the use it had anticipated, a number of trains were cut from the timetable.

As from 1st September 1858, the timetable allowed for trains stopping at the newly-opened station in Seend. By 1879 the horse-drawn coach services and the canal were both badly hit by the competition from the railway. Devizes was once served by as many as 50 coaches. By 1859 it had just two, the *Aurora* and the *Star,* and these ceased in November 1862 with the opening of the Berks & Hants Extension Railway. Omnibuses and flies

Castle Class 4084 Aberystwyth Castle with an up Bristol to Paddington train in 1940. The first coach, a 'concertina' all third, is being used as a strengthening vehicle due to extra passengers. (D.Seaton)

Star Class 4043 Prince Henry passes Pannier Tank 3780 shunting in the shed line. This was a 12.22pm arrival from Bristol to Reading in 1940. The small building in the background beneath the cliff was the station paint store. (D.Seaton)

Father Christmas outside Devizes station to meet the children in 1963. The station footbridge is in the background. (D.H.Morris)

Father Christmas was still managing to arrive in the town by train and was met at the station by a pony and cart, on which he was driven around the town, scattering bright new half-pennies, before taking up residence at Charles Sloper's Christmas Bazaar.

To a number of the regular engine drivers, the Branch was known as the 'Suicide Line' because of the number of patients from the Mental Hospital at Pans Lane who took their own lives under the wheels of a train. This invariably occurred by a stile at Longfields, which was the line's nearest point to the hospital. Funeral Directors J.J.Stevens & Sons were known to keep a suitable box tucked into the base of the embankment at this spot.

Devizes porter, Jack Allen, remembers an incident in the 1950s which caused a delay to the 4.43pm to Bristol. The train was the 2.35pm from Paddington, which, on this occasion, failed to arrive at Devizes until 5.00pm. A lady's handbag was found on the engine, having belonged to a female patient from the Roundway Psychiatric Hospital who had committed suicide when struck by the engine as it passed through Stert. Jack Allen and a policeman went back to the scene of the death on the shunting engine to retrieve the body. This was one of a number of incidents to occur on this stretch of the line over the years. A similar tragedy a few years earlier had involved No.5423,

with driver H.J.Bates and fireman F.C.Bailey, on the 10.50am Devizes to Patney & Chirton passenger service.

The 1950s were also the time for the popular 'London Night Out'. A 4.30pm excursion to London could be taken, to see a West End show and have a meal, before racing back to Paddington to catch the late train home. On the August Bank Holiday Monday of the station's centenary year in 1957, seaside excursions were on offer, Weston-super-Mare being one of the destinations, departing:

Devizes	7.55am	11s.6d.
Seend	8.05am	10s.9d.

Sudden cuts in train services were implemented during 1958, and the starting points of some services began to be altered. Following the summer of 1960, the 6.00pm from Paddington was withdrawn, and from September 1961, the 2.35pm went as well, which meant that Devizes had lost its last weekday express from London and through train to Bristol.

Serious concern was now growing locally because of the diminishing service which the railway was providing, and, as a consequence, the Devizes RDC held a meeting with British Railways in Bristol in October 1961. This proved fruitless however, and the committee was told that not only were services being reduced, but also that closure was a distinct possibility within a few years.

5974 Wallsworth Hall, wrong road at Devizes station with a Weymouth excursion in the late 1950s. In the background are Hinxman's premises and lorry. Note the catch points and the cattle dock line with its wash-down facilities. (F.Merrett)

A selection of tickets from Devizes station. (D.H.Morris)

Pannier Tank No.6408 with a two-coach train outside the signalbox in 1961. (D.H.Morris)

Due to a land subsidence between Patney and Chirton and Lavington stations on the main Paddington to West of England route, it has been necessary to close the down line and impose a speed restriction of 15 m.p.h. on the up line. The distance affected is approximately 200 feet and it is anticipated that 1,000 tons of filling, mainly stone, will be required in the early stages to restore the 50 ft. high embankment carrying the lines.

The cause of the slip is thought to be the exceptionally wet weather of last Winter and remedial works have been carried out on the site for some time past in order to maintain the timetable of summer services on this heavily occupied section of track. Recently, however, the rate of earth settlement increased and in the early morning of 21st August a slip occurred which necessitated action to restrict the movement of trains in the area.

Photographs by courtesy of B.B.C.

Restoration work will continue night and day and the techniques developed by the Engineer to deal with this work will ensure the quickest possible restoration of services on both lines, although a restriction of speed will apply over the affected area for some time.

The work will proceed with a minimum interference to traffic but is, of course, dependent on the stability of the embankment after the stone filling has been carried out.

Alternative routes for passenger and freight trains are available via Devizes and also via Swindon and Melksham. The former is only a single line not normally open during the night but special arrangements have been made to keep this section open throughout the 24 hours as the principal diversionary route. Owing to the severity of the slip, however, it will be necessary in the initial stages also to occupy the up line for intermittent periods in order that the stone filling can be tipped from wagons at the site. When this takes place the longer alternative diversionary route via Swindon and Melksham will be brought into use for trains normally running over the main West of England line.

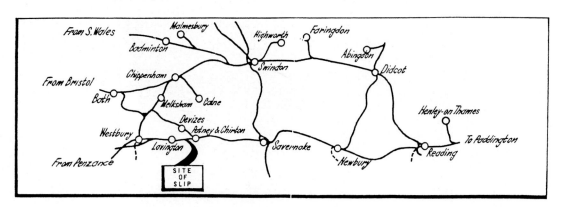

Delays are bound to continue until normal working is resumed and the inconvenience to passengers is regretted. In the meantime our staff will be ready to give you the latest information and assist in every possible way.

An event took place on the night of 22nd August 1961 which the people of Devizes, and, in particular the railway staff, hoped would secure the future of the branch. A serious embankment slip occurred on the main line near Lavington, just east of Crookwood signalbox, at 83 miles, 40 chains. The embankment on this stretch of line, running through gault clay, had been a source of trouble over a good many years. A slip had occurred soon after it was constructed in 1900. At this point the 45-foot-high bank has a slope over 120 feet long from top to bottom, with a stream passing under it in a 6-foot brick arch culvert. On this occasion a bog had formed upstream from the culvert, on the downside of the line, against the toe of the bank. The section of bank had shown signs of movement for some time, and it had been decided to remedy this by grouting. Work had started in May but stopped in August, owing to a plant breakdown. Considerable movement of the down line was evident, resulting in a 5mph speed restriction. This culminated on 22nd August with the down line being closed at 4.00am after movement of some 10 feet, leaving the track suspended over a 180-foot length. The up line was closed except for trains bringing ashes and stone. A circuit of 'Mermaid' side-tipping wagons was arranged between Frome Quarry and the site. In excess of 10,000 tons of stone, ash and fly was needed. Obviously this total closure seriously affected the busy summer timetables.

It was to last for several weeks with all trains diverted via Swindon, Melksham and Holt Junction, and in particular over the Devizes Branch (see the BR (Western Region) notice opposite). The *Wiltshire Gazette* of 24th August wrote of the claims of people living in homes close to the line at Pans Lane, who were suffering sleepless nights from the continued rumble of passing trains. It was reported that the usual 16 passenger and 4 freight trains over the branch each day had more than doubled. Tuesday of that week was believed to be the first time in living memory that the *Cornish Riviera Express* had passed through the town. Other crack expresses seen were the *Royal Duchy*, the *Torbay Express* and the *Mayflower*. To cope with the increased traffic the signalbox was once more 24-hour manned, having for a number of years been closed from 9.30pm to 5.10am during weekdays.

The branch, of course, was unable to accept 'double red' King Class engines because of the weight restrictions on some of the bridges, so, for any of these in use, it was necessary for them to be routed via Swindon. Another problem was the 12-coach length of some expresses. This was too long for the loop at Devizes station, which caused operational difficulties, especially where trains crossed there. The main down line between Patney and Lavington was re-opened to traffic on Monday 25th September (five weeks after its closure), the up line having been re-opened the previous Friday.

Warship D837 and the Cornish Riviera passing the permanent way siding after the Lavington landslip in August 1961. (D.Lovelock)

A Warship with the Mayflower, passing the well-kept gardens in front of the permanent way Inspector's office in the summer of 1961. (F.Cutting)

D822 waits with an up through train in August 1961, with an LNER coach as first vehicle. Note the great excitement caused by the diversion. (D.Lovelock)

2-6-2 Class 4500 No.4567 shunting the Holt to Devizes pick-up goods in Devizes station in the summer of 1961. (D.Lovelock)

Train-spotting at Devizes increased in popularity after the landslide closed the main line. Identified boys in c.1961 include Eric Meadows, John Webb, ? Hayward, ? Roberts-Phare, Leon Smith, Garth Webb, Jimmy Hislop, Kevin Dew, Anthony Mitchell, Jeffrey Musiol, David Woodruff, Brian Normington, Michael Smith, Peter Escott, ? Merritt, Peter Bishop, Terry Williams, Barry King. (Wiltshire Gazette & Herald)

Another group of trainspotters sitting on the old GWR bench amongst the neat flowerbeds by the platform gate entrance form the centrepiece for this happy scene, c.1959. (D.H.Morris)

Further cuts in service were introduced from 5th March 1962, one of the most damaging being the closure of the branch on Sundays. This had a serious effect not just on the public but, in particular, on military personnel returning to the camps of Salisbury Plain and also on the station staff.

The local paper reported that the cuts involved 'four trains, including the popular 6.30pm to Paddington. Station-master, Mr E.J.W.Major, said it meant that station workers would lose a considerable amount of their earnings'. The cuts as a whole lost the branch a total of nine through trains connecting with Reading and Paddington. It was apparent that BR's policy in cutting out the well-used services was their covert way of making the line unviable, resulting in inevitable closure.

The branch in its time carried many of the famous, including British and American Generals during the war years; Sir Winston Churchill; Royalty; and even The Beatles. On Saturday 19th October 1963, another famous visitor was 4-6-2 *Flying Scotsman*, now preserved, and a rake of ten Pullman coaches on a 21st anniversary Ian Allan Rail Tour. It carried 400 enthusiasts on an excursion from Paddington to Ilfracombe, together with Mr Alan Peglar, the owner of the engine. British Rail had taken it out of service in January of that year. Crowds of people had gathered at Devizes to see the visitor which pulled in 30 minutes late, and at Holt Junction some 300-400 witnessed the single-line staff handed over to the signalman as the train slowed. The tour transferred to the Southern Region for its return to London Waterloo.

By the summer of 1965, the branch and its services were almost dead. With the Devizes signalbox closed, one single line meandered between Holt and Patney. An example of BR's apparent aim to lose passengers was the 9.46am Westbury to Patney being held at Devizes station for 24 minutes from 10.16am to 10.40am, which effectively prevented it making a connection at Patney with the 10.28am Westbury to Newbury. This train would leave Patney at 10.45am with the Devizes train pulling in a few minutes later.

Much attention was paid to the Flying Scotsman, ex-LNER No.4472, on Saturday 19th October 1963, hauling a train of Pullman coaches on an Ian Allan Rail Tour from Paddington to Ilfracombe. (F.Merrett)

DMU service B2 in the main platform with a freight train of mineral wagons in the background.

Diesel Multiple Units (DMUs) had been introduced in the early 1960s. When they became a permanent feature and steam locomotives no longer needed to run around their coaches, the passing loop in Devizes station was removed. This coincided with the closure of the signalbox, so Devizes ceased to exist as a block post and it became necessary to amend the timetable to accommodate the single line that had been formed. The 06.25am Trowbridge to Devizes ran empty coach stock (ECS) from Devizes to Patney. When the 06.58am Trowbridge to Paddington SX/Reading SO had cleared the branch at Patney, the DMU of the 06.25am Trowbridge ran back from Patney to Devizes (ECS) to form its next working, the 08.00am Devizes to Westbury SX/Warminster SO. The 17.45 Westbury to Devizes SX ran ECS to Patney because it could no longer pass the 17.36 Newbury SX at Devizes. The 18.30 Devizes to Westbury SX was therefore withdrawn as the DMU went ECS Patney to Westbury instead.

When the line closed in 1966, weekday local up trains to Devizes numbered five, two of which continued in service to Patney. In addition a 10.30am departed Devizes, arriving Patney at 10.40am. Down trains from Devizes totalled six,

of which five started from Patney. On Saturdays there were three up trains to Devizes, arriving Patney at 10.10am. Seven down trains left Devizes, three of which started at Patney and an 11.35am from Patney terminated at Devizes at 11.45am. Most of these services were worked by DMUs.

The 19.36pm Newbury to Westbury on Saturday 16th April 1966 was the final service train to pull out of Devizes to a boisterous farewell from 100 or so, gathered there to witness it. The DMU, driven by Gerald Steer of Westbury, left on time at 8.57pm with just over a dozen passengers. It was bedecked with streamers, rockets were fired and the two-tone klaxon was repeatedly sounded. Reg Chave was the porter on duty that evening and wore his GWR uniform for the occasion. Edward Major, the retired last resident Station Master of Devizes was there to see off the final train as was Mr William Pike, Area Manager from Chippenham station. Alan Mead and his wife caught the train at Pans Lane; he had worked at Devizes station for almost 20 years. When the train had disappeared into the darkness and the crowds had left, Reg Chave turned the key of the Booking Hall door and closed the station for the last time.

Service B2 leaves Devizes for Holt on the last day of service, 16th April 1966. (P.Fry)

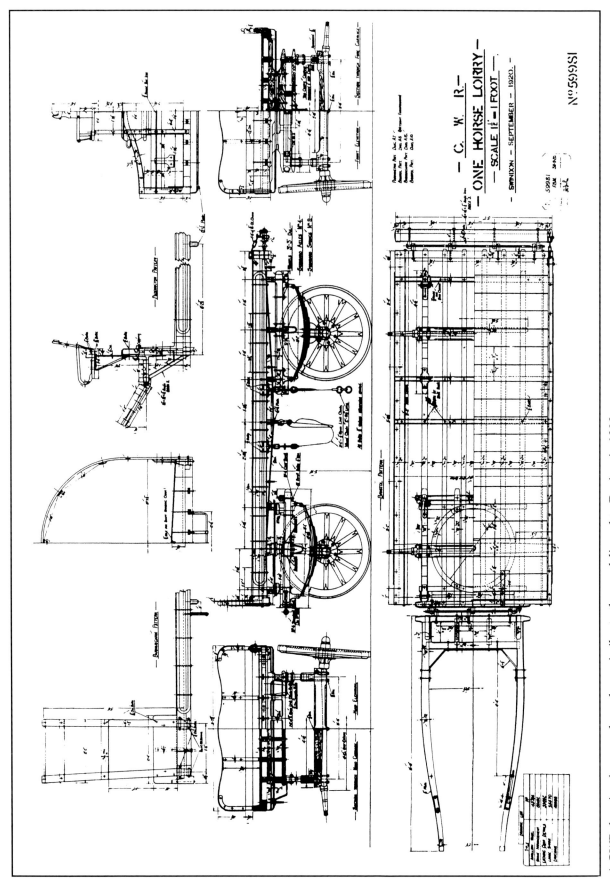

A GWR drawing for a one-horse lorry similar to the one delivered to Devizes in 1908.

where the type of goods being received made it practical. From this, delivery notes would be prepared and allocated to the various lorry drivers or at this time the horse and cart deliveries within the town area. Complete trucks of goods received were dealt with by the mileage checker with details being recorded on advice notes which would be posted to the receiver. The notes would also indicate any demurrage charges (for storage over time allowed) and the time limit for collection. The goods were also recorded in a Mileage Book and had to be signed for at the time of collection.

Loaded wagons kept in the goods yard for more than two days would have a wagon demurrage charge levied and these were accounted for by the clerks, many of whom during the war were local ladies, evacuees or wives of military personnel.

The weighbridge and office was an important and busy part of the goods yard workings and Eric Slade who started work as a weighbridge boy there in 1939 (the previous one, Philip Hawkins being in the Territorials, having left to join the Wiltshire Regiment) found he had plenty of work to do. He worked a 48-hour week which included 4 hours on Saturdays from 8.00am to 12.00noon. His duties would comprise cleaning the weighbridge office and lighting the fire; sorting invoice and delivery notes; addressing advice notes and demurrage charges; recording postage and taking the mail to the post box on the upside platform at the end of the day. These duties were in between the constantly arriving and departing lorries that he weighed on the bridge.

In the July to September period of 1939 at 1.45am, the Bristol goods, having classification 'K', would leave East Depot (Monday excepted), arriving in Devizes at 4.02am having been assisted from Holt Junction by a banking engine. At 4.25am it would leave for Reading. On Mondays only departure from Bristol was at 2.00am arriving Devizes at 4.22am and leaving for Reading at 4.50am. Local goods guards, Bill Bishop and Sid Woolacott, would pick up the train at Holt or Devizes and work 'double home' to Reading returning to Devizes on the

No.7923 runs in with a Reading to Trowbridge goods. The chalked 'M19' on the smokebox has possibly been left following use on a troop train. (D.Lovelock)

down goods the following day. This down goods from Paddington (E Class), arrived Devizes at 5.35am, leaving for Bristol at 6.00am (Mondays excepted). The Reading to East Depot (K Class) ran daily, arriving in Devizes at 10.39am and leaving for Bristol East Depot at 11.35am. At 3.57pm a train of milk empties (C Class) left Slough for Westbury stopping at Devizes at 7.25pm. An 8.05pm from Paddington to Bristol Kingsland Road (C Class) stopped in Devizes at 10.50pm for 15 minutes to pin down brakes. This 8.05pm also ran on Sundays as did a train of milk empties (C Class) leaving West London at 2.45pm for Westbury via Devizes.

Freight handled during the war years at Devizes was considerable and varied. The agricultural business of T.H.White received tractors and combine harvesters. Some of these were lend/lease provisions sent from the U.S.A. The tractors arrived heavily greased, presumably being deck cargo, and the combine harvesters were crated. On arrival at the station they were unloaded using the station crane and taken on the lorries to the company premises. The station crane was a real workhorse in these times, being used continuously throughout each day. The Paddington goods would bring in food and general provisions for the shops, or specialised materials for town businesses. From Avonmouth fertilisers arrived for use by the farmers and these were distributed around the farms using the railway lorries. Engine driver Jack Newman from Westbury remembers the linseed from the farms in the Salisbury area arriving at Devizes for the new flax factory in London Road before being sent out again in large coils on five-plank open wagons. The factory was opened for the war effort by the Board of Trade and continued in use until 1953/54. During the war years many of the girls working there were from the Land Army. The station lorries delivered and collected from the factory.

From Theale in Berkshire, shale was delivered for use as hard-core at the local army camps. Rubble from the blitzed centres of Bristol and Plymouth also arrived for the same use. The unloading and transportation of these materials was carried out by the railway staff, using army lorries. They were assisted by Italian POWs and also by private contractors. All of the material was used for the construction of hardstandings for military vehicles and equipment, much of it at Hopton Barracks.

Transport in use for collection and deliveries was both horse-drawn and motorised. Two shire horses and a Welsh cob were used for dray work in the town; in addition there was a Scammell three-wheel tractor and trailer, one 8-ton and two 2-ton lorries. These were AEC and Thornycroft, one of which had a gate change. All of them were started by handle although one did originally have a self-starter. This was removed, however, in order to standardise the lorries. At times when extra transport was needed, lorries would be borrowed from Bristol or Swindon. At the end of the working day, all the station lorries were fitted with dummy plugs to prevent them being commandeered.

Devizes and district had a number of 'buffer depots' which were used for bulk storage of food stocks such as tea, sugar, corn-beef and dried milk. Such depots were at Westbury, Cheverell, Chittoe and the stables at Bishops Cannings. This was government contract work with the stocks being taken to the depots by the railway lorries and collected again at a later date for despatch by rail.

Bert Miles was one of the regular Devizes drivers using a horse and dray on town deliveries. One time when he was on sick leave, another driver, Tom Newton, took his horse out on the town run and found it would not continue past *The Dolphin Inn*. After a period of time trying to coax the horse, the landlord, Major Harry Norman, appeared at the door and advised Tom to enter. This he did and after a short while he returned to the horse and dray which happily continued with the deliveries. Bert's secret was then revealed to all his colleagues at the station.

Station foreman Bill Newman, shunter Eric Slade, station foreman Percy Bond and shunter Tom Newton in Devizes goods yard in 1943. (E.Slade)

The downside yard was approached from the upside yard via a level board crossing, manned in working hours from the small hut beyond. The notice on the right reads 'All Down Goods & Mineral Trains Must STOP DEAD Here'. This was in preparation for the descent of Caen Hill. This was the site of the accident on 12th June 1943 recounted on the previous page. (I.D.Beale)

further freight arrives. This is signalled at 3.45pm and passes through the station with 66 "Pool" petrol tanks, probably empties bound for Avonmouth. The engine, painted light green with a red buffer beam is a brand new '38' Class 2-8-0. It does not stop, pausing only briefly at the Stop Board at the head of the incline.

The railway and its trains, of course, were prone to attack from enemy aircraft and guard Sid Woolacott on one occasion sheltered in the 4-foot beneath his van when the Reading to Devizes goods was raked with machine gun fire. His injuries were a lump on the head from hitting his steel helmet on the side of the van.

The weekly *Wiltshire Gazette* came out on Thursdays and batches were sent out by rail to the surrounding areas. Ken Axford, whose father Ernie was one of the Devizes permanent way gang, worked for the paper and was required to deliver them on hand trucks to the station. He recalls that controlling these on the incline of Station Road was a considerable strain, the hand trucks tending to run away with the weight of the papers. Ken remembers also the German POWs calling at the press office for materials with which they were supplied to print their own camp magazine.

One of the occasional duties of the station staff during the summer months after the war was to feed or release racing pigeons at stated times after they had arrived by train.

By the winter of 1946, the Bristol (East Depot) freight was departing at 1.45am as was the Reading to Bristol. After nationalisation, a slightly later departure from Bristol brought the train into Devizes at 4.15am, and later on at 6.00am, where it was picked up by goods guards Dave Nash and Sid Woolacott working the double-home duty. Arrival for them back in Devizes on the next day was around 9.00am. Dave remembers in 1957 being asked to work his rest days for a few months because of a shortage of guards.

LMS 0-6-0 No.3603, on loan to Westbury shed, seen with a pick-up goods in Hillworth cutting during 1940. (D.Seaton)

The racing stables at Beckhampton on the A4 between Chippenham and Marlborough were sending horses to race reetings from Devizes station at this period. Sheep were still being moved by rail as well, from Devizes to Reading and Bristol. Barley and wheat was being collected from the farms using the station lorries. It then went by rail from Devizes to the docks at Avonmouth. In the opposite direction sacks of cattle cake were arriving for the firms of Bibby's and Silcock's. The railway vehicles used for collection and delivery in the mid 1950s were a one-ton van on town parcels driven by Fred Parsons, a three-ton Thornycroft for Bromham and Rowde area deliveries driven by Joe Davis, a three-ton Austin for the Lavington area driven by Tom Curnick, and a three-ton Scammell on the town goods driven by Joe Burbidge.

One of the early Scammells had half doors in the cab with no windows above them which was not liked by the drivers in the winter. This was rectified when motor driver Bert Brown bet Jack Cotton the cartage clerk that he wouldn't be able to back the Scammell into the goods shed. Jack having just returned from war service where he had driven army vehicles, took up the challenge and duly wrecked the side of the vehicle. It was sent away to Slough workshops and came back repaired and with a window fitted but only in one of the doors. The drivers wanted Jack to try reversing again in the chance that the other side might get a window fitted but he decided one attempt was sufficient. A BR mobile crane was attached to the station during the 1950s being used at other stations on the branch for unloading coal. One of the drivers, Jimmy Caswell, remembers that the rear-wheel steered vehicle was not easy to handle.

One Saturday morning in the 1950s, just after 6.00am, shunter Bob (Bonzo) Lewis, who liked driving the engines, had been allowed to take the Bristol goods into the goods shed. With the tank engine inside, he was a little heavy-handed opening the regulator and blew a large hole in the shed roof. A number of pigeons in the roof at the time were blown through the hole in varying conditions.

Another shunter, Joe Giddings, talking to the *Devizes Gazette & Herald* reporter Terry Gaylard in April 1986 (20 years after closure), recalled that

The 'Four Shunters'. From left to right – unknown, Bob (Bonzo) Lewis, Sid Woolacott and Stan Hillier. Bob Lewis apparently carried a little weight and obtained his nickname from a circus train passing through Devizes displaying an elephant on the side with the name 'Bonzo'. (S.Smith)

one tank engine, 0-6-0 PT No.8744, 'didn't like Devizes station'. This engine, which came from Westbury, was continually being derailed and this prompted a number of enquiries. The engine crews tended to blame the track alignment and the PW men would accuse the engine of being at fault.

During the early 1950s the oil storage depot in the down yard was used when Regent Oil moved in. It is thought that they were using the tanks previously owned by the Russian Oil Products Co. which had been out of use for a number of years.

Access to the downside goods yard was by way of crossing the main line west of the station from the upside yard. The crossing keeper for the access road to the down yard had a small hut at this position from where he would emerge to wave a flag when a train was due. One of his other duties was to sort the used passenger tickets before sending them for audit at Aldermaston each month.

1955 was the time of a prolonged national railway strike which inconvenienced passenger traffic on the branch but not so food supplies to local shops. Fishmongers were not affected as their supplies, which normally arrived by rail, came instead by road at no extra cost and in less time. Fish cafés in Devizes were inconvenienced in the early days of the strike but one sold fried sausages instead.

Around 1958/59, Hinxman's moved their office and storage arrangements from the upside to the downside yard by the petrol tank area. In the upside yard there was a wash-down area for lorries. This was between the weighbridge and the goods shed. Ron Church, Hinxman's foreman, recalls that coal merchants were forbidden to use this facility. It was used for washing down railway vehicles and tanker lorries from the petroleum companies. They however had to pay the railway for the use.

At this time fuel oils from Avonmouth were arriving in Regent tank wagons for P.J.Card & Son. These were shunted into the upside goods yard from where Card's lorries would transfer the oil. The lorries had been adapted for easier direct

Pannier Tank No.4067 shunting a pick-up goods on a beautifully crisp snowy day. On the left, note the fire buckets at the end of the permanent way Inspector's office, near the junction with the 'Bear' siding. Below is a view of the downside yard from the island platform. (S.Haynes)

loading. The firm continued to receive its oil by rail until the goods traffic ceased at the end of 1964.

The *Working Time Table of Freight Trains* (Bristol District), from 15th September 1958, provided for such things as maximum loads, maximum speeds of trains through junctions and time allowances. How these applied to the branch is shown in the tables on the following three pages:

161

Maximum Loads for Main Line Freight Trains—

SECTION From	SECTION To	WORKING LOADS — Maximum number of wagons to be conveyed except by Trains specially provided for in the Service Books or by arrangement	Group A — Class 1 Traffic	Class 2 Traffic	Class 3 Traffic	Empties	Group B — Class 1 Traffic	Class 2 Traffic	Class 3 Traffic	Empties	Group C — Class 1 Traffic	Class 2 Traffic	Class 3 Traffic	Empties	Group D — Class 1 Traffic	Class 2 Traffic	Class 3 Traffic	Empties
DOWN.																		
Patney	Devizes	60	22	29	44	55	25	33	50	63	27	36	54	68	36	48	72	90
Devizes	Bradford	60	37	49	74	93	43	57	86	100	47	63	94	100	62	83	100	100

SECTION From	SECTION To	WORKING LOADS — Maximum number of wagons to be conveyed except by Trains specially provided for in the Service Books or by arrangement	Group DX — Class 1 Traffic	Class 2 Traffic	Class 3 Traffic	Empties	Group E — Class 1 Traffic	Class 2 Traffic	Class 3 Traffic	Empties	Group EX — Class 1 Traffic	Class 2 Traffic	Class 3 Traffic	Empties				
DOWN.																		
Patney	Devizes	60	39	52	78	98	43	57	86	100	47	63	94	100	...	...	...	...
Devizes	Bradford	60	68	91	100	100	75	100	100	100	82	100	100	100	...	...	...	...

ASSISTED TRAINS.—The load for trains assisted up inclines, except where otherwise shewn, will be the maximum load for the train engine plus the maximum load the assistant engine can haul, as shewn in the Maximum Load table, but if there is only one Brake Van and the assistant engine is at the rear, an additional wagon of Class 1 traffic or two empty wagons, not exceeding a total tare weight of 14 tons, may be conveyed in lieu of the second Brake Van for each assistant engine used. Assisted Trains must not exceed the working loads unless authorised, and no train must exceed the equivalent of 100 13-ton wagons. The instructions contained herein do not in any way affect or remove the prohibition placed by the Chief Engineer on the working of certain types of engines over certain sections of line, although loadings may be given in the table for engines over portions of line which are prohibited for them.
*—Via Westbury Loop. †—Via Frome Loop. ¶—For maximum loads for C, D and E trains, worked by " Castle," 47XX, 49XX and 43XX engines, see page 158.

B162 Maximum Loads for Main Line Freight Trains—

SECTION From	SECTION To	WORKING LOADS — Maximum number of wagons to be conveyed except by Trains specially provided for in the Service Books or by arrangement	Group A — Class 1 Traffic	Class 2 Traffic	Class 3 Traffic	Empties	Group B — Class 1 Traffic	Class 2 Traffic	Class 3 Traffic	Empties	Group C — Class 1 Traffic	Class 2 Traffic	Class 3 Traffic ¶	Empties	Group D — Class 1 Traffic	Class 2 Traffic	Class 3 Traffic ¶	Empties
UP.																		
Bradford	Holt Junction	53	21	28	42	53	24	32	48	60	26	35	52	65	34	45	68	85
Holt Junction	Bromham and Rowde	50	17	23	34	43	19	25	38	48	21	28	42	53	27	36	54	68
Bromham and Rowde	Devizes	50	10	13	20	25	12	16	24	30	12	16	24	30	17	23	34	43
Devizes	Patney	60	18	24	36	45	21	28	42	53	22	29	44	55	30	40	60	75

SECTION From	SECTION To	WORKING LOADS — Maximum number of wagons to be conveyed except by Trains specially provided for in the Service Books or by arrangement	Group DX — Class 1 Traffic	Class 2 Traffic	Class 3 Traffic	Empties	Group E — Class 1 Traffic	Class 2 Traffic	Class 3 Traffic	Empties	Group EX — Class 1 Traffic	Class 2 Traffic	Class 3 Traffic	Empties				
UP.																		
Bradford	Holt Junction	53	37	49	74	93	42	56	84	100	46	61	92	100	...	...	...	...
Holt Junction	Bromham and Rowde	50	27	36	54	68	33	44	66	83	33	44	66	83	...	...	...	...
Bromham and Rowde	Devizes	50	17	23	34	43	20	27	40	50	20	27	40	50	...	...	...	...
Devizes	Patney	60	30	40	60	75	37	49	74	93	37	49	74	93	...	...	...	...

NAME OF PLACE	DIRECTION OF TRAINS		Miles per Hour
	From	To	
CASTLE CARY TO BEDWYN			
Castle Cary Junction	All Up Weymouth Line Trains between ... to 129m. 55c. ...	Overbridge and Signal Box, 129m. 65c.	35
At Castle Cary	Up Main Line between 115m. 50c. and 115m. 32c.		60
Between Bruton and Witham, 125m. 40c. and 125m. 0c.	Main Line	... ...	65
Witham	Wells Branch	Main Line	10
Between Frome and Witham at Blatchbridge Junction, 116m. 58c. and 116m. 51c.	Main Line		50*
Frome Station	Main Line	Radstock Branch	10
Frome...	Up Trains through Station and Middle Junction ...		30*
Frome and Westbury (at Clink Road Junction), 114m. 45c. and 114m. 38c. ...	Main Line		50
Fairwood Junction and Westbury South between 111m. 20c. and 110m. 60c. ...	Main Line		40*
From 110m. 35c. to 110m. 10c.	All Up Trains over curve		45
Westbury South	Frome (Up Main)	Salisbury Line	15
Westbury South	Salisbury Line (Up)	Frome Line (Up Main)	15
Westbury North	Salisbury Line	Trowbridge	15
Westbury North	Frome	Patney and Chirton	30*
Westbury North	Salisbury Line	Patney and Chirton	15
Westbury North	Frome	Trowbridge	30
Westbury North and Heywood Road East Junction, 94m. 65c. and 94m. 44c.	Main Line		40*
Hawkeridge Junction and Heywood Road West Junction	All Trains		15
Patney and Chirton	Devizes Branch	Up Main	15
Patney and Chirton	Up Main	Bay Platform	10
Patney and Chirton	Devizes Branch	Bay Platform	10
Patney and Chirton	Bay Platform	Up Main	10
Grafton East	All Up Trains 68m. 50c. to 68m. 10c. ...		60
SAVERNAKE AND MARLBOROUGH			
All Up and Down Trains between 16m. 20c. and 16m. 35c.		... ...	40
All Up and Down Trains between 18m. 50c. and 18m. 40c.		... ...	45
All Up and Down Trains between 19m. 20c. and 19 m.p.		... ...	40
HOLT JUNCTION AND PATNEY AND CHIRTON			
Holt Junction...	To or from Devizes Line...		15
Devizes	Up and Down Lines through Loop Junction at each end of Station		10
Seend	Single Line facing junction to Down Sidings Devizes end of Station		10

All Red Group Engines to reduce speed as specified when passing over the following Bridges:

Mileage of Bridge.	Maximum Speed.	Mileage of Bridge.	Maximum Speed.
87m. 35c.	40 m.p.h.	89m. 14c.	30 m.p.h.
88m. 17c.	40 m.p.h.	93m. 40c.	30 m.p.h.

B156   Time Allowances for Freight Trains—

DOWN	Point-to-Point Allowances					UP	Point-to-Point Allowances				
	C Head Code	D Head Code	E Head Code	F Head Code	H.K Head Codes		C Head Code	D Head Code	E Head Code	F Head Code	H.K Head Codes
	Mins.	Mins.	Mins.	Mins.	Mins.		Mins.	Mins.	Mins.	Mins.	Mins.
BATHAMPTON TO PATNEY											
Bathampton	—	—	—	—	—	Patney and Chirton	—	—	—	—	—
Limpley Stoke	—	—	—	—	10	Devizes	9	9	9	9	12
Freshford	8	9	9	9	1	Bromham and Rowde ...	—	—	—	—	—
Avoncliff Halt ...	—	—	—	—	—	Seend	—	—	—	—	10
Bradford-on-Avon ...	—	—	—	—	6	Holt Junction	15	20	20	20	10
Bradford Junction West ...	8	9	9	9	4	Bradford Junction North ...	3	3	3	4	5
Bradford Junction North ...	1	1	1	1	1	Bradford Junction West ...	1	1	1	1	—
Staverton	—	—	—	—	—	Bradford-on-Avon ...	—	—	—	—	4
Holt Junction	3	3	3	4	5	Avoncliff	—	—	—	—	3
Semington	—	—	—	—	—	Freshford	7	8	8	8	3
Seend	—	—	—	—	10	Limpley Stoke	—	—	—	—	1
Bromham and Rowde ...	—	—	—	—	4	Bathampton	8	9	9	9	10
Devizes	21	22	23	24	11						
Pans Lane Halt	—	—	—	—	—						
Patney and Chirton ...	9	9	9	9	12						

BANK ENGINES RUNNING LIGHT

POINT-TO-POINT TIMES

	No. of Minutes		No. of Minutes
Corsham to Box	8	Severn Tunnel East Box to Severn Tunnel West Box...	8
Cranmore to Witham	15	Severn Tunnel West Box to Severn Tunnel Junction and shunting clear	3
Mells Road to Frome	15	Patchway to Pilning Junction	7
Filton to Dr. Day's	10	Wootton Bassett Incline to Trowbridge...	48
Filton to Stapleton Road	8	Trowbridge to Westbury	9
Warminster to Westbury	11	Westbury to Trowbridge	9
Upton Scudamore to Westbury	8	Savernake (Low Level) to Westbury	55
Brewham to Westbury	28	Devizes to Holt Junction	18
Brewham to Castle Cary	14	Trowbridge to Bradford-on-Avon...	8
Thingley Junction to Trowbridge	25	Andoversford to Charlton Kings	13
Wootton Bassett Station to Trowbridge	47		
Pilning Junction to Severn Tunnel East Box	4		

SHUNTING ENGINES   B197

STATION	Engine No.	Starting Time	AUTHORISED HOURS							Total per Week H. M.	PARTICULARS OF WORK
			Mon.	Tues.	Wed.	Th.	Fri.	Sat.	Sun.		
Devizes	1	11.45 a.m.	5¼	5¼	5¼	5¼	5¼	1¼	—	27 30	Works 10.30 a.m. Holt Junction to Devizes (arr. 11.30 a.m.) and 5.10 p.m. SX, 1.50 p.m. SO, Devizes to Melksham.

There were, in addition to the foregoing, rules and regulations on 'Assisting Trains Between Holt Junction and Devizes'. When an up freight or empty stock train had more than a single load and it was necessary for a banking engine to assist the train engine from Holt Junction, the assisting engine had always to be placed and coupled up at the rear. This had to be attached at Holt Junction and detached at Devizes by the guard. Freight trains requiring such assistance had to come to a stand at Holt Junction and Devizes for the purpose. The driver of the assisting engine had to keep a good look out for signals and be prepared to act in conjunction with the driver of the train engine and, when running over sections of the line which were on a falling gradient, had to exercise the greatest care to ensure the train engine alone worked the train and the assisting engine kept buffer to buffer without assisting. Assisting engine drivers reaching the summit of the Devizes incline had to exercise care in running from there to Devizes station. Passenger trains being assisted between Holt Junction and Devizes were required to have the assisting engine attached at the front.

When ballast trains were worked in the section between Devizes and Patney & Chirton, the engine had to be at the Devizes end of the train.

The amount of freight necessitated an engine from Westbury being allocated to Devizes on a daily basis and this continued until around 1960.

A local paper reported in 1960 that a Devizes butcher, Robert Douse, by striking matches to attract the engine driver's attention, saved three cows that had strayed up the raised embankment onto the line at Nursteed Road. The train was heading into Devizes from Patney & Chirton. The butcher presumably had the safety of the train at heart as opposed to a quick profit!

During 1962, Blue Circle cement trains started using the branch on their journey from Kent to South Wales. It was hoped locally that this would provide a life-line for keeping the branch open but this was not to be and the trains had ceased running within two years. As with the trains of today leaving the Somerset quarries, the cement trains of the sixties required powerful locomotives for the numerous heavy trucks hauled. The BR Standard 9F 2-10-0s and 2-8-0s, ex-War Department, were used and they must have been the heaviest ever on freight hauling over the branch. There were some occasions when the trains did not run through to South Wales but terminated at St Philip's Marsh, Bristol. The return to Kent was not made over the branch but by way of the Bristol to Reading main line.

During the 1960s there was an amalgamation of the coal businesses in the town. The Totnes, Devon, firm of F.J.Reeves took over Hinxman's in November 1962 and by the following year the company was known as Reeves, Maslen & Hinxman. Later still this changed to F.J.Reeves(Devizes) Ltd,

Builders and Coal Merchants. The firm was still bringing in large quantities of coal by rail during 1963 but freight traffic generally had waned with BR's policy of centralisation. The last Devizes freight train ran on 30th October 1964; it was a local goods and it left for Westbury with 0-6-0 PT 57XX No.3735 crewed by driver Frank Newell, fireman Mike Pickford and goods guard Harold Tanner.

Wartime/Military

The military presence in the area during the greater part of the branch line's existence provided it with considerable traffic in passengers, equipment and provisions and at no time more so than during the two world wars. From the turn of the century however, there had been increasing military use of Salisbury Plain for the establishment of camps and for training purposes.

In 1901 the Midland & South Western Junction Railway, which ran north to south across the Plain, together with the GWR, signed an agreement which allowed for trains to run on each other's tracks in the locality. In the picture below, MSWJR 4-4-0 No.7 heads a troop train into Devizes station with stock from the same company. The picture is thought to have been taken in the early part of the First World War, c.August 1915. In the opposite direction, the GWR carried troops to Ludgershall, and freight deliveries of hay and straw from Devizes were taken for the horses of the artillery regiments. Troops accompanied by a regimental band left the camps in Devizes for the front, marching to the station to board the trains for the coast. Canadian troops billeted in the town fetched their stores from the station using horse-drawn wagons. Without radio and up-to-the-minute newspapers, the station staff received war news written by the London clerks on invoices. 'Zeppelins over the City' was one such message. During the Great War, the GWR itself provided

MSWJR 4-4-0 N0.7 and troop train arriving at Devizes, c.1915. Special dispensation was made for wartime working of stock between the GWR and MSWJR. (J.Hale)

HM Forces with 25,474 personnel of which 2,436 lost their lives. Four men from Devizes station were amongst those and their names are recorded on the War Memorial at Bristol Temple Meads station; from the Traffic Department: R.G.Biss, P.S.A.Edwards and F.J.Park; from the Engineering Department: W.Hutchins.

An event which drew large crowds between the wars was the annually staged Tidworth Tattoo with the Devizes Branch playing its part in transporting members of the general public who were attending. Crowded excursion trains were worked from South Wales and Bristol via Devizes.

With the outbreak of the Second World War the railways of Britain came under the control of the Railway Executive Committee, appointed by the Minister of Transport. One of its first tasks was the planning of a programme for evacuating from London and district to the safety of the country, some half million children and adults involving the running of 4,300 special trains. The adult evacuees were mothers of the younger children and the others were school teachers. Each child was provided with a gas mask and had a name and address label attached for identification purposes to their coat collars.

There were three entraining stations in London on the GWR from which evacuation trains departed, these being Paddington, Acton and Ealing Broadway.

A programme had been prepared based on an evacuation period of four days. The branch only had Devizes with Patney & Chirton as scheduled station stops for these trains and they were all to depart from Ealing Broadway. Devizes was programmed to receive 1,600 evacuees on the first and fourth days and 800 on each of the second and third days. Each train was required to be made up of no more than 12 coaches and was required to convey 800 passengers. The departure and arrival times of the Devizes trains were:

1st day	depart 9.43am	arrive 11.45am
1st day	depart 4.51pm	arrive 6.55pm
2nd day	depart 9.07am	arrive 11.10am
3rd day	depart 9.07am	arrive 11.10am
4th day	depart 9.07am	arrive 11.10am
4th day	depart 2.45pm	arrive 4.50pm

After detraining at Devizes, empty stock would continue to Trowbridge or return to Acton.

The evacuation programme commenced on 1st September 1939 and as was the case with the first

NOTICE
TO RAILWAY PASSENGERS

NOTICE IS HEREBY GIVEN

that, due to the National Emergency, the following alterations in Passenger Train travel, as applying to the Railways in Great Britain, will come into force on and from MONDAY, 11th SEPTEMBER, 1939:-

1. **Passenger Train Services.**
   The Passenger Train Services will be considerably curtailed and decelerated. For details see the Company's Notices.

2. **Cancellation of Reduced Fare Facilities.**
   Excursion and Reduced Fare facilities (except Monthly Return, Week-end, and Workmen's tickets) will be discontinued until further notice.

3. **Season and Traders' Tickets.**
   Season and Traders' tickets will continue to be issued.

4. **Reservation of Seats, Compartments, Etc.**
   The reservation of seats and compartments, and saloons for private parties will be discontinued.

5. **Restaurant Cars and Sleeping Cars.**
   Restaurant Car facilities will be withdrawn, and only a very limited number of Sleeping Cars will be available.

By Order
11th September, 1939.   THE RAILWAY EXECUTIVE COMMITTEE.

The Railway Executive Committee issued this notice on 11th September 1939, putting the country's railways on a wartime footing.

few days of World War One, the railways were put to the test with the whole country being on the move. There were still families returning from holiday in early September, foreign visitors were returning to their countries, military personnel and equipment were being mobilised, government officials were being dispersed and priceless national artefacts were being sent to various places around the country for safe storage.

Following the experiences of 1939 the prepared evacuation programme was amended. By February 1940, when evacuation from London again took place, the number of scheduled trains for Devizes was reduced to the following, with departures from Paddington station:

2nd day	depart 1.10pm	arrive 3.05pm
6th day	depart 3.40pm	arrive 5.52pm

The trains carried 800 persons and 300 persons respectively. After detraining, the stock was returned to London. The train to Devizes on the 6th day completed the evacuation programme at that stage of the war.

The initial movement of evacuees to places of relative safety was by no means the last as there was a continuing need throughout the years of the war, but the final large-scale programme came in 1944 when flying bombs were targeting London and the South East.

The efficiency and organisation of the branch and its staff was to be evident during 1940 when they found themselves confronted with one major task after another. It began with the winter of 1939/40 when severe weather conditions with a day of steady rain followed by a sudden heavy frost brought traffic and communications to a standstill. Thick layers of ice brought down telephone and telegraph wires. There were failures of block instruments, of electric train staff circuits and points became frozen solid. The difficulties necessitated time-interval working on the branch and on other lines around Salisbury Plain.

Ernie Ross who at the outbreak of war was sent from Bristol Temple Meads to Devizes as a Class 4 shunter arrived for work at 6.00am on the first morning of the severe conditions to find the Devizes signalman unable to switch in the Seend box and other boxes unable to release tokens from the instruments. It was necessary then to resort to pilot working, which Ernie Ross had to inaugurate by making his way along the line to Seend. This he did with the help of two gangers and using one of their trolleys. The frost was so thick on the rails that they needed to scoot this down the steep incline of Caen Hill bank. On reaching Bromham & Rowde Halt at the bottom of the incline, the porter on duty signed the forms acknowledging pilot working. Ernie then went on by himself on foot to exchange pilot working forms with the signalman in Seend box. The Holt to Seend section staff had not been affected and so a train stood at Seend station waiting to proceed to Devizes which it was able to do on the arrival of Ernie Ross. He later boarded a second train back to Devizes, on arrival finding the station foreman acting as a pilotman on the Devizes to Patney section. These conditions on the branch lasted for three days and two nights.

Army camp construction in London Road, Devizes, was in full flow during 1939/40 with the materials arriving at the station and being taken by road to the camps. Much of the unloading and transportation was carried out by private contractors. The railway staff experienced problems with these contractors who, being on piecework, generated intense competition between the various lorry drivers. Ernie Ross recalls that when it was necessary to shunt the long siding in order to remove the wagons that had been unloaded and to move in further loaded ones, arguments became fierce. The men who still had wagons to be emptied refused to leave them in order to allow shunting to start whilst those waiting for their wagons to be moved would become very angry at having to wait. The rail staff would waste valuable time endeavouring to get the men out of the wagons and were abused for doing so. They of course were strictly forbidden to shunt with anyone in a wagon. After suffering these conditions for a period, it was decided by the engine driver and shunters to bend the rules in an effort to resolve the problem. After first warning the men in the wagons they were going to shunt them, they moved the train into Devizes Tunnel, engine first. When the engine and wagons came to a halt inside, the fireman put plenty of wet coal on and closed the dampers, which caused an immense cloud of thick black smoke. The draught of the tunnel carried this back to the entrance totally engulfing the lorry drivers in the wagons who couldn't even see to jump out. When the smoke cleared, the engine driver moved the wagons into the middle siding where the first empties were cut off. The lorry drivers were then given 30 seconds to get out before being returned to the tunnel for a repeat. It appears they didn't need telling twice and never again gave the staff any trouble. The local army camps were users of vast quantities of coal and this would also be moved from station to camp by private contractors.

The next mammoth responsibility to involve the station was 'Operation Dynamo', the machinery of which came into being on 26th May 1940 to assist the evacuation of troops from Dunkirk. The task involved moving thousands of returning troops from the coastal towns of Dover, Brighton, Margate, Folkestone, Ramsgate, Eastbourne, Newhaven, etc, to inland reception centres as quickly as possible. Devizes was one of these centres where war-weary troops were brought for rest and re-kitting. The troop trains left the ports for Addison Road station in London and from here trains were able to leave for various parts of the country.

Ernie Ross who was living in digs in Devizes was woken by a policeman just after midnight on 26th May and told to report to the railway station for further orders. On arrival at the closed station he was met by three army officers. He opened up the station, the waiting room of which was to be used as an office by the army. The colonel, army sergeant and Ernie Ross went into the signalbox to consult with the signalman and they were then told the news in respect of Dunkirk and that they were to receive train-loads of soldiers who had been rescued from the Normandy beaches. They were to be taken, on arrival at the station, to the Wiltshire Regiment Barracks and to the large training/transit camp that was still being built in London Road. The colonel required that the down trains arriving from London be brought into the up platform to allow direct access onto Station Road where vehicles would be waiting to move the troops. These instructions were passed on to the engine drivers by the signalman when they arrived at Patney & Chirton signalbox. Ernie Ross clamped and padlocked the down facing points and the up catch point and hand-signalled the first train 'wrong road', into the platform between 2.00 and 3.00am. Helped by a porter and local army personnel, the tired and dishevelled soldiers with their personal equipment were assisted from the train onto the lorries waiting at the roadside. The trains were full of uneaten food and men were dropping to the ground asleep while being escorted. Many were in a state of shock, some wet through, others had no clothes or boots and were wrapped in blankets. A good many were injured. When it was thought everybody had left the train it had to be searched for items left behind. Rifles and clothes were removed to the waiting room but on one of the centre corridor coaches the military men came across a sleeping 'Tommy' of no more than 17 years of age. He awoke suddenly, grabbing his rifle, but was restrained and assured that he was safely home in this country whereupon he broke down and cried, presumably in relief. Five similar specials arrived before Ernie Ross ended his shift at 2.00pm. Because of the requirement that they should all use the up platform, a certain amount of disruption was caused to the normal daily service. Down trains continued to use the usual platform but up trains used the back platform. Although Ernie was on duty again at midnight, there were no more Dunkirk trains during that shift.

At a later date, following the evacuation of St Valery-en-Caux, 'Operation Aerial' was put into action. Troops were landed at Plymouth and Southampton. Devizes received two more special trains, the first containing British soldiers and the second French. The latter, after being cleaned up and fed, left again by train for Southampton Docks and eventual return to French soil. The Devizes station staff found this move hard to accept.

One of the men returning from Dunkirk who found himself at Devizes station was Ian Samuel, an officer of the 6th Field Ambulance Unit. He had been returning to Margate on the Dutch vessel *Patria* and on docking was taken to the Dreamland leisure centre for feeding. Following this he boarded the train to Addison Road station in London where they detrained and were again fed. Together with his unit's colonel, J.Hyatt, he was loaded onto a train not knowing the eventual destination. In time they arrived at Devizes, the colonel's home town, and his wife having heard that troops from Dunkirk had been arriving at the station, was there on the off chance of meeting him. It appears she had little difficulty on the platform of seeing him as she was 6' 1" tall and he was 6' 7". Both men were taken to the Wiltshire Regiment Barracks and given the red carpet treatment. After 16 hours sleep and re-kitting, Ian Samuel went by taxi on 48 hours leave to his home in Hereford. The journey there and back was not made easy as the road signs had been removed in order to confuse possible invaders. On returning to Devizes with his wife, accommodation was impossible to find as other people had had the same idea. He had reason however to appreciate the local taxi man's hospitality as he took them into his home and provided them with a bed. It was the only bed in a one-bedroom flat. Breakfast was on the table next morning and on their departure the Devizes man would not take payment. Being unfit for military service, it was this man's contribution to the war effort.

As a result of the sad sight of the Dunkirk troops, another contribution to the war effort was made by the local firm of Chivers who erected a marquee on Devizes Green as a facility in which troops could arrange entertainment for themselves.

Following Dunkirk and occupation of countries across the English Channel, invasion of Britain in the early years of the war was always a strong possibility. Measures were introduced to combat such a threat, one of which was the formation of the Local Volunteers (Home Guard). Thousands of serving railway men joined the various units; the Devizes weighbridge boy Eric Slade enrolled with the 4th Wilts H.Q. Company. These men were used to guard railway property, in particular important bridges and the Fish Bridge at the bottom of Caen Hill was such a structure.

Throughout 1940 the movement of troops and equipment around the country was constant which created congestion on the railway. So much stock was tied up with these movements that local coal supplies were being affected. Ships arriving with materials were being held in dock because they were unable to unload and the lack of refrigerated vans meant food could also not be unloaded at the dockside. By October the situation was so bad that one of the decisions taken by the Railway Executive Committee was to put all of the private owner wagons with the exception of special ones, into a common user pool. This was achieved and eventually eased the problem.

1940 ended for Devizes station with another massive influx of people. On the Monday and Tuesday of Christmas week, relations of evacuees in the town were arriving all day long to visit them. In addition some evacuees were travelling to London to spend a few days at home. Soldiers on leave were also arriving and leaving from the station.

Devizes was host to numerous nationalities during the first half of the 1940s; some were friends, some were foes, some were even friendly foes and it was the Italian POWs that came into this category. They were camped mainly in Devizes Castle overlooking the railway station. Being so close, the railway staff became acquainted with some of them. They were not permanently locked up, but were put to work on the farms in the area and lorries would call at the castle daily to take them to their respective farms. The Italians were remembered for their skill in making intricate things with their hands such as jewellery and lighters. One of the Italians in Devizes who became renowned was known as 'Primo'. As he was able to speak good English, he was used as an interpreter and his particular skill was in repairing watches. He disappeared from the area one day, taking with him numerous watches he had been asked to repair and he was never seen in the town again.

The attack on Pearl Harbour by the Japanese on Sunday 7th December 1941, heralded the Americans' entry into the war. Americans began to arrive in the British Isles from January 1942 with their numbers building up rapidly from May onwards. Wiltshire, Berkshire and Hampshire formed the heartland of the U.S. Army in this country. The American sent over in May 1942 with the task of preparing camps, airfields, warehousing and the various military requirements of the arriving forces was Major-General John C.H.Lee. He was a regular visitor to Salisbury Plain as two of his Service of Supply District Headquarters were at Wilton and Tidworth. Guard Walter Tanner remembers a hair-raising journey when he travelled light-engine with a Westbury crew on Locomotive No.6000 *King George V* to Newton Abbot to bring General Lee back to the Plain. Walter recalls also that food rations left on troop trains tended to become perks of the train crews. There was one occasion when the troops had disembarked and the train was running back empty through Woodborough where Walter lived; the train driver slowed down to allow a large box of 'K' rations to be pushed out which later in the day Walter was able to retrieve. The contents were enjoyed by the Tanner family for several days.

As is known the Americans were pretty well self-sufficient; the quality of their uniforms, food and equipment, together with their pay and conditions, were far superior to that of the British servicemen. They soon became popular and the people of Devizes, in particular the children and young girls, made them welcome. They were camped at Prince Maurice and Waller Barracks. There was a good American field hospital at Waller and on The Green in Devizes were two Nissen huts manned by the American Red Cross. Armoured vehicles, tanks and jeeps arrived by the train-load at the station where they were off-loaded onto the cattle dock before being taken to camp. The Americans supplied their own mobile crane for doing this. Early on, the 4th Armoured Division found it was taking a long time to unload these trains at the short cattle dock and having seen the military platform at Patney station, made a request to unload there instead. This was approved but when tried, the platform, which was basically of timber construction, collapsed under the weight of the tanks so the train had to return to Devizes. The Americans then asked to unload from the trackside between Patney and Stert but this permission was withheld by the Railway Company because of the disruption it would have caused to single-line working.

cat which was being returned on the next train. Jack Cotton, a cartage clerk at Devizes, recalls one occasion when the cat was found in the goods shed drunk. It was lying on its back with its feet twitching, beside a leaking cask of Guinness awaiting collection by Wadworth's Brewery. It slept for a long time but fully recovered. The cat had a favourite sleeping place which was Jack's 'In' tray on the desk. It only had three legs so the station staff clubbed together to have an artificial one made and fitted but it was not appreciated by the cat who was able to get about easier on just three.

Not all the POWs were German. Lil Painter recalls the arrival at the station of some Polish troops who with completely blank faces were staring from the carriage windows.

Other nationalities finding themselves at Le-Marchant POW Camp were Latvians, Lithuanians and Czechs. The majority of prisoners arrived in a filthy and smelly state with the result that the railway carriages had to be cleansed as well. When the Channel Islands were re-captured, however, the Germans who all came to Devizes were in immaculate condition as their commander had issued complete new uniforms for his men before surrender. Also they arrived clutching wooden suitcases full of Jersey butter and other food. Needless to say, they had to give these up to the camp guards.

On one occasion the RTO at Devizes Station rang the POW camp and requested transport for a prisoner who was too old to walk the distance. He was 78 and told his captors in good English that he had been too young for the Prussian War, too old for World War One but had been pressed into service for World War Two.

Goods driver Bert Brown recalls that together with the station drivers, they sat in their vehicles all one evening, awaiting the arrival of a train from which they were told some of the POWs would need taking to the camp. With the arrival of the train however, a fleet of coaches from P.J.Card & Son arrived and these were used instead of the railway lorries.

The inevitable aspect of war is the death of the country's young men and women, and its effect on the civilian populations of the large towns and cities. Devizes was not immune from this during the war years with a number of military personnel killed in action being returned for burial. When they were brought in on the train, they would be taken to the far end of the up yard, past the goods shed from where the bodies would be collected by the local undertakers. The same procedure applied in the case of civilian fatalities.

The man who had successfully guided the station through the war years with all the added responsibilities and different procedures was Station Master Dennis O'Donoghue. He had been upgraded to Class 1 because of this. There was an occasion, however, when he did find himself in trouble. During the war, fires were not allowed in station waiting rooms because of the shortage of fuel. He had found a way around this by having coals removed from passing engines and placed in the grate for the comfort of passengers. A lady passenger was so pleased with the warmth she experienced that she wrote to the GWR to compliment them and consequently the Station Master was rebuked.

The extra staff, particularly in the goods office, who were employed to assist with the additional workload were reduced after the war when trade returned to normal.

With the end of the war in sight, Devizes Town Council held a meeting at the end of January 1944 to discuss ways in which they would like to see the town develop. They decided at the meeting to set up a co-ordinating committee who would look at, amongst other things, slum clearance, housing for service personnel returning from the war, road widening, a by-pass road, and with the increase in air travel, the provision of a civilian airport. The question was asked: was a single line railway sufficient? It was thought that this would hazard the building of an airport in the town. The meeting also expressed the need to do something with the canal which the railway company would probably be pleased to get rid of. It had become a health hazard and needed much repair if it was ever to be used again.

Local people will note from the above points that the only probable success was the removal of the slums. As for railway improvements, British Railways were to become more concerned with getting rid of it than they were with the hazardous canal. After major renovations over a number of years by the Kennet & Avon Canal Trust the canal, with its flight of locks at Caen Hill, was re-opened by the Queen in 1990 and is now one of the major attractions of the town.

A slight accident occurred at the station in August 1946 when one of the eight coaches of a Paddington to Trowbridge furlough special (No.18.F.37), fouled the platform on arrival. The

Signalmen Rowley Reeves and Bert Clack in Devizes signalbox in June 1965. (J.Summers)

Porter Reg Chave seen clipping the points on the up line in 1961. (F.Cutting)

Devizes station staff on the platform outside the signal box in 1922: from left to right; (back row) R.Brown, C.Dunsdon, H.Bush, Jim Nash, George Stiles, W.Chapman, W.Knee; (third row) G.Warry, Fred Clack, G.White, Bill Cox, F.Cotterill,

F.Scrivens, Charlie Hillier, Mr Bennett, H.Clark, Jack White, R. Elliott; (second row) W.Ellis, Miss Dickenson, Johnny Gall, Mr Titball, Station Master J.J. Eaton, Mr Harding, Mr Launchbury, Miss Staniforth, George T.Nicholson; (front row) Arthur J. Bungay, Bill Perrett, E.Underwood, Sam H.Hitchcock, Bill Brooks, Charlie Wish, Harvey Lodge, Tommy Truckle (who also appears in the picture on page 174). (B.Brooks)

The Devizes station football team playing in the local Southbroom League in 1921: left to right: (back row) E.Nettleton, F.Cotterill, Bill Nutland, Harry Lodge, Mr Harding, W.Penny; (centre row) William Perrett, Eric Willis, Tommy Edwards; (front row) Jack White, F.Scrivens, Bill Cox, Charlie Wish, E.Ford. (B.Brooks)

Where a large body of men work together they generally enjoy the activity of team work and in addition to the station's first aid teams, Devizes station also had sufficient young members of staff in the 1920s to be able to field their own football team in the local Southbroom League. In later years a team completed in the inter-station skittles tourament in which they were champions one year during the 1950s when they travelled to Bristol for the finals. Ganger Ernie Sly from the Savernake low level gang recalls that Bill Noakes the district permanent way engineer and Devizes signalman Bill Brooks had their own sporting interest. There was an occasion in the 1950s when Bill Noakes told Ernie he was going into Devizes for a haircut and would see him later. He did have his haircut but also went to Bath Races with Bill Brooks where they had a good day. Bill Brooks was good at book-keeping and figures; it seems this extended to the horses as well.

By the mid-1930s the station staff had been reduced to 30 (7 clerical and supervisory positions and 23 on wages) but this increased again with the outbreak of World War II to 33 (7 clerical and supervisory and 26 wages) with a wage bill of £11,000 by the end of the war. The staff from 1939-45 comprised:

Station Master	1	Booking clerks	3
Parcel Clerk	1	Goods Clerks	6
Station Foremen	2	Shunters	3
Passenger Porters	4	Drayman/Motor Drivers	4
Drayman (Parcels)	1	Goods Checker	1
Goods Foreman	1	Goods Porters	4
Weighbridge Boy	1	Crossing Keeper	1

These figures of course were often adjusted to accommodate circumstances at the time and they do not include permanent way gangs, signals & telegraph staff, signalmen or travelling personnel such as guards and ticket collectors.

The following pages give some brief career details of just a few of the railwaymen who served at Devizes station during these busy, exciting and sometimes dangerous few years.

Permanent way staff receiving the 'Best Kept Length Award' for the district at Devizes station, c.1956: from left to right; (back row) Charlie Elliott, Charlie Brown, Reg Beake, Ernie Sly, 'Tortell' Flippance, Ted Hilliar, Ted Goodman, Percy Powell, Sid Matthews, A.G.'Ivor' Maslen; (front row) George Nash, Walter Prictor, David Jones, Bill Noakes (District Engineer), Bill Phillips (Assistant District Engineer), Dick Bailey, Vic Kimber, Arthur Gregory. (D.Nash)

Sid Woolacott was a member of staff with a railway pedigree, his father having been a goods guard and four of his brothers also being railwaymen. Sid came to Devizes in 1939 replacing Maurice Raymond as a goods guard. He joined the Southern Railway as a junior clerk at 14 before transferring to the GWR at Yeovil three years later. He progressed there as a porter, shunter 1st Class and finally a goods guard. He spent 26 years at Devizes and it was with great sorrow that Sid witnessed the decline of the branch. Prior to his redundancy in 1965, his duties had been downgraded to porter, parcels clerk and to the issue and collection of tickets. Like signalmen Bert Clack and Rowley Reeves, he had taken considerable interest in maintaining the ornamental flower beds and was proud when they won the 'Best Kept Station Award'. Sid worked on the railway in total for 51 years and unfortunately saw little retirement as he died within months of leaving. The railway was Sid's life and his family were of the opinion that he was unable to live without it.

Weighbridge boy Eric Slade joined the station in 1939 on the recommendation of one of the chief clerks, Ted Major, later to be Station Master at Patney & Chirton and also at Devizes. Eric was paid a wage of 15s. per week with stoppages of 2d. Whilst as a boy employee he received an annual rise of 5s.. Later in his service he carried out the duties of porter and also the delivery of the town parcels using a horse-drawn parcels van. He left Devizes for Yatton in 1945 and went on to Bristol (East Depot) as a Class 3, and later Class 1 shunter where again he dealt with the goods traffic for Devizes. From 1949-55 he was at Temple Meads before leaving the railway. Eric's brother Dennis worked in the weighbridge office and as a porter for a short time from 1943. Their family connection at the station was signalman Bill Brooks who was an uncle.

Another local railway family were the Bishops; Bill the father was a goods guard, his son Clarence a district relief signalman whose home station was Westbury. The daughter Kath joined the staff as a

Porter/parcels clerk Sid Woolacott in front of the Devizes nameboard at the time of his retirement in 1965. (S.Smith)

Eric Slade, weighbridge clerk, outside the weighbridge office in 1940. (E.Slade)

Eric Slade's letter of appointment as a lad porter, dated 2nd October 1939. (E.Slade)

Eric Slade's certificate of enrolment with the Home Guard while serving at Devizes station. (E.Slade)

Retirement presentation to yard foreman Charlie Hillier in October 1959 : from left to right; (back row) Jack Yates, Clarence Bishop, Les (Shack) Wiltshire, Ken Welsh, Joe Giddings, Joe Chapman, Jimmy Caswell; (front row) Bob Diskett, Arthur Boulter, Len Brown, Alfie Wiltshire, Charlie Hillier, Station Master Edward Major, Kath Bishop, Gladys Millard, Jack Allen. (Wiltshire Gazette)

booking clerk in 1940 and worked at the station until 1965 when she transferred to Temple Meads knowing Devizes was to close.

Motor driver Len Brown who appears in the photograph of the 'Station Centenary Birthday Cake Ceremony', joined Devizes station in 1931. He started on the railway in 1925 as a lad porter at Marlborough High Level on the GWR. One of his jobs, he remembers, was to guard the many bicycles, brought on the trains returning the Marlborough College boys from their vacations, from pilfering of pumps and lights. Having served as a porter and motor driver for almost 40 years, he was made redundant by BR in 1964 and left to work for Wadworth's Brewery. That company employed a number of ex-railwaymen at this time.

In 1931 there were still telegraph linemen and signal linemen, later to be known as signal & telegraph linemen. Harry Dyer and Alf White were signal linemen at this time with their home station at Devizes.

One of the men who worked in the goods office before and after World War Two was Jack Cotton who started work there in 1936 as a learner (apprentice clerk) before moving to Bridport as a junior clerk. He then returned to Woodborough on the Berks & Hants to become the first and only senior clerk to serve the station, having been appointed

to deal with the materials arriving for use in the rebuilding of RAF Upavon. On completion, he left for Bristol Temple Meads as a tail traffic officer in 1940, being responsible for everything carried at the rear of a passenger train, such as pigeons, guns for the army, food, general provisions and even coffins carrying civilians killed in air raids. He received call-up papers for the army while at Temple Meads in 1940 but entry was deferred for 6 months whilst he taught a woman the tail officer's job. After the war, Jack returned to Devizes as a cartage clerk until 1950 when he moved to Chippenham goods depot as chief clerk (outwards). At this time the wages of railway staff had fallen well below what could be earned in private industry so later in the year Jack left British Railways with regret. Jack's sister Gwen was also at Devizes as a passenger porter during the war.

Another station recruit during the war years was Dave Nash who started there in 1939 as a lad porter. He went to Melksham in 1943 as a porter and a year later to Frome as a shunter. He used to cycle to Frome from his home in Bromham near Devizes. He was pleased when later that year he returned to Devizes as a district relief porter. In 1945 he became a signalman in Seend but returned to his post as district relief porter at Devizes in 1946 before becoming a goods guard in 1948. The railway made him redundant from this position in 1962 but he was able to take a post at Chippenham as a shunter/guard. In 1964, as with others on the railway, he left for the improved wages available in industry. A duty Dave recalls with pleasure whilst a porter at Devizes, was the town deliveries he undertook using the horse and dray.

A familiar figure at Devizes station even before he became one of the staff was Joe Giddings. He was a young enthusiast who could not have been happier that when he was taken on by the GWR in 1942 as an 18-year old porter. At this time he was told by the Station Master that he would have a job for life. Joe would have a go at anything to do with the railway, including driving the shunting engines in the goods yard, against regulations of course. The Station Master's pledge proved false, however, when in 1964 Joe, then a shunter, was made redundant. He was very resentful that the work he loved was taken from him.

During the war years a good many women had been employed at the station carrying out a variety of work in posts normally filled by men. The positions covered included ticket collectors, booking clerks, weighbridge clerks, porters, goods clerks, parcel clerks and guards. With the end of hostilities and the return of male staff following demobilisation, most of the women were required to leave the railway although a few of the single ones remained. Some of these ladies are still resident in the town today and remember vividly their wartime service at the station. After the war the staff numbers actually increased. In 1951 the total work force was 40 but reductions in 1964 halved that figure when freight traffic was lost to the station. From the 20 staff then employed, the complement was later reduced again. Edward Major retired in 1964 and was the last permanent Station Master. A duty he enjoyed before retiring was the cutting of the station centenary cake. This had been baked by the wife of Alan Mead, himself a clerk in the goods and booking offices and was inscribed

WITH BEST WISHES
TO THE DEVIZES STAFF
1ST JULY 1857-1ST JULY 1957

Celebration of the Devizes station centenary: left to right; (back row) Arthur Boulter, Gerald Taylor, Ken Sheppard, Joe Burbidge, Rowley Reeves, Joe Chapman, Reg Chave; (centre row) Maurice Brown, Jim Martin, Charlie Hillier, Pete Reardon, Bert Clack, Les Wiltshire, Joe Giddings; (front row) Len Brown, Gwen Cooper, Gladys Millard, Station Master Edward Major, Dennis Ayres, Bob Inchley, Jack Allen. (Jean Summers)

Signalling

It is thought that the single-line branch was initially worked by timetable/crossing orders. In January 1873 the single line between Newbury and Hungerford was worked by train staff, between Hungerford and Devizes by disc telegraph and between Devizes and Holt by pilotman. This was known still to be operating in February 1876.

In 1877, possibly at the same time as interlocking signalboxes were built, the train staffs and tickets system, assisted by disc block telegraph was introduced on the entire single-line portion.

Block working provides for a section limit being imposed on trains passing in the same direction between two adjoining boxes but on single-line workings, where the requirement was for trains to travel over the same rail but in opposite directions, it was necessary to have additional safety features to prevent the possibility of trains entering the single-line section from opposite ends at the same time. The train staffs and tickets system was then used, with the block being supplementary. This was the preferred system at the time as the combination speeded up the passage of trains on a single line whereas a single line worked by just the staff could lead to considerable delay. The 'staff and ticket' would allow trains to pass over a staff section in the same direction in succession providing train schedules were being monitored and the staff for the section being entered was held by the signalman at the entrance to the section.

In 1893 the electric train staff was introduced, probably of the Webb & Thompson type, with the train staff and ticket system being abolished. This was a considerable advance on the previous system as far as facilitating the working of traffic and preventing from human error. Normally there were no delays caused by a staff being away, and the removal of a second staff was impossible until the first one had been entered into the apparatus at the next box on the line.

With the electric train system, if more trains travelled, for example, on the up line than on the down, the number of staffs would accumulate in the instrument. In such circumstances the telegraph lineman would use a special key to open the instrument case, lift the lock and remove the relevant number of staffs for returning to the adjoining signalbox. This practice was recalled by Ian Hibbard who remembers seeing the staffs returning to Holt Junction signalbox from Seend by the first down train on Monday mornings.

The two original boxes at Devizes, one adjoining the goods shed and one at the tunnel entrance, were of 20- and 16-lever provision respectively but the one on the platform that replaced them in 1897 was of 39 levers extended with a 45-lever horizontal tappet frame in March 1911. Later still an additional lever '0' was added making a total of 46 levers. The Type 5 box was 24-hour manned by signalmen Class 1 and classified as a Light Cross Country Line. The up starter signal was at the end of the platform on which the signalbox was positioned. From 1923 the box became Class 4.

By 1931 two track circuits had been provided to the rear of the Down Home and Down Inner Home signals. An additional track circuit was later installed on the back platform. Finally track circuits were provided in lieu of locking bars for the facing points at either end of the station.

At this time the area covered by the Devizes-based signal lineman was from Patney & Chirton to Melksham via Devizes. The telegraph lineman based at Devizes covered Hungerford West exclusive to Holt Junction for branch apparatus, Patney & Chirton to Westbury North exclusive, the Marlborough Branch and Grafton loops. He attended faults on through wires from Hungerford testing point to Holt Junction, with the Newbury lineman co-operating for testing purposes when required.

One summer's day during the 1930s, one of the tokens from the electric train staff system was lost. The section involved was between Patney and Devizes for which section at the time the token colour was blue. On arrival at Devizes of a down train, the signalman noted, when being handed the ring carrier by the fireman, that it was empty. The footplate was searched to no avail but the signalman in the box at Patney was able to confirm the token had left there. It was necessary to operate pilot working and this continued all the next day while gangs of men searched the lineside for the missing token. It was not found and so authorisation was given to adjust the token machines and return to normal working. It was eventually found during the autumn by two boys playing near the line.

Communication between the shunters and the signalbox was by electric bell of which two were fixed at the west end of the station, one on the lamp post near the catch point on the up side of the line and the other on the telegraph post near the down siding points on the down side of the line. Only the person in charge of shunting was

Three-quarter view of the signalbox with a clear view of the various station signs on the up platform. (I.D.Beale)

The gates to the signalbox locking room. (J.Gander)

The square-post up starting signal with track circuit diamond and the harp-framed gas lamp standing at the east end of the island platform in 1954. (I.D.Beale)

Signalman Bill Brooks winding the clock and resetting it to Summer time in 1938. (B.Brooks)

185

authorised to use the bell signals. After sunset or during fog or falling snow, or when the signalman was unable to see if the main line was clear, the person in charge of shunting, on completion, was required to inform him that the line was clear.

The tunnel formed part of the shunting operation in the down yard and for communication between the shunters and enginemen, a klaxon horn was provided in the tunnel at the Patney end of the yard. This was operated from a plunger fixed on a lamp post near the hand points lever to the down sidings. The signal gantry at the tunnel mouth incorporated a special shunt signal for traffic advancing into the tunnel between shunts.

The following are the Rules and Regulations applying to shunting operations at Devizes in 1933 and which remained the same in the 1958 instructions:

The siding connection to the down line is seen clearly behind lampman Charlie Tilley. (B.Brooks)

Shunting Operations – Devizes Station is at the summit of a gradient of 1 in 52, falling immediately at the Holt Junction end of the yard towards Holt Junction, and it is of the utmost importance that every person when carrying out shunting operations should exercise the greatest possible care in the movement of vehicles on the Main Lines.

The points at the trailing end of the crossover leading from the Single Line to the Up Platform Line at the Holt Junction end of the yard are so set as to fall normally open towards the No.1 Goods Siding, and act as safety points. They are self-acting, but they can be held by a lever in the Signal Box, and are so arranged to afford protection to any vehicles which might otherwise run uncontrolled on to the Single Line.

No vehicle must under any circumstances be allowed to stand on the Up Main Line outside the self-acting catch points at the Holt Junction end of the Station.

Before shunting operations are carried out which necessitate the occupation of the Up Platform Line at the Holt Junction end of the Station, and while vehicles are standing at the Up Platform without an Engine attached, the Up Facing Points at that end of the Station must be set for the Down Line and must remain in that position until the operations have been completed, except in the case of traffic taken off a Down Freight Train and placed on the Up Platform Line by the Train Engine. In the latter circumstances immediately after the Train Engine has re-crossed to the Down Line, the facing points must be set for the Down Line and must remain in that position until the Up Platform Line is clear.

The Goods Siding at the Reading end of the Station on the Up Side has a connection with the Down Line only. Shunting operations with this Siding from or to the Running Line must only be carried out when the Engine is at the Holt Junction end of the vehicles being moved.

In cases where it is necessary to shunt vehicles from the Up Line to the Down Sidings over the connection leading from the Back Platform Line at the Reading end of the Station, whenever possible this must be done by having an Engine or Brake Van with a man in it leading towards Holt Junction, but if it

186

is not possible to arrange this, under no circumstances may a vehicle or vehicles be propelled from the Up Line for the Down Sidings until the necessary Points have been set for the movement, and the Shunter in charge will be responsible for seeing that those Points and appropriate Disc are set before he allows the vehicles to pass over the connection leading from the Single Line. Similarly, in the case of vehicles from the Down Sidings for the Up Line and thence to the Goods Yard, the connection leading from the Back Platform Line at the Reading end of the Station must remain set for the Sidings until the vehicles have come to a stand on the Single Line beyond the Up Line connection which must be altered for the direction of the Up Line before the vehicles are allowed to move back.

Vehicles must not be moved over or allowed to stand on the Down Line, neither must vehicles be attached to a Down Train standing at the Platform unless an Engine is attached to them at the Holt Junction end, except as follows:-

Vehicles required to be detached from Down Passenger Trains, unless an Engine is available to take them across to the Up Platform Line, or place them in a Siding **while the Train is standing at the Down Platform**, must in every case be placed on the Up Line or be propelled into the Down Side Sidings by the Train before they are detached. A competent Shunter or Porter must in all cases be in charge of and properly secure the vehicles, either by the hand-brakes or hand-scotches and sprags.

When Down Freight Trains require to detach traffic this must be done, as far as possible, by the Train Engine and wagons being detached and sent ahead, and the vehicles must then be taken off by the Shunting Engine, which must place them in the Up Sidings. Before the Train Engine is sent forward a sufficient number of brakes must be put down on the wagons to ensure the Driver bringing them to a stand without difficulty. The brakes of the two leading wagons, next to those detached, must be put down, firmly secured, and a sprag placed in the wheel of the first vehicle, so as to prevent the Train moving forward. If the Shunting Engine is not available the Train

Engine must place the wagons in the Down Sidings either at the Holt Junction or London end of the Station, unless the nature of the traffic makes it desirable for the wagons to be put in the Up Sidings, when this may be done by the Train Engine. While the latter movements are being carried out the leading vehicles of the Train standing on the Down Line must be secured by the brakes and sprag as shewn above.

Up Freight Trains with a single load, if requiring to do work, must on arrival at Devizes be placed in No.1 Siding clear of the Main Line before the Engine is detached or any shunting movement performed. If double-load Trains are too long to be placed in No.1 Siding, the Engineman and Guards must be careful to draw the Train in over the incline as far as possible, clear of the Siding Points over which the work has to be performed and when brought to a stand, the Guard must at once tightly apply the brake in the van, and the Engineman of the Assistant Engine must also use all the brake power at his command to prevent the Train receding. Before detaching the Train Engine the Guard must advise the Driver of the Assistant Engine the number and character of the vehicles which will be left on the van, and if these are numerous or heavy he must agree with the Engine Driver upon what number of wagons it will be necessary to put down brakes, and then act accordingly.

Every effort must be made to get Up Trains clear of the self-acting points when they arrive so that they can fall to their normal position and thus prevent the possibility of vehicles running away down the incline.

The Down back Platform Line is available for Up or Down trains and is signalled accordingly. Any Down Train may run to this Line as required, but only the following Up Trains:- (a) An Up Passenger Train when an Engine is available to stand in rear of the Train while on this road. (b) Auto Car but no vehicles must be detached from the Car while standing at the back Platform Line, unless removed by an Engine. (c) Freight or Milk Train when it cannot be accommodated in the Up Sidings, but no detaching must take place unless an Engine is at the rear of it. If no Engine is at the rear of the Train it must remain stationary until drawn ahead to be shunted to the Up Line or into a Down Siding. (d) Passenger or Empty Stock Train not requiring to call or assisted by Engine in rear; such Engine to remain on same Line until departure of Train. The regulations for working over the Down Platform Line will also apply to the back Platform Line.

The Guards of all Trains (including Passenger, Freight and Mineral) stopping at Devizes must be careful to put on and secure the hand-brakes before leaving their vans.

When two Trains are approaching the Station from opposite directions at the same time, the Up Train must be given precedence.

To be available for immediate use, two sprags, two hand-scotches, and a brake-stick must always be kept on hand at each end of the Down Platform.

On 12th July 1959 six signals were renewed, comprising: Down Main Home, Down Main Starting, Back Platform to Down Main Starting, Back Platform to Up Main Starting, Up Main Starting and Up Distance. Some of these can be seen in the photograph below.

The September 1958 to June 1959 *Western Region Working Timetable of Freight Trains* shows that the signalbox at Devizes on weekdays was open from 5.10am to 9.10pm and on Sundays in shifts from 7.10am to 8.00am, 11.00am to 12.30pm, and 4.30pm to 9.30pm. The signalmen of the period were Rowley Reeves and Bert Clack but with the retirement of these two stalwarts, British Railways took the opportunity to close the box completely as from 4th July 1965. The removal of the passing loops and sidings soon followed, making a complete single line from Patney & Chirton through to Holt Junction which, in turn, meant that only the up platform at Devizes was then used. The box, however, had for a brief period in 1961 returned to 24-hour working when the Lavington embankment slip had provided the branch with a train service reminiscent of its former glory.

The new round-post signals are seen here in August 1964, after the east end siding has been lifted. (D.J.Hyde)

Great Western Railway.

VISIT OF THE PRIME MINISTER
TO
Hardenhuish Park
CHIPPENHAM
On Saturday, June 12

TRAIN SERVICE AND FARES

LEAVING				AT							RETURN FARES.			
											Third Class.		First Class.	
				a.m.	a.m.	a.m.	p.m.	p.m.	p.m.	p.m.	s.	d.	s.	d.
BRISTOL—														
Clifton Down	..	..	..	—	8 53	10 28	—	12 28	3 28	—	3	5	5	8
Redland	..	..	..	—	8 56	10 30	—	12 30	3 30	—	3	5	5	8
Montpelier	..	..	..	—	8 59	10 33	—	12 33	3 33	—	3	4	5	7
Stapleton Road	..	..	..	—	9 4	10 37	—	12 37	3 37	—	3	3	5	5
Lawrence Hill	..	..	..	—	9 9	10 41	—	12 41	3 41	—	3	2	5	3
Temple Meads	..	..	..	6 40	9 35	10 55	12 20	1 20	4 8	—	3	1	5	2
KEYNSHAM	..		..	6 49	—	11 7	—	1 33	4 20	—	2	6	4	2
BATH	..	..	..	7 7	9 54	11 24	1M16	1 52	4 36	—	1	8	2	9
BATHAMPTON	..	..	..	7 13	10 19	11 30	1M22	—	4 42	—	1	4	2	3
BOX	..	..	..	7 20	10 27	11 40	1M28	—	4 50	—	1	0	1	8
CORSHAM	..	..	..	7 30	10 38	11 53	1M38	—	5 0	—	0	7	1	0
SWINDON	..	..	..	7 35	9 20	11 15	12 48	1 20	2 3	3 12	2	1	3	6
WOOTTON BASSETT	..		..	7 45	9 30	11 25	12 59	1 30	—	3 22	1	5	2	4
MALMESURY‡	..	..	..	7 13	9 18	11 3	—	1 15	—	3 5	1	8	2	9
DAUNTSEY	..	..	..	7 56	9 40	11 35	1 10	1 42	—	3 32	0	9	1	3
SALISBURY	..	..	..	7 20	—	—	12 55	—	—	—	5	1	8	6
WILTON	..	..	..	7 27	—	—	1 2	—	—	—	4	9	7	11
WISHFORD	..	..	..	7 33	—	—	1 8	—	—	—	4	5	7	4
WYLYE	..	..	..	7 42	—	—	1 17	—	—	—	3	10	6	5
CODFORD	..	..	..	7 50	—	—	1 25	—	—	—	3	4	5	7
HEYTESBURY	..	..	..	7 57	—	—	1 31	—	—	—	3	1	5	2
WARMINSTER	..	..	..	8 9	—	—	1 41	—	—	—	2	7	4	4
WESTBURY	..	..	..	8 48	10 6	12 16	1 53	2 7	3M52	—	2	0	3	4
TROWBRIDGE	..	..	..	9 3	10 35	12 28	2 4	2 30	4M35	—	1	6	2	6
MARLBOROUGH (High Level)	..			—	9 5	—	12 35	—	—	—	4	9	7	11
SAVERNAKE (Low Level)		..		—	9 31	—	12 57	—	—	—	4	1	6	10
PEWSEY	..	..		—	9 40	—	1 6	—	—	—	3	5	5	8
WOODBOROUGH	..	..		—	9 47	—	1 13	—	—	—	3	0	5	0
PATNEY AND CHIRTON	..			—	9 55	—	1 19	—	—	—	2	9	4	7
DEVIZES	..	..	..	8M5	10 6	—	1 30	—	3M30	—	2	2	3	7
SEEND	..	..	..	8M19	10 15	—	1 39	—	3M42	—	1	7	2	8
HOLT JUNCTION	..	..		9 11	10 42	12 36	2 11	2 38	4M43	—	1	2	1	11
STAVENTON HALT	..			—	—	—	—	2u24	4M39	—	1	3	—	
BROUGHTON GIFFORD HALT				—	—	—	—	—	4M46	—	1	0	—	
MELKSHAM	..	..		9 20	10 50	12 44	2 18	2 50	4M50	—	0	10	1	5
BEANACRE HALT	..			—	—	—	—	—	4M54	—	0	8	—	
LACOCK HALT	..	..		—	—	—	—	—	4M59	—	0	5	—	
CALNE	..	..	..	9 20	10 45	1 45	2 40	5 0	7 12	—	0	9	—	

189

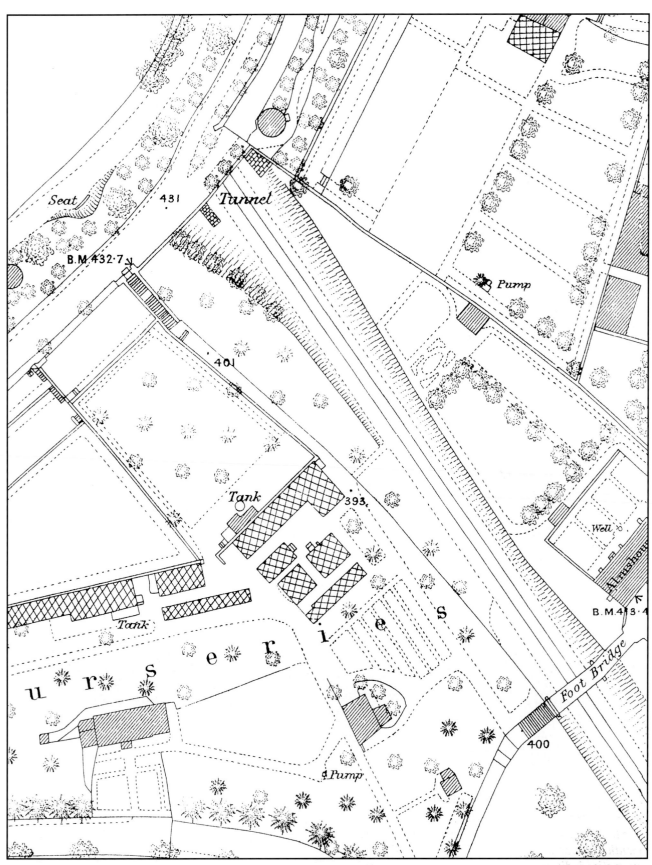

An extract from the 1886 O.S. 25" to 1 mile map, showing the east end of Devizes tunnel and the footbridge to Hillworth.

7. Devizes Tunnel

The tunnel was built in 1862 to form part of the Berks & Hants Hungerford to Devizes connection. At 190 yards long by 40 feet wide, it ran underneath Devizes Castle and had a 20º radius of curve. Whilst initially the tunnel housed a single track, it was constructed allowing for a future capacity of two tracks, and in fact the O.S. map of 1886 shows twin lines entering from the west end, of which one terminated inside at a buffer stop. The foundation of the tunnel walls had to be carried some 20 or 30 feet below the existing surface of the castle's moat and down to the level of what was probably the original moat before the castle's elevation. During the excavation a number of Roman artefacts were unearthed. The mouths of the tunnel were formed with grey stone crenellated portals to blend with the castle itself at the wish of the castle owner. The lining was of masonry except for the portions at the Devizes station end (approximately 1 chain long) and the Pans Lane end (approximately 20 feet long) which were brick-lined. A wooden footbridge crossed the mouth of the tunnel at the west end, forming a right of way from the castle grounds to the station, just below which was an underbridge for Snail's Lane which was used as an access road.

Before work started on the tunnel, the BHER entered into an agreement dated 14th July 1861 with William Brown, one of the tenants occupying property in the castle grounds. The excavation below part of the property, it was thought, might render that part unsafe for habitation. It affected only the part used by the tenant so the agreement was for him to vacate for three months whilst the excavation took place and for this the railway paid him £30 compensation. The servants remained in the part of the premises which it was considered would not be affected by the works.

In 1880 the War Office requested from the railway a report on the tunnel which was thought to be for weight and clearance details for the movement of military equipment on the line.

The tunnel mouth with the 'Bear' siding and telegraph lineman's hut in the foreground. The wooden footbridge just above the mouth can be seen behind the yard gas lamp and permanent way hut. The castle property which had to be vacated during the excavation is directly above. In the foreground is a trolley used by the permanent way staff for moving equipment. (J.Gander)

On Tuesday 21st August 1888, the firm of Debenham, Tewson, Farmer & Bridgewater, auctioneers and land agents of 80 Cheapside, London, sold Devizes Castle by auction. The property was sold tenure freehold with the exception of about half an acre of leasehold renewable in perpetuity at a nominal rent. The tunnel was the freehold of the GWR but the surface part of the East Moat Field was leased to the vendors at 5s. per annum.

This was the time when the tunnel housed twin tracks, one of which terminated within. The date when this short length with buffers was removed is not known but they had gone before the Second World War when local reporter Terry Gaylard, together with friends, were invited by the driver of a tank engine to ride on the footplate through the tunnel to pick up more goods trucks. Terry remembers being in big trouble on arrival home afterwards looking like a chimney sweep. Although the tunnel was only 190 yards long, he says that it seemed longer as the trains, being close to the station at that point, were always travelling slowly.

Signalman Rowley Reeves and Bert Clack had a theory that when up trains passed through the tunnel, if the smoke from the engine came back out on the station side, it was a sure sign that it was going to rain.

Between the wars, a Down (Outer) Home signal was installed on the downside of the single track and on the Devizes station side of the Hillworth Road bridge. This was at 617 yards, worked from lever '0' at the signalbox. It was track-circuited to 200 yards to the rear of the signal (in order to detect waiting trains).

Immediately outside the eastern end of the tunnel was a footbridge originally built of sleepers. It was referred to locally as 'Wooden Bridge' even after it was replaced in 1954 with one of metal and concrete costing £615.11s.4d. This formed part of a walkway via St John's Churchyard to Hillworth and was a favourite place for young train-spotters to congregate. The walkway lies on the route from Devizes Castle taken by those to be hanged when the gallows stood at Hillworth. The bridge, now owned by Railtrack, remains in use to this day.

5973 Rollestone Hall enters the east portal of the tunnel with a down four-coach train in the 1950s. (Trevor J.Saunders)

At the east end of the tunnel was a footbridge which was a fine vantage point for photography. This postcard view of the castle shows the crenellated portal and allotments at the turn of the century.

The wooden footbridge at Estcourt Hill with two girls posing for a postcard photographer. A Distant signal at the tunnel mouth had been removed by 1923 and replaced by an Outer Home signal positioned nearer to and west of Hillworth Road bridge. (Paul Gilson collection)

About half a century after the photograph showing the allotments by the tunnel mouth, 28XX Class 2-8-0 No.2811 with the 10.40am Saturday Only Bristol to Reading, leaves the east end of the tunnel. (Trevor J.Saunders)

0-6-0 Pannier Tank 5416 emerging from the tunnel with the 11.02am Devizes to Patney & Chirton service in May 1959. (J. Spencer-Gilks)

5014 Goodrich Castle pulling out of the tunnel with the 11.22am Bristol to Paddington stopping train on leaving Devizes at 12.26pm in 1940. (D.Seaton)

On the 1923 O.S. map on the next page, a footpath from Hillworth Road to St John's Church is shown crossing the line in view of the wooden footbridge. This was the vantage point for Douglas Seaton's series of train photographs in the early years of the Second World War. The white gate in the fence with a trespass notice can be seen in front of the 2-6-0 and concertina composite coach on a down train in the snow of 1940. (D.Seaton)

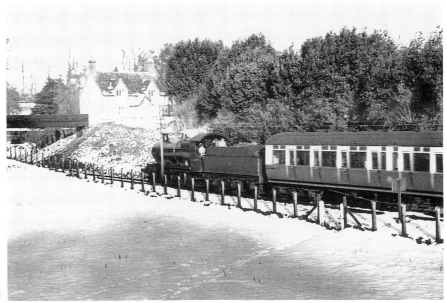

The white gate for the footpath is clearly visible in this 1940s scene as LMS 0-6-0 No.3096, on loan to the GWR and shedded at Westbury, passes with an up goods train. (D.Seaton)

4085 Berkeley Castle in 1940 on a 3.05pm Bristol, 4.39pm Devizes for all stations Patney to Reading, due to arrive at Paddington at 7.50pm. The first carriage is a corridor clerestory type, now without roof boards in wartime. (D.Seaton)

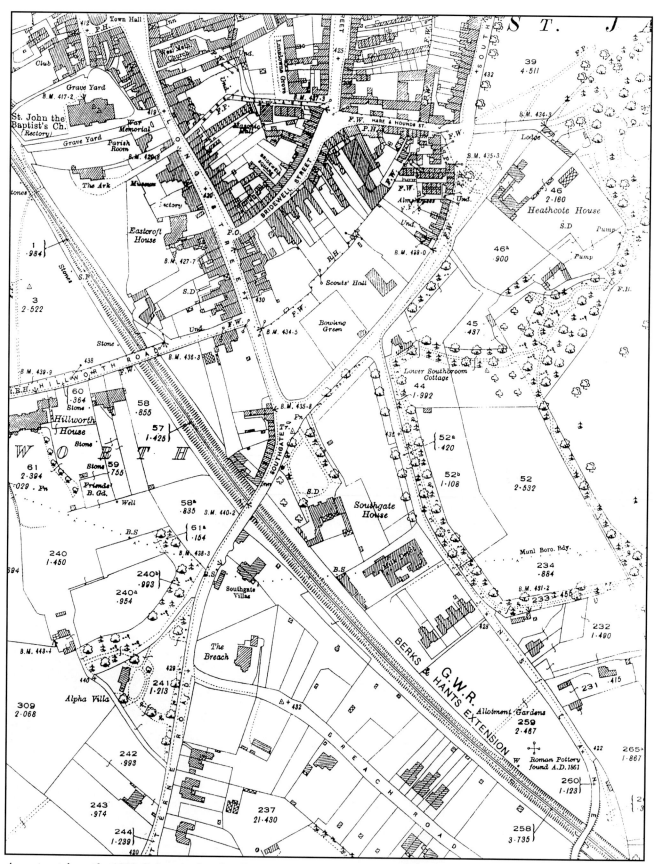

An extract from the 1923 O.S. map showing Pans Lane crossing the Devizes Branch just south-east of the future halt.

8. Pans Lane Halt

When the Berks & Hants Extension from Hungerford to Devizes opened on 4th November 1862, the nearest station to Devizes on the line was at Woodborough, a distance of seven miles. Requests had been made for an additional station at Patney, but the GWR was of the opinion that Woodborough was sufficient to provide the service. At the turn of the century, however, Patney obtained its station with the opening of the new line to Westbury.

A station closer still to Devizes opened on 4th March 1929 in the parish of Roundway. This was to be known as Pans Lane Halt. The station site was in a cutting that, when originally excavated for the Berks & Hants Extension, produced a number of Roman relics, the site having been the centre of an extensive Roman settlement in the second century A.D. It appears that this area was known by the early inhabitants as 'Punctuobice', and when the station was being built, it was suggested to the railway authorities that it be given this name. This was turned down on the basis that it was too long a title for so insignificant a station. One of a number of skeletons discovered when the cutting was excavated had with it two perfectly preserved small urns which were donated to the Devizes Museum. Further skeletons were discovered later when the station platforms were being built, and it is known that at least one

of these was reburied in the station embankment. It has been suggested that the area's name originated because of the numerous finds 'panned' up there over the years. When the GWR offered tenders for the construction of the station buildings, they referred to the site as 'Pans Lane Bridge'. When the halt was built there were only a few houses in the immediate vicinity, but a proposal was made for the Borough of Devizes to expand, and the provision of a station, it was considered, would achieve this. Other than residential property, the Devizes Isolation Hospital and the Wilts United Dairies were within a short walk of the new halt.

Station Buildings

Pans Lane Halt consisted of one platform, 208 feet in length, positioned on the down side of the line. It had a gravel surface, held in position by a wall of railway sleepers, and on it was a corrugated-iron waiting room. The cost of its conctruction was £196. A wooden permanent way cabin and a fixed distant signal were sited just off the Devizes end of the platform, but the signal was removed at some stage. Also at the west end was a whistle board warning train drivers of their approach to the tunnel.

Only passenger traffic was dealt with at Pans Lane, and the entry was by way of a flight of timber steps and a pathway from the road bridge, lit by two oil lamps. A Tilley lamp lit the station

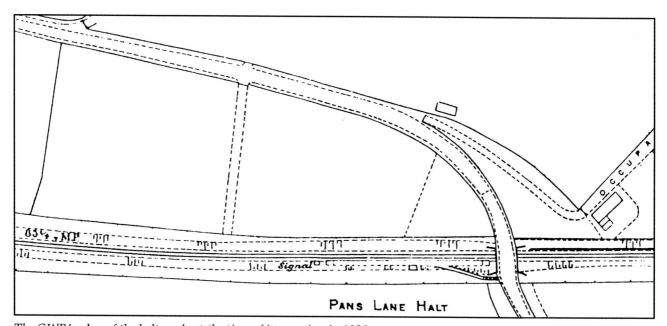

The GWR's plan of the halt made at the time of its opening in 1929.

A postcard view, c.1900, of the future site of Pans Lane Halt taken from the overbridge. The factory in the background is that of Wilts United Dairies. The locomotive passing the fixed distance signal is an 0-4-2T hauling four coaches.

and this was serviced daily by a porter from Devizes. The guard of the last down train calling at the halt was required to extinguish the lamp and take it to Devizes station.

Passenger Services

During the 1930s, auto-trains came into their own on the branch where short distance stopping trains were needed. These, unlike railmotors, were made up of a carriage or set of carriages with a small steam locomotive at one end. At the opposite end, the train was capable of operation from the windowed end of the carriage, so this facility avoided the need for the engine to run around the train at a terminus, which it could not do unless a passing loop was provided. Pans Lane, with a single line through it, was such a station. In the latter part of 1953 eight of the twelve up weekday services were auto-trains and, as Pans Lane was a station without run-round facilities, it was used as the starting point and terminus for some of the local trains such as the 5.52pm from Trowbridge, arriving at 6.25pm.

During 1940 the 2.45pm from Paddington was reintroduced. Having formerly run as an express, it now stopped at all stations between Newbury and Devizes, which it reached at 5.11pm, terminating at Bristol Temple Meads at 6.20pm. This service did not last for long and was withdrawn again from October 1941. This left the branch with no down trains between the 2.05pm from Newbury, terminating at Devizes at 3.17pm, and the 6.30pm Devizes to Westbury auto-train. From 6th October, Pans Lane was temporarily closed by the GWR although stops were made when necessary. The evening auto-trains from Trowbridge were now terminating at Devizes. In the timetable commencing 25th September 1939, the two down Sunday trains, the 9.05am and 5.30pm from Paddington to Trowbridge, would stop at Pans Lane if passengers made a request to the guard at Patney & Chirton. Such a request was made to Reg Clarke who was the guard on one occasion just after the war, but knowing that the steps up to the road level from the platform were steep and of timber, he felt that with the amount of heavy rain at the time they could be slippery and dangerous so he politely refused the request. The passenger's view of this has not been recorded.

The withdrawn 2.45pm from Paddington was later reintroduced as the 2.35pm and George Behrend in his book *Gone with Regret* observed:

either you knew what was so funny about the 2.35pm train from London with 'Paddington, Bristol and Weston-super-Mare' on it or else you found out in the neighbourhood of Pans Lane Halt. Pan laughed loudest of all! The train left Paddington's Platform 1 carrying the 'Paddington, Bristol and Weston-Super-Mare' headboards, as did most of the Bristol trains not working through Taunton. The unsuspecting passengers would board the train without showing their tickets and on departure, good time would be made to Reading and Newbury. Here, as later on at Devizes, there would be a leisurely three minutes for station staff. At this stage it would be realised by some, an irate Sir Winston Churchill being one, that they had not, as thought, caught a fast express train but were on the dreadful stopper that would take 3 hours 22 minutes to complete the journey. Passengers not having previously used this particular train could become really concerned when after leaving Patney & Chirton on the main line, they found themselves on a single line and at Pans Lane Halt.

The platform was too short to take a complete train, being sufficient for only two coaches. Passengers other than those on the two-coach local trains, were required to travel in the two rear cars and drivers pulling into the halt had to make sure these coaches were stopped alongside the platform. Guards of all trains calling there had to ensure they collected tickets from all the passengers getting off. These tickets then had to be presented to the Station Master at Patney & Chirton in the case of up trains and to the Station Master at Devizes in the case of down trains.

As Pans Lane was an unstaffed station, it was necessary for passengers boarding the train there to buy tickets from the guard or in the case of those travelling the short distance to Devizes, at the station on arrival.

Despite early hopes, Pans Lane was not to prosper. From its opening in March 1929 until the end of that year it sold 1,476 tickets at a total income of £85. By 1933, ticket sales had dwindled to 672 with, for the first time, two season tickets, all providing an income of £54. The station was used mainly by people living in the area and visitors to the nearby Roundway Hospital.

Although vast quantities of local milk was sent daily to London, the Wilts United Dairies factory in Pans Lane was producing butter and cheese until its closure in 1940; it all went from Devizes station as the halt did not have the access and facilities for freight handling.

Trains were calling again at Pans Lane after the Second World War with the BR Summer Timetable of 1953 showing two up trains daily and three on Saturdays. There were three down trains daily from Monday to Saturday inclusive with more scheduled to call at the halt on Sundays. The same year BR agreed to provide an additional four stopping trains but indicated the future of the halt would depend on the popularity of these services.

In the early 1960s, the timetables showed local and London trains stopping everyday except for Sundays, but in the final timetable leading up to closure, Pans Lane Halt was omitted.

had been
ore solid
h line.
s previous
s adequate
ney Bridge,
ed with the
to the local
indicated
still to be
command
ddition, to
good road
dients, the
ble. Patney
ready had a
particular'.
ne GWR by
n Hill, vicar
responding
ne proposal
oint where
Devizes line
nd into the
entrance to
to Andover
d best serve
, Easterton,
on from the
on, Bishops
north side.
e proposal,
table access
mount they
g the station
15th April
authorities
e approach
engineer's
e work and
nates were
led a bridge
and one for
sing instead
ach roads.

Hill's proposed
Stert Junction

PANS LANE HALT.

The Platform is 208 feet in length, situated between Devizes and Patney. Passenger traffic only is dealt with.

As the platform will not accommodate a complete Train, but only two coaches, passengers other than by rail motor cars for Pans Lane must be confined to the two rear coaches, and in drawing up at the Halt care must be taken that these coaches are stopped alongside Platform.

Guards of Trains and Rail Motor Cars calling at Pans Lane will collect Tickets from passengers alighting there, and hand same to the Station Master at Patney and Chirton, in the case of Up Trains, and to the Station Master at Devizes in the case of Down Trains.

To ensure Passengers travelling in the last two coaches, and to avoid passengers alighting at Halt without Tickets, care to be taken by Station Masters that passengers joining Trains at their Stations enter those coaches and are in possession of Tickets.

RAIL MOTORS, DEVIZES TO PANS LANE AND BACK.

A Rail Motor Car may work from Devizes to Pans Lane, and return from there to Devizes under Electric Train Staff Regulation 8(a).

When an Engine is used attached to a Motor on a service which normally includes a trip from Devizes to Pans Lane and back, this portion of the journey must be cancelled and other means provided to convey any passengers. The Station Master at Trowbridge must arrange to advise Devizes by wire when an Engine is being used attached to a Rail Motor.

Instructions for railmotors calling at the halt, from the 1933 Working Timetable.

The downside platform entrance, station signs and footbridge steps. Note the signalbox beyond the west end of the down platform. (R.Priddle)

The footbridge and nameboard in 1951 after the canopy has been removed. Note the three neat flowerbeds on the island platform. (R.Priddle)

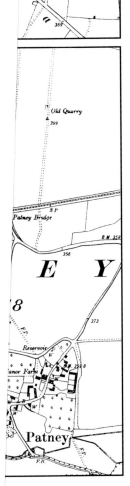

Walking across to the island platform its upper construction can be seen. (R.Pope)

Descending the stairs to the island platform waiting room, one could always study the posters. (R.Pope)

Two rear views of the signalbox overlooking the loading dock. The lower windows were to the locking frame room. (R.Pope)

(below) Lampman Charlie Tilley stands outside his hut and store at the far west end in 1935. (W.Tanner)

(above) The corrugated-iron hut in the left foreground, previously used for milk traffic is now in use by the lampman for maintenance. The hut previously used for that purpose is visible in the centre distance, now tarred black for the permanent way gang. By this date – August 1958 – the signals are on metal round posts, having previously been wooden. The water tower built during the Second World War is visible on the right in front of Patney Copse; it was the source of the station water supply. (R.Carpenter collection)

The permanent way department's hut at the east end of the down platform, seen from the road bridge in 1966. Note the grindstone to the left and the extension at the rear of the hut as compared with the photograph on page 205. (D.J.Hyde)

On completion of the new line from Patney to Westbury, where it joined with the Wilts, Somerset & Weymouth route, the station at Patney was opened for goods traffic from 29th July 1900 and for passengers from 1st October. Westbury station was built at this time and between the stations on the new line two more stations were opened to serve local needs at 'Lavington' and 'Edington & Bratton'.

In July 1909 a military platform was completed on the north side of the up island platform running parallel with the perimeter fence. It was constructed with railway sleepers, having an earth and stone surface, 650 feet long and 18 feet wide. The reason for its provision was to allow a suitable location for the detraining of a large force of Territorials who took part in an army exercise on Salisbury Plain on Sunday 1st August. The size of the platform was important as it was necessary for the troops and equipment to be off-loaded promptly so that the train could be moved away to allow the next one in. The trains came from London and had to cross the up main and branch line to enter coaches first into the single-sided military platform that terminated at a buffer stop. There was access from the platform directly onto the roadway from where the troops crossed in a

southerly direction over the railway bridge, passing through the villages of Patney and Chirton before reaching Salisbury Plain. The military platform had the same standard of oil lighting installed as the rest of the station. It is thought that as a result of traffic movements for the exercise and the certainty of future military use, the GWR authorised the installation of a new cross-over rail at the London end of the station, to allow the down trains, after unloading, to be put back onto the up line for immediate return to London. No evidence has been found, however, that this cross-over was ever installed. Another cross-over was introduced at this time connecting the two lines between the military and the up bay platform.

Major track work took place during 1936 when the complete line from Patney & Chirton to Holt Junction was adapted for heavier engines. The entire permanent way was renewed, with alterations in parts, at a cost of £7,583. Renewal of the signalling at Bromham, Seend and Devizes was also carried out at the same time at a cost of £825. Point connections at Patney & Chirton were renewed in 1946 for £265, and a few years before this, in July 1942, the road access to the station was improved at a cost of £32, with the materials arriving by rail from Freshford.

Looking west from the footbridge the military platform can be seen on the extreme right. Its signal is 'off', indicating a shunting movement by the locomotive seen waiting at the up main platform. At the down main platform can be seen an up milk train, the last four vehicles of which are low siphons and a four-wheel brake van, alongside the milk dock. Several milk churns are waiting by the then base for the milk traffic. (Mowat collection)

(left) Another view of the same military goods train as in the previous photograph. A Dean Goods hauls sheeted wagons loaded with tracked vehicles. (Mowat collection)

(right) The photographer has now moved to the road bridge to watch the train reverse from the up yard, through the military platform and apparently as far as the buffers to drop off the brake van. In the background may be seen the covered section of the footbridge, with the uncovered part for the public footpath on the right. The separate access road to the military platform can be seen on the right-hand side. (Mowat collection)

(left) Eastwards from the footbridge, the end of the military siding is seen in the 1920s with its separate road access alongside. To the right before the road bridge is a run round loop to assist in shunting, without fouling the main line. (Mowat collection)

(right) In this 1953 photograph, the track of the military platform is still in position as is the stone part of the platform edging. The timber edging had been removed 12 months previously. The bay platform used by the branch-line trains is seen on the left. (M.Luffman)

During 1947 a new brick building with a flat roof for use as a parcels office and messroom was built on the down platform at the east end of the existing buildings. This provision, together with the essential services, cost £567, and it replaced a corrugated-iron building. One of the essential services was the telephone with an exchange number of Chirton 250.

A timber fogman's hut stood on the down side of the line near the Down Home signal until a spark from a passing engine caused it to be destroyed by fire on 25th August 1947. Leading porters Jim Perry and Charlie Tilley tried to extinguish it with water, but were unable to get close enough because of the severe heat.

The staff at Patney & Chirton always took pride in its maintenance. The Ladies' Waiting Room often had fresh flowers on the table and the platform gardens were well tended with interesting floral displays. In fact they won the 'Best Kept Gardens Award' on five occasions, and after the last presentation the staff asked the judges to make the award to a different station the following year. There was an occasion when the *Torbay Express* stopped at the station to pick up Sir Brian Robertson, Chairman of the British Transport Commission, who was returning to London. He was so impressed with the floral displays and general upkeep that he remarked to Edgar Cross, the Station Master: 'This is one of the stations we must keep'. The Station Master saluted him as the *Torbay Express* pulled out.

Passenger Services

With the station opening for passenger services on the 1st October 1900, the first arrival was a local 6.45am Trowbridge to Pewsey. Its departure time from Patney was 7.31am, Woodborough 7.40am and Pewsey at 7.47am. The first down train left Patney at 9.53am. This was the 6.30am from Paddington to Bristol Temple Meads arriving at 11.35am. Both of these trains passed over the branch, but there was also a local service on the new line between Patney and Westbury running weekdays only. This comprised four trains in each direction daily, calling at the intermediate stations of Lavington and Edington & Bratton. The first of these arrived at Patney from Westbury at 9.45am, departing on the return journey at 10.00am.

Patney & Chirton station in 1953 showing the down main platform with its flat-roofed staff accommodation east of the platform buildings and the island platform with its well-kept flowerbeds. (M.Luffman)

In addition to the new line services, Patney station received daily five up and five down weekday trains using the branch, and six on a Thursday, which was Devizes Market day. On Sundays two trains in each direction called at Patney.

Services to and from Patney did not change significantly in the next twelve months except for the introduction of slip coaches released off the 9.35am and 5.10pm London to Weymouth expresses.

Probably the most famous train to pass through Patney was the *Cornish Riviera Express*. It appeared with the introduction of the first regular Paddington to Plymouth non-stop service, via the Berks & Hants Line, on 21st July 1906. It was not long before it too was formed with slip coaches, released at Westbury for Weymouth, and Taunton for Ilfracombe and Minehead.

In the 1908 summer timetable cheap tickets to Devizes every Saturday were available from the local main-line stations between Pewsey and Edington & Bratton. These could only be used on one train, and in the case of Patney & Chirton, it was the 5.40pm departure. The 3rd Class return fare was 7d. and passengers could return by any train on the day of issue, which, at that time of day, did not give them many options. The last local train back from Devizes was the 7.22pm.

The station traffic was busy, of course, through the First World War years, much of it being military. Conveyance of passengers after this period remained fairly constant until the end of 1928. During that year 6,968 tickets were sold at £954, plus two season tickets at £1.10s. each. From then on ticket sales reduced year by year and did not pick up again until 1942 and even then the returns were only 4,133 and 8 season tickets. The downward spiral started again from 1946 and in the early 1950s the figure hovered at around 3,000 tickets per year. The decline was partly as a result of local train withdrawals by BR who indicated at the time that people were increasingly using trains for long-distance travel rather than local journeys. Notwithstanding this, the June/September 1953 timetable showed a total of 24 regular weekday trains stopping at Patney. The mornings were the busy time with 15 trains before 12.00 noon. The first of these was the up 6.25am from Trowbridge, terminating at Patney at 7.08am where it formed the 7.20am down, terminating in Devizes at 7.32am. It waited there until 8.05am before departing for Westbury with an all station stopper. The first up London train in the morning from Patney departed at 7.50am. This was the 5.45am from Bristol Temple Meads, 7.15am off Trowbridge, arriving in Paddington at 10.15am. The first down train from Paddington calling at Patney was the 7.05am, stopping at all stations to Patney, where it arrived at 9.50am. It then took the branch, stopping at Devizes, Seend and Holt Junction. It left Holt at 10.18am along the Wilts, Somerset & Weymouth via Bradford Junction to call at Bradford-on-Avon and Bath Spa, before terminating at Bristol Temple Meads at 11.08am.

A couple of incidents occurred at Patney at this time, involving passenger-carrying trains, which could both have turned out to be worse than they were. The first was really a case of over-familiarity involving the arrival of a local train at Patney from Devizes. This type of train, referred to by the local inhabitants as the 'Patney Puffer', was supposed to pull into the bay platform on the up side of the line but the signalman knowing there was no main-line train scheduled at the time of its arrival, would allow this particular service to run into the main up line platform. Consequently the engine drivers became familiar with this routine. The day came however, when because of a special running, signalman Bill Brooks switched the branch train into the regulation bay platform. The engine driver, not expecting this, maintained his speed for a straight approach to the main-line platform. He found himself rounding the curve of the bay platform with the train being thrown against the platform's edging due to the excessive speed. Fortunately it remained on the rails, but the carriage stock received considerable damage.

Another incident involved a main-line train, also occurring during the 1950s. At that time there was a farm crossing just east of Patney Bridge; on this occasion farmworker George Strickland was crossing when his tractor became stuck with its trailer still standing on the lines. Fortunately, Station Master Edgar Cross noticed this from the platform and knowing the train was due, quickly informed the signalman who was able to stop the oncoming train until the line was cleared.

A more humorous accident has been recalled by Robert Kemp, a Devizes tailor, who remembers Mr Higginbottom, a tall man, travelling between Patney and Devizes in a non-corridor coach. He found he had been sitting on an ants' nest and being alone in the compartment, he took off his trousers and shook them out of the window. In the slip stream, however, they were blown out of his hands. On arrival at Devizes he was able to borrow a pair from the porter, who was, inevitably, very short.

Brown Bouverie Gas Turbine No.18000 rushes through Patney on the down Cornish Riviera in 1951. On the left can be seen the branch token catcher net with the military platform behind. (Wiltshire Gazette)

216

9. Patney & Chirton Junction

On leaving Pans Lane, the branch followed a gentle curve towards Patney, crossing first Sleight Bridge near Stert, which, when it was being demolished in March 1970, defied 300 sticks of gelignite before giving way to the bull-dozer. Leaving Stert, the line passed over two small lane bridges and the underbridge at 82 miles, 75 chains which straddled the A342 Devizes to Andover road. The roadway dipped considerably here and frequent flooding occurred under the bridge. The bridge itself, originally built in 1862 of wrought-iron main girders, timber deck and brick abutments, was reconstructed in 1941 because of corrosion to the girders. The estimated cost of the work was £2,260. Two hundred yards from the underbridge the A342 crosses Lydeway overbridge, under which runs the Paddington to Westbury main line. This bridge was subject to severe damage in 1935 when rain water seepage caused a partial collapse. The branch then ran parallel with the main line until joining it approximately a quarter of a mile west of Patney & Chirton station.

The two villages of Patney and Chirton lay in the picturesque Vale of Pewsey. Discounting the military use of Salisbury Plain, the area's industry is primarily farming, as it was with the coming of the railways in the latter part of the 1800s. The station mainly handled farm produce. When the railway first passed through Patney in 1862, however, no station was provided. The GWR received requests for such a provision but turned them down on the basis that nearby Wood-borough station was adequate to serve the needs of the area. After the eventual provision of Patney station the village itself developed northwards towards the station.

Station Buildings

The new line under construction between Stert and Westbury by Messrs Pauling & Co was making rapid progress by April 1898. Work had been delayed before this when subsidence of a 12-foot culvert at Crookwood had buried an immense quantity of materials. This had been overcome by rebuilding it on a more solid foundation closer to the existing branch line.

By this time the GWR had changed its previous opinion that Woodborough station was adequate and were considering a new one at Patney Bridge, which was near the junction to be formed with the lines to Westbury and Devizes. In a letter to the local press, however, the General Manager indicated that the final site for the station was still to be settled. The GWR wanted the station to command the new line and the branch, and, in addition, to have good road access. Lydeway had a good road but, because of differing levels and gradients, the engineering difficulties made it unsuitable. Patney Bridge, whilst close to Woodborough, already had a road, albeit 'not leading to anywhere in particular'. Another site had been suggested to the GWR by local officials, with the Rev Dr Hamlyn Hill, vicar of Urchfont and a man of high profile, corresponding with the company on their behalf. The proposal was for the station to be sited at the point where Swinlake Drove crossed the existing Devizes line continuing north past Hatfield Farm and into the Etchilhampton road. The southern entrance to Swinlake Drove was from the Devizes to Andover Road. It was argued that this site would best serve the villages of Wedhampton, Urchfont, Easterton, West Lavington and Market Lavington from the south side of the line and Etchilhampton, Bishops Cannings and All Cannings from the north side. The GWR agreed to the merits of the proposal, but felt that the cost of providing suitable access roads would add considerably to the amount they were prepared to pay for constructing the station there. They wrote to Hamlyn Hill on 15th April asking for the possibility of the local authorities undertaking the construction of the approach roads. Later still they sent their engineer's report of the estimate for drainage work and metalling of the roads. Two estimates were provided, one for £3,200 which included a bridge over the line with raised approaches, and one for £2,308 which provided for a level crossing instead of a bridge to connect the two approach roads.

(left) Extracts from the O.S. map of 1901, showing the Stert to Westbury line under construction. Hamlyn Hill's proposed site for the station was where 'Stepping Stones' are marked at the left-hand edge of the lower map. The original Stert Junction signalbox is also marked 'SB' on the north side of the line, half a mile west of Patney Bridge.

Unfortunately for these villages and probably also for the railway company the necessary finance was not forthcoming from local sources, so the station was built at Patney, a village whose inhabitants in 1927 numbered only 127.

The building of the station commenced in 1899, at 81 miles, 7 chains from Paddington, slightly west of the existing Patney Bridge, from where initially it took its name, and was to a design similar to many standard GWR stations built at this time. It was named 'Patney & Chirton Junction' soon after opening to avoid confusion with 'Putney Bridge' in London. Two platforms were built, with the down one, 500 feet long, housing the main buildings. These, from west to east, comprised a General Waiting Room, a Booking Office, a Ladies' Waiting Room and a Gent's W.C., built in red brick with a slate roof.

Approaching the Lydeway bridge over the Andover road, by the Clock Inn, in the 1950s, is a Hall Class locomotive hauling the afternoon Newbury to Westbury train consisting of a corridor third, brake composite and a 'B' set. This view clearly shows the difference in gradient between the main line and the Devizes Branch. (Trevor J.Saunders)

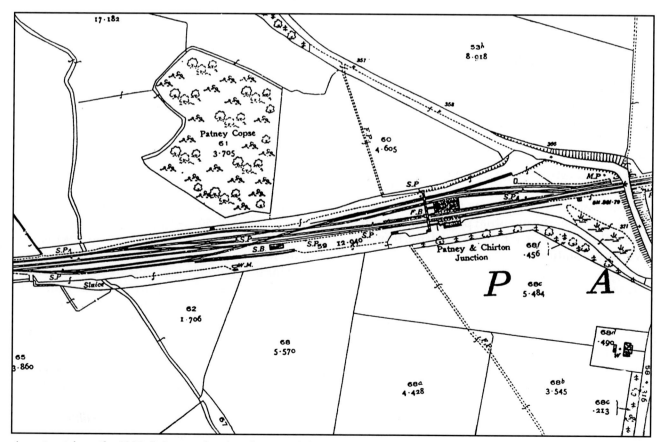

An extract from the 1939 O.S. map showing the up and down sidings at Patney & Chirton station.

A postcard view, soon after opening, showing the approach road, station buildings and permanent way hut in the foreground. The covered southern half of the footbridge can be seen, but the northern section from the island platform remained uncovered for all its life, serving as a public footpath.

A standard wooden canopy extended from the buildings over this part of the platform. From the roadway an approach road led to the main station entrance at the east end of the building. The up island platform, 400 feet long, had the same accommodation except for a Booking Office. This left a platform space between the General and Ladies' Waiting Room. Wooden canopies covered the platforms on both sides of the buildings. A covered footbridge gave access to both platforms and the bridge included a flight of steps from both sides of the track as it formed part of a public right of way. The canopy only covered that part of the footbridge over the main lines and the staircases to the down and island platforms.

The signalbox, with internal measurements of 49'6" x 11'6" x 11'5", was west of the downside platform, its materials matching the station buildings. The box displayed a cast-iron nameplate 'Patney Bridge Signal Box' until the renaming of the station, when a new plate was cast to display 'Patney & Chirton Junction Signal Box'. Bill Brooks, the last signalman in the box, purchased this from BR on closure of the branch but its whereabouts is not now known. Close to the box on both sides of the track, tablet catchers were erected for trains using the branch line. The cost of building the station with all of its facilities, the signalbox and additional trackwork amounted to £10,692.15s.6d.

The station did not have water cranes and in the early days domestic station water came from a bore-hole sunk on 20th June 1900. There was no fresh water at the station until 1950 when an Agreement (No.75121) was signed on 28th June with English Farmers Ltd for a supply from a new water tower built during World War Two by Rendell's, the Devizes builders, on the up side of the line in the field by Patney Copse.

At the rear of the signalbox was a 23-wagon goods siding into a loading dock which was added in 1904. This, together with a roadway and extension of a bridge over a nearby culvert, cost £1,386.16s.1d. Close to the dock was the weighbridge and its office. Opposite the mileage siding by the branch line there was a corrugated-iron lampman's hut; this later changed to a tool store for the permanent way gang when the facilities for the lampman were moved to a similar hut on the down platform. At the east end of the up platform stood a timber hut with a ground frame and at the same end of the down platform was a timber platelayers' hut.

On 30th April 1921 all is clean and tidy. The nameboard with its central support overlooks the main station and island platform building. The enamel sign attached to the fence beyond advertises 'Pears Soap'. Notice the oil lamps, the wooden platform seats and the screens around the Gent's W.C.s (LGRP)

This 1962 view makes a useful comparison with the previous photograph. Note the changes in the lamps, seats and paintwork, as well as on the footbridge which has now lost its canopy. (C.Maggs)

These and the following photographs of the station buildings provide (with the drawings in the Appendix) a useful guide to the standard station design of 1900. Starting with the road-side view of the main building (left), passengers entered through the iron gate on the left. The first three windows were to the booking office and waiting room; the next two were for the clerks and Station Master; then the Ladies' waiting room and toilet, with the Gentlemen's lavatory at the end. The flat-roofed building at the far eastern end was for parcels and the staff messroom, built in 1947. The rail-side views (above), with the main entrance top right and the Ladies' waiting room bottom left, show the glazed canopy which always gave plenty of light. (R.Pope)

The downside platform entrance, station signs and footbridge steps. Note the signalbox beyond the west end of the down platform. (R.Priddle)

The footbridge and nameboard in 1951 after the canopy has been removed. Note the three neat flowerbeds on the island platform. (R.Priddle)

Walking across to the island platform its upper construction can be seen. (R.Pope)

Descending the stairs to the island platform waiting room, one could always study the posters. (R.Pope)

Two rear views of the signalbox overlooking the loading dock. The lower windows were to the locking frame room. (R.Pope)

6960 Raveningham Hall is at the up platform on a stopping service on 14th May 1956. The ground frame hut is clearly seen at the platform end. In the foreground is the loop for the former military siding. (M.Boizvell)

By 1961, the station did not appear to be making much money. The June General Coaching Account for fares shows total receipts of £125.0s.3d.

£118. 19s. 11d	Passenger Tickets
17s. 8d	Bicycle/Dog Tickets
£2. 10s. 2d	Parcels Forwarded
6s. 0d	Car Parking
£1. 0s. 0d	Money Found
8s. 8d	Telephone Calls
1s. 0d	Timetable Sale
15s. 3d	Transfer Vouchers
1s. 7d	Miscellaneous

The station was unstaffed as from 8th November 1965 and closed with the branch in April 1966. At that time six passenger trains a day in each direction were stopping at Patney; there was no Sunday service. These weekday services were:-

DOWN TRAINS

09.26	(08.30 Newbury-Devizes-Westbury)
11.35	Devizes-Westbury
13.26	(12.30 Newbury-Devizes-Trowbridge)
18.33	(17.36 Newbury-Devizes-Westbury)
20.42	(19.36 Newbury-Devizes-Westbury)
21.00	Westbury via Lavington (connection from 19.36 Newbury).This service preceded the 18.55 Kensington Olympia-St. Austell Motorail along the main, the London to Cornwall train being booked to wait at Patney from 21.00 to 21.20 hours.

UP TRAINS

07.10	(06.50 Westbury-Lavington-Newbury)
07.32	(06.58 Trowbridge-Reading SX/ Paddington SO)
10.40 arr.	(10.30 Devizes-Patney)
10.49	(10.28 Westbury-Lavington-Newbury)
16.20	(15.20 Westbury-Devizes-Newbury)
20.15 arr.	(20.30 Westbury-Devizes-Patney) This last up train of the day ran five minutes later at times when the 17.05 Seaton Junction-Kensington milk train was running.

When the 7.36pm Newbury to Westbury left Patney for the branch on Saturday 16th April 1966, George Gay from All Cannings and his nephew were the last passengers to board the last train.

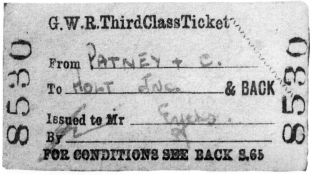

A return ticket from Patney & Chirton to Holt Junction.

Freight Traffic

As the station was in an area of prime farming land the majority of routine freight handled was agricultural. In the latter part of the 19th century a number of smaller farms in the Pewsey Vale had been amalgamated into larger units. This resulted in a number of big business farmers who developed their farms by mechanisation. Arthur Stratton was one of these. He and his family were from Woodborough and farmed 3,000 acres in and around nearby Alton Priors. As a result of poor harvests and foreign competition, these big business farmers, having bought up several smaller units, converted them to dairy farming. This milk was sent to London from the stations in the Vale: Lavington, Patney & Chirton and Woodborough. One farm at least, Cross's Manor Farm at Etchilhampton, had its churns labelled with a brass plate showing the station name 'Patney & Churton'. One of these plates with the incorrect spelling of Chirton still survives today. Frank Stratton, having promoted mechanisation in farming, lost his life to a machine when he was run over in 1918 by a steam engine in Woodborough station yard. Milk production in the area continued to flourish and just prior to World War Two, 51.5% of Wiltshire's milk was sold as liquid milk, mainly in London. Although there was mechanisation on the large farms, milk deliveries to the station were by horse and cart. The milk was brought to the station early in the

A brass plate from a milk churn used by one of the local farms. Note the mis-spelt station name. (R.Priddle)

morning. At Patney there were only two luggage trollies and these were used by the first farmers arriving with the milk churns. The latecomers had to roll their 17-gallon churns by hand over the crossing to the up platform where they were loaded into the milk vans. During the 1920s and early 1930s the outward milk handled was considerable and brought the railway good revenue. One of the best years at Patney was 1930 when Forwarded Milk Traffic for the year was 46,721 churns with receipts of £2,542. The next two years were good, but then a rapid drop took place in 1933 with only 893 churns being sent from this particular station at an income of just £88. Road transport was starting to encroach at this time. Other kinds of freight handled also began to diminish.

Livestock came in and went out of Patney although there was not a designated dock. Problems were often experienced with the loading and unloading of the animals, as the downside loading dock or the upside military platform had to be utilised as appropriate. It was not unknown for animals to escape. Between the wars the station was averaging approximately 50 livestock wagons a year which included both in and out traffic.

The average tonnage of coal for the same period was just over 600 tons per year. The coal would supply the local villages and in Chirton it could be obtained from Fussell's Garage who were coal dealers as well as car dealers. Percy Fussell also ran a taxi service from the station. Unless you were going to Patney itself, when you got out of the train it could be a long walk to any other destination. Coal arriving in railway wagons would be unloaded using railway labour and equipment. Coal distributors had to provide their own transport for collection from the station. Smaller items of general merchandise and parcels for despatch would be taken to the station by private means where they would be weighed and paid for. In-coming goods could be collected or alternatively, delivered to the customer by the railway parcels vans which were allocated to a number of stations and areas as part of the country lorry service. Patney was serviced by the Devizes-based vehicles. It was not unknown for some of the smaller packages to be delivered by the Patney station staff on their way home after duty.

The years of the Second World War did not see a surge in freight traffic in Patney and in fact the decline that was apparent in 1933 had continued, The total tonnage for 1933 had been 2,758 tons; ten years later in 1943 it was down to 1,873 tons. There was a slight improvement in the years immediately after the war, with outward freight including straw from the local farms for use by the army at Tidworth and livestock to market, together with rabbits from Alexander's Farm at Lydeway, these having been caught on and around Salisbury Plain. These left Patney in the Guards Van of passenger trains and were destined for the

The signalman's view of the downside yard and loading dock in 1956. (Trevor J.Saunders)

markets and hotels of London. Urchfont farmers George Potter and Dennis Ellis used the station for sending crops of sugar beet by rail to the sugar factories in Bury St Edmunds, Kidderminster and Ely. Dennis used the station during the 1940s and 50s and delivered the crop by tractor and trailer. He would receive permits from the sugar factories which determined the amount of sugar beet he could send on a particular delivery. The 10- and 16-ton wagons would be in the loading dock and Dennis would drive his tractor and trailer up to them and transfer his load manually, using a pitch fork. He recalls the wagons were not always in the load-dock in which case he would hitch his tractor to the wagons and pull them in himself. He also recalls the GWR had a 30-cwt lorry manned by three railway men who would collect sugar beet from the outlying farms. It took these three as long to unload their lorry as it did the farmer transferring his load by himself. The engine would arrive at Patney hauling a train load of sugar beet collected at other stations and the Patney wagons would be connected. Dennis's father also used Patney station for sending his eggs to market.

Incoming freight would arrive each morning on the 4.30am from Paddington carrying fish, meat and general groceries for the shops in Devizes. In July 1953, when unloading fish boxes from this train, porter Fred Cowdrey's left hand was pierced by a nail from a box. The national newspapers arrived via the branch to be collected by Jim Hale from Urchfont and Mrs Burry from All Cannings. Before World War Two, coal was brought into the station for the business of Mullins, the coal merchant at All Cannings; this business was later taken over by Tolsen's. Up until 1964 car parts for Fussell's Garage in Chirton together with small parcels were regularly arriving, with small parcels leaving as well. On 11th June 1948, Agreement No.71945 was signed as an indemnity allowing a Charles Carey to discharge kerosene from the dead end siding. Even a bed arrived in April 1953 on the 4.35pm from Newbury. When being weighed in on arrival, it fell off the scales onto porter Cowdrey who it would seem was accident-prone. Porter Harold Burry also had problems unloading fish boxes in 1961. He was standing with one leg on the four-wheel platform trolley and one leg in the fish wagon. He received a back injury when the trolley rolled away and he fell out of the wagon.

Harold Burry also recalls that many a time the china clay traffic en route from the Cornish mines to London would be put off at Patney and Wood-

The early morning stopping goods arrives at Patney in 1947, behind a 2-6-0, which is passing the east end ground frame and up starter. (P.Brown)

borough with hot axle boxes where the clay, which was like talcum powder, had seeped from the sacks through the wagon floorboards onto the axles. Porter Jim Gunthorpe says another reason for this was that often the sacks would be loaded in just one corner of the wagon, the rest being empty, and the weight of the sacks over one wheel would cause the overheated axle boxes. When, later, the china clay was sent in tankers the problem was resolved.

Freight working ceased at Patney & Chirton as from May 1964.

Wartime/Military

Patney & Chirton station's association with the military began following construction of its military platform in 1909. This was much used throughout World War One when the army had large numbers of horse-mounted troops and artillery. There were times when the fields round the station were used as temporary rest camps prior to the troops being marched onto Salisbury Plain.

The 6th Manchester Regiment detraining onto the military platform (opened on 1st August 1909) en route to West Down Camp on Salisbury Plain for exercises in summer 1910. They had travelled from their depot at Ashton-under-Lyme in Lancashire & Yorkshire Railway coaches with their horses conveyed at the rear in horse boxes that appear to be from the LNWR.

Sunday 1st August 1909 saw the start of a huge Territorial Army exercise on the Plain involving almost 40,000 men brought on trains from London. The Wessex Division, made up of Wiltshire, Somerset, Hampshire and Dorset units plus the London Territorial Division, detrained at the three stations of Amesbury on the London & South West Railway and at Lavington and Patney & Chirton on the GWR. The first long and heavily-laden trains left Paddington and Waterloo stations principally, a little after midnight, followed by a regular sequence of trains all departing at appointed times. The trains conveyed in addition to the troops, horses, guns, transport wagons and vast amounts of ammunition. The horses required special attention, not being trained military horses in the main but animals hired from London bus companies. On that day the two railway companies moved the following:

Officers and men	29,000
Charges and Troop Horses	6,000
Field Guns	90
Machine Guns	36
Ammunition Wagons	130

In addition there were bicycles for the Bicycle Corp, baggage carts, ambulance wagons and various other items of equipment. The guns and wagons were carried on open trucks, the officers' horses went three to a horse box, and the troop horses were eight to a cattle truck. As an example, one field artillery train arriving at Patney conveyed 6 officers, 180 other ranks, 6 officer's charges, 100 troop horses, 1 cart, 4 field guns, 11 ammunition wagons and 1 ton of baggage. On arrival at the station the operation of detraining was handled with precision to allow completion before the next arrival. The 140 troop trains were in addition to the regular August Bank Holiday passenger traffic. The troops got off on the down platform and marched over the footbridge to the other side.

All the arrangements at Lavington and Patney stations were the responsibility of Charles Kislington, District Superintendent of the GWR, and his assistant T.Williams. They were aided by 100 railway employees. Whilst the trains were backed up to a loading dock at the end of the military platform at Patney, the railway workers preferred to unload the wagons from the side as

opposed to running over the length of the train and out at the end. The trains kept arriving at Patney throughout the day and although the weather had been fine at first, it later changed to rain. This did not stop the local people from flocking to the station and onto the surrounding lanes to view the arrivals. The fields served as a rest camp and the lanes leading to the camps on Salisbury Plain became a sea of mud with the passage of troops and wagons.

After two weeks of training, the procedure was reversed and the railway was used to return the troops and equipment to the metropolis. This and following exercises turned into reality a few years later when Britain entered the war in September 1914. Patney station was a hive of activity for troops arriving for training and encampment on the Plain prior to leaving for the war zones. A large convoy of Canadian and Newfoundland Troops arrived at Plymouth and Devonport on 14th October. Some 500 Newfoundlanders lay at anchor in Devonport Harbour on the SS Florizel until Tuesday 20th October when they disembarked to board a fast train for a five-hour journey to Salisbury Plain, arriving at Patney station shortly after midnight. From the station they marched to Pond Farm Camp which they reached at 3.00am. This tented camp was a few miles north-west of Stonehenge. During the march from the station in pouring rain many of the men felt the effect of 17 days on board ship and sea-sickness from times when their small ship was buffeted in rough seas. Their arrival in Wiltshire coincided with an exceptionally wet spell of weather. From then until the middle of February 1915, nearly 24 inches of rain fell, there were high winds and it was cold. The tents were of little protection and a number of the troops died in the terrible conditions before their mission had begun.

As with Devizes, Patney station lost a member of staff in the Great War. This was H.Bridewell and his name appears on the war memorial on Platform 3 at Bristol Temple Meads.

Flying during the war years had really been in its infancy, but it produced many fine pilots whose exploits became legendary. The pilots of the RFC were a colourful addition to trench warfare and the rules of engagement with their counterparts were on a strictly gentlemanly basis. A need was seen to develop this and so the RAF was formed on 1st April 1918, born of an amalgamation of the RFC and the RNAS.

RAF Upavon became the home of the Central Flying School and the young pilots who trained there through the twenties learnt to fly better than anywhere else in the world. They were encouraged to work hard, play hard and be happy individualists. One of their exploits in the 1922 era concerned the Cornish Riviera which around midday each day passed through Pewsey station on the Berks & Hants heading west, just a few miles from the airfield at Upavon. As it steamed along the line through Woodborough and Patney at about the same cruising speed as the Avro 504K, the trainee pilots would formate on the engine just a few feet from the cab. On one of the occasions the train crew, who obviously did not like the game, started throwing lumps of coal at the aircraft. It had not previously occurred to the airmen that their practice was not appreciated by the railwaymen. Being the gentlemen that they were, a group of the pilots ordered a large hamper of food and drink from Harrods which they had sent to 'the crew of the Cornish Riviera – c/o Paddington station, with compliments of the C.F.S.' The next time one of Upavon's planes went near the train, it was greeted with much waving and smiles from the footplate.

The C.F.S. in later years produced many of the pilots who were to serve with the RAF during the Second World War. How was Patney & Chirton effected by this war? Probably not to the same extent that it was during 1914-1918. September 1939 saw the arrival of the first evacuees from London. They got off the train at the station with their identity labels attached to their clothes. Children from the same families were generally kept together where possible. The majority of the children were separated from their parents for the first time in their lives but some entire households left the city for the comparative safety of the countryside. Initially each household who had an evacuee was paid 8s.6d. per child, per week. Chirton village looked after enough children to warrant having two schools. The local children attended their usual school and the village hall was the school for the children from London. Their teacher, who came with them on the train, was Mr Green. For the majority of evacuees, it was their first experience of visiting the countryside; some took to it, others didn't. Some had never even seen farm animals before and the whole experience was a new way of life. A number of them arrived on the train with only the clothes they stood up in and were a sorry sight. One such lad was provided

with new clothes by his guardians and even paid pocket money. He enjoyed life in Chirton to such an extent that when the time came for his return to London he did not want to go and threatened to jump off the train. He was placed in the carriage under the watchful eye of the vicar who ensured he arrived home safely.

Many of the troops taken off the beaches at Dunkirk in May 1940 passed through Patney station. Both up and down trains on their way to Devizes slowed or stopped en route with their shocked, tired and injured passengers.

W.J.Gough was the Station Master of Patney at the outbreak of hostilities and on retirement he was replaced by Ted Major, a chief clerk from Devizes. In addition to his position at the station, he was also a lieutenant training the Chirton Army Cadet Force whose members came from various villages in the area. At this time also he was learning to drive and would practise along the station approach road and into the goods yard. The day came when he lost control of the car which careered out of control onto the tracks. Fortunately the cadet force were there at the time and were able to lift the car to safety for him. Ted kept his car in a shed at the station, paying the GWR 10s.6d. per annum for rent.

An incident of interest involving the station and its staff occurred on 14th March 1944, following the crash of a German Junkers 88 near the canal bridge at All Cannings at 11.30pm. The aircraft had left Brussels at 9.45pm to bomb London but on its approach to the city one of its engines failed. The bomb load was jettisoned and it proceeded on one engine but this caught fire and the pilot, Hans Schonleiter, gave the order to abandon aircraft. One of the four-man crew landed near the main Devizes to Upavon road at Chirton. He then walked down the lane from Chirton into Patney where he gave himself up to porter Wally Gray who was on the station platform. The German handed over his gun and was taken into the signalbox where he was given a cup of tea by signalman George Carpenter. He waited in the box until collected by the Devizes police. Of the other crew members, one was arrested by the American army at Tidworth, one at Bulford, and the body of the pilot, who had presumably baled out too low, was found two days later in a field at Patney with his parachute around him. His grave is at Haycombe Cemetery in Bath.

The following month a battalion of American soldiers with 175mm guns, lorries, caterpillar tractor units, equipment and stores arrived by rail and was unloaded onto the military platform. They were dispersed onto Salisbury Plain in preparation for onward movement to the South Coast ports in readiness for the D Day landings on 6th June. One of the caterpillar units, while crossing Patney Bridge, struck the parapet wall and the marks it left are still visible today. The bridge was obviously well built, as one would have expected it to be badly damaged when struck by such a vehicle.

A POW camp was built in Patney which housed mainly German and Italian men. Whilst it was only some 500 yards from the station, the prisoners were not moved by rail. They would be brought to the village by lorry from Devizes where they had arrived by train. During their captivity these men were used for labour on the local farms. A few remained after the war and are still living locally.

Staff

George Grant was the first Station Master to be appointed at Patney, in 1900, carrying out his duties until 1912 when he was replaced by John Derrick. His daughter Evelyn was a booking office clerk at Patney through the war years and married Charlie Tilley, the lampman. John Derrick retired in 1927 and became the landlord of the *Three Horseshoes* in Chirton.

The station strength through the years until 1949 was ten, thereafter being reduced to eight. The ten comprised:

Station Master Class 4	1
Leading Porter	1
Porters Grade 2	3
Signalmen Class 2	3
Signal Lampman	1
Goods Shunter Grade 4	1

Charlie Tilley, the signal lampman, was well known in the district. His job was to walk the line between Savernake and Holt maintaining the railway's lamps. He worked to a schedule which covered different sections each day on a rotating basis. He would often be seen wearing a bow tie as part of his railway uniform. He knew a lot about nature and the local country-side, and catching rabbits beside the line was one of his specialities. After Charlie retired, Harold Burry became the lampman for a time.

A First World War picture of the station staff shows, from left to right, back row: unknown; J. Miles, porter; Ernie Cox, signalman; Alec Tilley, porter; George Stone, porter; front row: unknown; John Derrick, Station Master; Evelyn Derrick, booking clerk; and Bert Green, porter. (GWR Museum, Swindon)

A staff photograph taken on the bay platform in 1952 with the branch 'push and pull' auto-train as a backdrop. From left to right: Walter Hillman, guard; Tom Parker, driver; Walter Tanner, relief porter (from Woodborough); Harry Giles, signalman; Edgar Cross, Station Master; Jim Perry, porter; and Bert Casely, fireman. (W. Tanner)

A group photograph on the down line in summer 1952. Standing from left to right: porters Jim Perry and Reg Gidding lampman Charlie Tilley; seated is Station Master Edgar Cross. (Wiltshire Gazette)

W.J.Gough succeeded John Derrick as Station Master in 1927, remaining until the mid-1940s when Ted Major took over. He, in turn, became Station Master of Devizes in 1957. The last appointment to Station Master at Patney took place in 1947 when Edgar Cross replaced Ted Major. Patney's last Station Master had joined the GWR in April 1913 as a junior clerk at Devizes. In addition to his station duties, Edgar was a good servant to the local community, his door always being open for those seeking help and advice. One of his official duties worthy of note was to stand on the platform in his best uniform and salute the Royal Train whenever it passed through Patney. While this would not seem to be unreasonable during the daytime, he even carried out the duty, if necessary, in the middle of the night. After he retired in 1962, the station was covered by reliefs, with many of the station duties being undertaken by Harold Burry who was porter there from 1953. When the station became unstaffed in 1965, Harold was moved to Newbury until he retired in 1973.

Signalman Bill Brooks, who served at Patney box from 1947 until 1966, was the man on duty on Saturday night, 16th April 1966, signalling the last official train onto the branch. Having closed the box after its departure, he closed the chapter on his own railway service. He had completed almost 50 years on the railway, retiring at 63.

Signalling

Stert Junction appears in the *Service Time Table* for October 1899. All trains stopped at that point, from where the new line to Westbury was being constructed, in order to hand over the single-line staff. Certain trains also picked up or put off contractors' traffic. From 1897, a signal cabin on the up side of the line (see the map on page 202) was in use at the junction until the main box was built. This temporary box at Stert was previously at Windsor and had a 17-lever frame.

The continuously-manned box at Patney & Chirton, being on a principal main line, was originally staffed by signalmen Class 1. The box, at 81 miles, 16 chains from Paddington, was fitted with a locking frame in 1900 that was a double-twist 81-lever type, the centres of each lever being $5^1/_4$ inches apart. When this box was out of

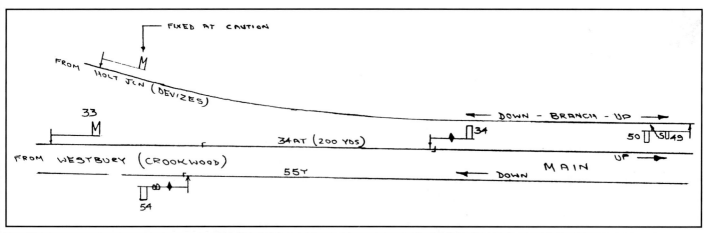

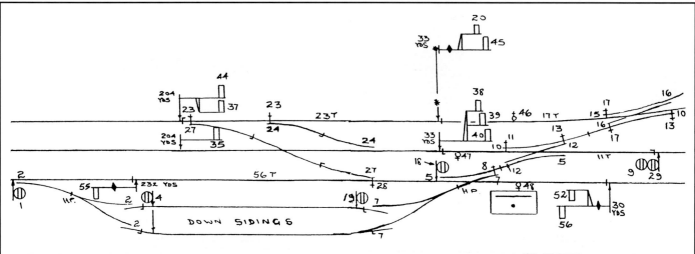

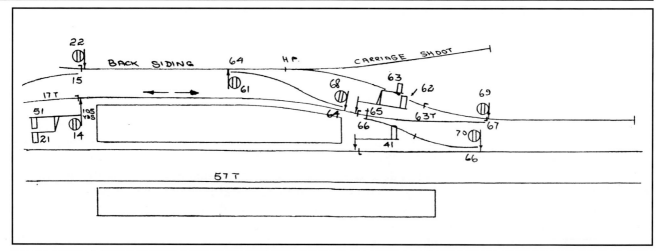

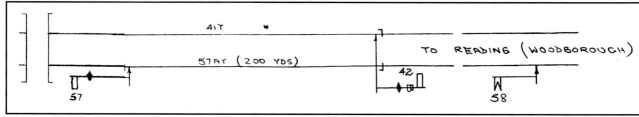

Patney & Chirton signalbox diagram, c.1956. (J.Morris, Signalling Record Society)

Patney signalbox on 16th February 1957, three months after refitting with a new frame. Bill Brooks mans the levers. (B.Brooks)

circuit the junction was always set for the main line. The track layout altered very little down the years. In 1904 an additional siding on the down side was added, running into the loading dock at the rear of the signalbox, and in 1909, the siding into the new military platform on the up side was added.

In early 1919, the electric token instrument in the signalbox, which had been in use since the opening in 1900, was renewed at a cost of £235. In 1923 the box was Class 2. By 1931, six track circuits had been installed to the rear of the Home, Inner Home Starting and Advanced Starting on the down line, and to the rear of the Up Home and Up Advanced Starting signals. The track circuits to the rear of the Home signals were interlinked with the block instruments. The track layout remained fairly constant until 1935 when the branch line loop on the up side was taken out of use, as was the military siding and back bay to the up siding in 1964.

On 11th November 1956 the signalbox was refitted with a 70-lever, 5-bar, vertical Tappett frame (of standard GWR design), with the levers only 4 inches apart. At the same time the box was rewired, new Western Region commutator blocks were brought into use and one pull only was added to the 'line clear' release on the Up and Down Main Advanced Starting signals. The new frame was one of the first to have levers working the running signals in the middle of the frame and not, as was the usual practice, to have them at each end.

A signalman on the single-line branch had to be aware of the time taken by a train to pass between one signalbox and the next. He would, for example, decide whether he could allow a freight train to pass over the single line, perhaps between Patney and Devizes, within sufficient time to clear the line without interrupting a subsequent passenger train scheduled on the same length of track. To assist him to determine the time required for the passing of various types of freight train, a table was produced, as overleaf.

	Ruling Gradient 1 in	Allow for STOP N	Allow for START N	'POINT - TO - POINT' ALLOWANCES.						
				C.	D.	E.	F.	H	J	K
		Min.	Min.	Min	Min	Min	Min		Min.	
PATNEY TO BATHAMPTON.										
Patney & Chirton	-	-	1	-	-	-	-		-	
Devizes	100 F.	1	1	9	9	9	9		12	
Bromham & Rowde	52 F.	-	-	-	-	-	-		-	
Seend	79 F.	2	1	-	-	-	-		10	
Holt Junction	66 F.	1	1	15	20	20	20		10	
Bradford Jct. North	167 R.	-	-	3	3	3	4		5	
Bradford Jct. West	120 F.	-	-	1	1	1	1		1	
Bradford-on-Avon	115 F.	1	1	-	-	-	-		4	
Avoncliff	186 F.	1	1	-	-	-	-		3	
Freshford	186 F.	1	1	7	8	8	8		3	
Limpley Stoke	242 R.	1	1	-	-	-	-		1	
Bathampton	115 F.	1	-	8	9	9	9		10	

Columns 4 to 7 show the time for vacuum-fitted freight trains of Codes C, D, E and F to travel between two boxes; column 8 shows the time taken for slower trains using loose-coupled wagons. For example, a Code D train would be allowed nine minutes to travel between Patney and Devizes with one minute for starting and one minute for stopping. Signalmen, in addition to requiring a good head for figures, needed to be reasonably strong and fit, particularly in a busy box where during a shift they were continually pulling the levers on and off. The Accident Book for Patney & Chirton shows that injuries to signal-men at work were not uncommon. In August 1954, district relief signalman Walter Atyeo, the father of Bristol City and England footballer John Atyeo, injured his back pulling the Up Distant. A week later Bill Brooks strained his left side pulling levers to the military siding. On 1st January 1956, signalman Walter Eggleton experienced the Facing Point Lock 45 lever stuck halfway during shunting operations, causing him to fall against the stove in the box, bruising his back. Harry Giles slipped on the wet wooden entrance steps on Boxing Day 1958 and strained a knee, and in March 1961 he received a groin injury while reversing No.2 Point for the second time after it had not closed properly at the first attempt.

Dismantling the timber military platform, the catchpoint and the wheelstops, with signalling alterations, was authorised in October 1951, with further signalling alterations taking place on Sunday 15th January 1956, when the Down Branch to Down Main Starting, and Down Branch Starting signals, positioned on the down side of the down platform for the branch line, were replaced. In both cases the siting of this work was at 105 yards from the signalbox.

A considerable number of further signalling alterations took place on Sunday 27th March 1960 when a new Down Main Distant of the colour light type was positioned on the down side of the Down Main, 2,326 yards from the box, together with an Up Main Distant on the up side of the Up Main, 1,850 yards from the box. The height of both signals was 12 feet. A new Up Branch to Up Main Home and an Up Branch Home of the semaphore type were positioned on the up side of the up branch line, 215 yards from the box and at a height of 20 feet. An Up Branch Inner Home on the up side of the up branch line, 33 yards from the box and at a height of 14 feet, was introduced, together with a disc leading to the back siding. At the same time the Up Main Inner Home, Up Main to Up Branch Inner Home, and Up Siding to Back Siding Inner Home Bracket signal was repositioned on the same side of the line, 162 yards further from the signalbox. Signals taken out of use were:

The following morning, D1010 returned to Holt via Patney & Chirton and the Royal Train, displaying headcode 1XO1, departed the branch at 8.55am en route for Castle Cary and a visit by the royal party to the Bath & West Show at Shepton Mallet.

The short stay had required considerable local support, with the Wiltshire Constabulary providing security at the station yard, the Post Office providing a telephone link for affairs of State should it have proved necessary, and British Rail's own planning which included a visit beforehand by the 'tamping' machine.

With the closure of Holt station, its obituary was recorded in the locally-produced *Holt Magazine* and, as it had not been possible to present a copy to Her Majesty during her brief stay, one was sent to the Palace resulting in a letter of appreciation from the Queen's Personal Secretary at the time, Michael Adeane. This received such

considerable publicity locally and in the *Daily Telegraph*, that the magazine had to be reprinted to cater for the huge demand from all over the country.

After the Royal Train had left Holt, a certain amount of 'royal rubbish' was observed by the track where the coaches had stood. Details of this also reached the offices of the national tabloids who duly published the story. Even Giles of the *Daily Express* produced a cartoon to embellish the matter.

This had not been the first royal visit that Holt had welcomed, for the Queen's grandparents, King George V and Queen Mary, had passed through the village on the Royal Train during the First World War, on their way to Trowbridge station to review the troops.

The Queen and Prince Philip also spent another night in Holt when, on 8th/9th August 1973, the Royal train stopped near Avonview Farm, on the

Class 52 D1010 Western Campaigner heading the Royal Train off the branch on the morning of 3rd June 1966. (J.Sawtell)

The Royal train passing through Holt station on 3rd June 1966 on its journey to Castle Cary from where the Queen and Prince Philip travelled on by road to the Bath & West Show at Shepton Mallet. (J.Sawtell)

Melksham to Holt section of the line, prior to a visit they were making to Bath.

Prince Charles must have come to hear of the tranquility of Holt as, before his marriage, there were occasions when he and Lady Diana Spencer were reported to have met, using the Royal Train which was stabled on the Bradford Junction triangle, a short distance from the closed Staverton station. On one of these meetings, Lady Diana was ushered through Holt station yard to join the train before it travelled the short distance to Bradford Junction.

The demolition trains arrived on the branch at the end of January 1967, comprising flat-bed wagons for the rails, 12 and 13-ton wagons for the sleepers and fittings, plus a brake van. There were two trains a day, hauled by Warship, Western or Hymek diesel locomotives. The lifting of the rails started at the Patney & Chirton end of the line and worked back towards Holt. To allow these trains to enter and leave the branch to join the main line between Bradford and Thingley Junctions, a temporary block instrument with two-lever ground frame was installed, to be operated by the crews. The station buildings remained until the double track was converted to single.

Approximately one mile of track was lifted each day by five site gangers using a tractor and hand tools. For two weeks the trains returned over the branch to Westbury after loading. At that time they stopped at Devizes where the station buildings, signalbox, footbridge and fitments were being razed to the ground. Contractors were also working on the track by this time, using their own ex-Air Ministry 0-4-0 Ruston diesel locomotive which kept breaking down and delaying the work. It was sent to Stothert & Pitt in Bath for repairs following which it continued its destruction on the Taunton to Barnstaple line. On 20th March it was replaced by another 0-4-0 diesel dating from 1939 when it

Modified Hall 4-6-0 No.6965 Throwley Hall coming off the Devizes Branch at Holt Junction on 2nd May 1965 with an LCGB tour. (D.Lovelock)

had been built by John Fowler of Leeds. This also eventually seized up. To speed things up, BR sent another gang to assist on the line. For a short time they added to the farce by removing the rail from the Holt end whilst the original gangers carried on from the Devizes end. When the mistake was realised, for some unknown reason they started to relay track from Devizes to Patney so the branch was then disappearing at one end and growing at the other. At this point Warship Class D835 *Pegasus*, 30 twelve-ton wagons, two brake vans and tons of scrap were isolated in the middle.

Lifting of the track was eventually completed by the summer of that year, except for the short stretch between Holt Junction and Whaddon Bridge which was retained for wagon storage. This was removed in the early 1980s.

Today the single line still winds its way through Holt en route from Trowbridge past the re-opened Melksham station to Chippenham. In addition to the occasional freight train and diverted HST, the line is used for an early morning South Wales & West Regional Railway service from Frome to Swindon, with a late afternoon return Swindon to Westbury service, a poor shadow of its former busy daily schedule.

Nothing now remains at Holt to remind us that this was once a busy junction station. The final act of amputation occurred on 27th February 1991 when the land and station approach were disposed of by British Rail at auction. Appropriately enough, it was acquired by local coal merchant, L.H.Arlett & Son, whose business continues to operate from the station site today.

The Demolition train coming off the branch at Holt Junction in early 1967. This photograph provides one of the few views of the permanent way hut in the fork of the branch junction at Cuckoo's Nest. (J.Sawtell)

A Hymek with brake third, brake composite and Enparts van crossing Whaddon Bridge on a summer evening in 1965. The van was used to carry spare parts to and from Swindon Works. (J.Sawtell)

A lineside view of Whaddon Bridge crossing the River Avon near Holt after lifting of the track. The 93¾ milepost is still in position. (J.Sawtell)

The River Avon in flood as Whaddon Bridge is demolished in 1967. (J.Sawtell)

One span of the bridge at Semington being removed by mobile crane on Sunday 5th January 1969. (J.Sawtell)

Semington Halt, the next station along the line, was demolished in 1967. The adjoining underbridge lasted for another couple of years until Sunday 5th January 1969 when its spans were removed in turn using a 36-ton mobile crane. They were cut up on adjoining railway land before being taken to South Wales by road for sale as scrap.

Today the raised embankment of the trackbed remains as does one of the bridge supports. The only other reminder of Semington's railway days is the house at the base of the embankment, once *The Railway Tavern* but now carrying the name *The Railway Farm* with its adjoining annexe, *The Siding*.

Seend's pleasant country station also closed on 18th April 1966. Of all the seven stations that served the branch, Seend station site today remains most readily identifiable as to its past. From the top of the road bridge carrying the lane over the

former trackbed, it is possible to stand by the wicket gate at the head of the steps to the station and look down at the two platforms. These are now owned by local farmer Fred Cundick whose cows stand waiting where once stood passengers. The goods yard, now owned by Tony Gay of Holt, remains in use, as do some other original aspects of the station furniture. In the playground of Seend School stands the former BR station nameboard and a rest can be taken on one of the platform seats in the local playing field. Mrs Campbell lights her driveway in Seend with one of the platform lamps as does Norman Parker in Amesbury. On buying his, he was twice stopped by the police on his way home inquiring why he was carrying a railway lamp post on the roof of his car. The lineside cabin from beneath the side wall of the road bridge now has a new home at the Great Western Railway

Fish Bridge, looking towards Devizes, as the two spans are lowered in February 1969. (T.Green)

By the time the line was closed, Devizes station was already in a sorry state. A number of the rails had been lifted and sold for scrap. Those either side of the down platform were gone and the footbridge steps had beezn boarded up. This effectively isolated the platform but did not in fact prevent it suffering from vandalism. The staff thought that the station buildings were to be sold, but this was probably rumour or hope on their part. In January 1967 the demolition train arrived, but its work was delayed by a landslip on the Pans Lane side of the tunnel. By March, however, demolition was well under way; the station buildings were razed to the ground, with the timber making large bonfires.

On 3rd October 1966, Devizes Rural District Council Planning Committee was given details of a £400,000 Wiltshire County Council road improvement scheme. A new junction, at Whistley Lane, where it joined the A361 at Caen Hill, was included. Mr John Spencer, clerk to the council, commenting on the proposal to remove the railway embankment and return the land to smallholders, asked whether this meant the railway was lost to Devizes for ever. Mr Fewster for Wiltshire County Council replied that with the superstructure gone, there was not much point in the railway. John Spencer said in reply: 'It is hoped in ten years' time the railways will realise their mistake'. The road improvements were carried through and the railway did not return. British Railways, probably more than any other factor, condemned the town to small-time development, not necessarily because it took the railway away, but because the town never properly achieved main-line status.

Nowadays, there is very little left in Station Road to remind us of what the site once was. There is a car park where the main platform buildings stood, and the upside goods yard is covered by a block of maisonettes. Only the outline of the tunnel mouth and the small brick and concrete bridge over the lane near the tunnel remain as part of the infrastructure.

A number of original items from the station have survived such as a station lamp and post, bought to illuminate the garden of ex-town councillor Don May who once lived in Station Road; a platform seat rests by a local tennis court; and former ticket office booking clerk at Devizes, Alan Mead, is the keeper of the 'Devizes Signal Box' nameplate. One of the station nameboards is displayed at the Winchcombe Railway Museum in Gloucestershire and one of the *Devizes Castle* name-plates from locomotive 7002 is in Keith Buckle's private collection. Station Road is still referred to as such and has been embellished by a recent development served by a road off it called Great Western Close.

With the closure of the line, the east end of the tunnel was boarded up and for a time was used as a lorry garage by a local firm. Although it had not filled with smoke since the end of steam workings almost 20 years before, smoke returned to the tunnel in 1978 when workmen drove a lorry in from the west end and proceeded to burn off a load of waste building material. With one end boarded up the tunnel became engulfed in smoke, trapping the two men at the east end. They were rescued by the Fire Brigade breaking through the boarding. Today the tunnel is in use as a gallery for the Wiltshire Shooting Centre.

Hillworth footbridge remains in use but is the subject of considerable local disagreement. There are those who would wish it kept and others who feel it an eyesore and an encumbrance to the handicapped by virtue of the steps at one end. These people would like to see it replaced and Railtrack too would be pleased to rid themselves of it. The position remains unresolved.

The bridge still carries Pans Lane over the cutting today, the road servicing the hospital and the expanding residential area. The part of the cutting where the station stood has now been filled in to provide the residents with extended gardens. Standing on the bridge, the 'Pans Lane Halt' letters from the original station nameboard can still be seen, just a few yards from where they were displayed for 37 years, adorning a garden shed.

Patney & Chirton closed after the departure of the 7.36pm Newbury to Westbury train on 16th April 1966. Signalman Bill Brooks handed over the Patney to Holt token and the DMU headed for the branch, disappearing into the darkness.

Early in 1967 lifting of the track and demolition of the buildings started. Only the up and down main lines were left straddled by the station footbridge forming part of a public right of way. The loading dock at the rear of the signalbox still exists, as does the farmer's water tower in the field on the up side that once supplied the station's water, though this too is no longer in use.

When the station was demolished, the trackbed between the position of the military platform and the rear of the up platform was infilled with the masonry from the station building. Many of the fittings, such as the station nameboards and posts, were likewise discarded. Some of the station and its fittings have survived. Local farmer David Snook sits on his patio of platform stones and watches the HSTs hurrying through Patney, while Bob Bailey, a former BR motor driver based at Marlborough station, rescued some station lamps and the bell apparatus from Patney signal-box. The Station Master's house is now in private occupation and while its address was once in Station Road, this has now been renamed as Woodland Road.

The bell-block from Patney & Chirton signalbox. (R.Priddle)

242

A DMU stands in the bay platform beneath the footbridge at Patney & Chirton on 4th September 1965. The flowerbeds and platform surface are already showing signs of sad neglect. (P.Fry)

With the passage of time, history might well record that the closure of that part of the Berks & Hants known as the Devizes Branch and other similar lines resulted from bad management and a negative attitude by the British Railways board. Instead of taking steps to attract custom, where lines were becoming uneconomical, it was easier to reduce and rearrange services, further reducing their usefulness to the travelling public. It was simple then for the Board to promote the need for closure.

It would seem that little or no thought was given to the long-term needs of the community, making it not so much a case of closure, but rather one of terminal extinction. Lines were ripped up, bridges blown up, buildings demolished and land sold. Unlike the moth-balling that is evident in some European countries, the Board's policy ensured that there would be no going back.

Once the closure decision had been made, the Commercial Officer for BR wrote, early in 1960, to the Registrar of Deeds and Records (WR) at Porchester Road, London, requesting reasons that might prevent closure. The latter replied that in respect of the Berks & Hants line; Berks & Hants Extension; Wilts, Somerset & Weymouth Line; and the Stert to Westbury Line, provisions in the deeds covering the stations on these sections, excluding Reading and Westbury, would not preclude the withdrawal of passenger, parcels and/or freight facilities, except for a list of agreements between the Railway and private companies and individuals. Many of these agreements had fallen into disuse by that time and it was probable that BR had little difficulty in terminating any of them.

When Dr Beeching's plans to withdraw services were published on Wednesday 27th March 1963, Council meetings were arranged to discuss the proposal and there were many bodies airing views as to why some sort of service should be retained. It was all a bit half-hearted, however. The Wiltshire Association of Parish Councils wrote Dr Beeching an eight-line letter regretting any closure and pointing out that the railway provided the only form of transport in severe weather conditions. It is doubtful that Dr Beeching was swayed by this singular reason.

The Devizes Trades Council held out little hope of retaining a passenger service but felt a freight service was still justified. Alan Mead from the booking office at Devizes station, who was chairman of the Council, on which he represented the NUR, had good reason to express his concern for the future employment of men on the railway who would lose their jobs. Many of these, of course, had devoted their lives to the railway and were no longer young men. Alan made the point that most stations gave employment to at least 20 people. British Rail defended the closures with statements such as the one made by Mr Dudley Hart, Manager of BR's Bristol Division, who said that 'the intention was to reduce passenger stations in the Western Region from 818 to 250'. As the stations to be closed were all small, not many staff were involved and redundancies would not be a problem. Freight would not be affected and BR would still collect and deliver in the areas covered. On the future of the station buildings, Mr Hart stated that if they lent themselves to development, they would be used but mostly only for storage.

There have, over the past few years, been various promotions to bring the railway back to the area of Devizes. First there was a call to re-open Lavington station, followed a few years later by a proposed Devizes Parkway at Lydeway. Both of these sites, of course, were on the main line between Patney and Westbury. It has been suggested that such provision would promote the development of Devizes as a town, with people able to commute to Bath, Bristol and Swindon. It is also suggested that there would be extra benefits from tourism. There are also views that a station two miles out of town would be a wasted resource. For the time it takes to drive to the station, catch the train, change at Westbury and arrive in Bath to work, it would be quicker and a lot easier to drive direct from Devizes. For those without cars an out-of-town site would require an integrated rail and bus system.

Wiltshire Gazette & Herald journalist Lynda Fleming suggested in February 1992 that Devizes needs its station close to the town centre. With this comment the story of the Devizes Branch would seem to have gone full circle.

British Railways Board

Transport Act 1962

Withdrawal of Railway Passenger Services

The Minister of Transport has given his consent to the Board's proposals to discontinue all passenger train services from the following stations:

Bromham and Rowde	Savernake for Marlborough
Devizes	Seend Halt
Holt Junction	Semington Halt
Lavington	Staverton Halt
Manningford Halt	Woodborough
Pans Lane Halt	Wootton Rivers Halt
Patney & Chirton	

These services will be withdrawn on and from Monday 18 April 1966

The official notice of closure. (Devizes Museum)

Reading, Newbury, Hungerford, Marlborough, Devizes & Trowbridge, 53

WITH TRAINS IN CONNECTION TO
Bath, Bristol, Salisbury, Frome & Weymouth.

For intermediate Stations between London and Reading, see pages 26 to 37, and for other Trains between Trowbridge and Bristol, see pages 54 & 55.
All Trains shewn below convey Third Class Passengers.

DOWN TRAINS. — WEEK DAYS / SUNDAYS

Reference to Branch Table	DOWN TRAINS.	1,2,P. A.M.	A.M.	A.M.	A.M.	P.M.	P.M.	P.M.	P.M.	1,2,P. P.M.	1,2,P. A.M.	P.M.
Pge. 26	LONDON (Paddngtn) dep.	6 25	9 10		10 20	1 5	3 55	5 15	5 15	6 45	9 0	4 55
	Windsor "		8 32		9 20	12 35	3 10			6 0	9 20	5 30
	Reading arr.	7 42	9 55		11 15	2 0	4 48	6 16		7 40	10 27	6 15
26,37	READING dep.		10 5	11 25		2 15	4 53	6 5	6 15	7 50	10 45	6 30
	Theale "	8 7	10 17	11 37		2 27	5 13		6 27	8 0	10 58	6 42
	Aldermaston "	8 16	10 26	11 46		2 35	5 13		6 36	8 10	11 6	6 50
	Midgham "	8 22	10 32	11 52		2 42	5 20		6 42	8 16	11 12	6 56
	Thatcham "	8 30	10 40			2 50	5 28		6 50	8 23	11 20	7 3
52	Newbury "	8 42	10 53	12 12		3 2	5 40	6 32	7 10	8 35	11 30	7 15
	Kintbury "	8 53	11 3	12 24		3 14	5 51		7 21	8 46	11 42	7 26
	Hungerford "	9 1	11 10	12 34		3 24	6 3	6 47	7 28	8 54	11 52	7 34
	Bedwyn "	9 14		12 45		3 35	6 13			9 4	12 3	7 44
	Savernake "	9 26		12 57		3 47	6 25	7 5		9 14	12 15	7 54
	Marlborough {dep. arr.	9 5 9 45		10 30	12 35 1 40	3 27 4 3	6 0 6 45	7 35		8 50 9 32		
	Pewsey dep.	Mxd 9 38		11 0	1 10	4 0	6 37			9 24	Mxd 12 28	8 5
	Woodborough "	9 48		11 10	1 19	4 10	6 46			9 32	12 37	8 13
	DEVIZES {arr. dep.	A.M. 6 30	A.M. 8 20	10 0	11 25 11 0	1 31 1 35	6 53 5 25	7 30 7 3	Newbury arr. 6 58 p.m.	9 44 9 47	A.M. 12 50 8 0	8 25 8 28
55	Seend "	6 38		10 14	11 8	1 46	4 33	7 14		9 55	1 2	
55	Holt "	6 46	8 55	10 22	11 17	1 53	4 40	7 22		10 3	8 30	1 12 8 43
54	TROWBRIDGE {arr. dep.	6 52 7 25	9 5	10 28 10 35	11 23 11 23	2 0 2 26	4 46 5 35	7 28 7 50		10 9	8 40 9 30	1 20 8 50 1 35
	Bradford "	7 38		10 45	11 37	2 33	5 14		8 30		9 40	1 44
	Freshford "	7 45		10 51	11 43	2 42	5 20		8 37		9 46	1 50
	Limpley Stoke "	7 49		10 55	11 47	2 46	5 24		8 43		9 50	1 54
	Bathampton "	7 58		11 4	11 56	2 55	5 34		8 56		9 59	2 2
38	Bath "	8 5		11 9	12 3	3 2	5 38		9 5		10 5	2 7
	BRISTOL (Temple Meads) arr.	8 40		11 30	12 30	3 25	5 28		6 12 9 33		10 40	2 35
	Trowbridge dep.	7	9 24	11 3		3 19	3 19	7 0	9 45			7 17
54	SALISBURY arr.	8 37	10 25	12 15		4 32	4 35	8 15	10 52			8 55
54	Trowbridge dep.	7	9 15	10 53	12 47	3 11	3 11	5 53	7 55	12 6	9 17	7 32
55	Frome arr.	7 39	9 52	11 38	1 10	3 57	4 0	6 18	8 17		9 41	7 69
54	Yeovil (Pen Mill) "	8 39	10 36	12 39	2 30	4 43	4 43	7 19	10 32	12 51	10 32	9 10
54	Bridport "	9 50	11 38	1 50	3 51	6 20	6 20	8 30			11 45	10 25
54	Dorchester "	9 37	11 25	1 38	3 21	5 44	5 44	8 7	11 17	1 33	11 23	10 6
54	WEYMOUTH arr.	10 0	11 45	1 55	3 33	6	6	8 25	11 32	1 52	11 40	10 25

UP TRAINS. — WEEK DAYS / SUNDAYS

Reference to Branch Table	UP TRAINS.	1,2,P. A.M.	A.M.	1,2,P. A.M.	A.M.	A.M.	A.M.	1,2,P. A.M.	P.M.	P.M.	Mxd Trn.	1,2,P. A.M.	A.M.
55	WEYMOUTH dep.				7 0		8 25	10 25	11 50	4 20	5 5			10 30
55	Dorchester "				7 20		8 44	10 42	12 12	4 41	5 23			10 55
55	Bridport "				6 40		8 3	10 25	11 57	4 27	4 45			10 36
55	Yeovil (Pen Mill) "		6 5		8 10		9 36	11 19	12 59	5 12	6 26			11 54
55	Frome "		7 15		9 7		10 6	11 54	2 15	5 49	7 32			12 56
55	Trowbridge arr.		7 34		9 27		11 9	12 9	2 33	6 9	7 56			1 19
55	SALISBURY dep.		6 5				10 10	10 10	1 54	4 40	7 56			8 10
	Trowbridge arr.		7 25				11 28	11 28	2 26	5 57	7 56			9 30
38	BRISTOL (Temple Meads) dep.		6 10				8 25	8 15	2 20	4 30	6 40			3 45
	Bath "		6 38				8 15	10 26	2 38	4 57	7 0			4 13
	Bathampton "		6 38				8 55	10 35	2 49	5 5	7 15			4 21
	Limpley Stoke "		6 45				9 3	10 44	2 57	5 13	7 25			4 32
	Freshford "		6 50				9 7	10 44	3 1	5 17	7 29			4 35
	Bradford "		6 57				9 12	10 51	3 7	5 23	7 35			4 43
55	TROWBRIDGE {arr. dep.		7 07 7 8	36			9 24 9 35	11 3 11 45	3 19 3 26	5 31 6 23	7 45 8 35	P.M. 8 35	6 0 6 5	4 52 5 15
	Holt Junction "		7 18				9 42	11 58	3 32	6 39		8 55	6 7	5 24
	Seend "		7 18				9 51	12 0	3 41	6 39		9 10	6 10	5 35
	DEVIZES {arr. dep.	A.M.	7 28 7 33	58 8 0			10 1 10 10	A.M. 12 10 11 35	3 53 3 57	6 49	8 29 8 33	9 25	6 20 6 32	5 47 5 52
	Woodborough "		7 48				10 24	11 48	4 11		8 49		6 45	6 7
	Pewsey "		8 1				10 30	11 58	1 10		8 59		6 55	6 17
	Marlborough {dep. arr.		8 45	8 5 8 45		8 5	10 30 11 15	12 35 12 27 1 40	4 12 4 50		8 50 9 32			
	Savernake dep.		8 21			9 35 8 10	10 51 11 3	12 14 1 22	4 31	P.M.	9 13 9 24		7 7 7 17	6 30 6 41
	Bedwyn "						11 3	1 31	4 44					
	Hungerford "		8 40			8 57	11 17	1 48	4 58	7 55	9 36		7 36	6 54
	Kintbury "					9 4	11 26		P.M.				7 44	—
52	Newbury "	A.M. 7 58	8 51			9 17	11 42	2 3	5 6	8 15	9 52		7 51	7 19
	Thatcham "	8 6				9 25	11 52	2 12	5 16	8 25			7 59	7 26
	Midgham "	8 12				9 32	12 0	2 19	5 23	8 32			8 6	7 33
	Aldermaston "	8 18				9 39	12 8	2 25	5 29	8 39			8 13	7 41
	Theale "	8 27				9 49	12 18	2 32	5 35	8 49			8 23	7 53
26,37	READING arr.	8 38	9 15			10 0	12 30	2 44	5 40	6 6	9 0 10 17		8 35	8 5
	Reading dep.	8 45	9 27			10 15	12 52	2 55	5 50	6 24	9 25 10 30		8 45	8 20
30	Windsor A arr.		10 5			11 46	2 13	4 28	5 57	7 45	11 10 11 10		9 50	9 20
	LONDON (Paddington) arr.	10 0	10 15			10 55	1 50	3 50	4 55	7 20	10 20 11 30		10 20	9 45

Salisbury and Weymouth Passengers to and from Devizes and Hungerford Line change Carriages at Holt, Trowbridge or Westbury. Passengers travelling from or to Paddington, Windsor do not in all cases leave Reading by the same Train as the London Passengers. Enquiry should be made at Reading.

For Horse and Carriage arrangements see pages 136 and 137.

ROUTES FOR RETURN TICKETS.—Tickets to the West of England available via Swindon or Hungerford.—Passengers travelling from or to Paddington, Victoria, Battersea, Chelsea, West Brompton, Kensington, or Stations East of Reading, to or from Trowbridge, Bradford, Yeovil, Dorchester, Weymouth, and other places on the Wilts, Somerset, and Weymouth Branch, also to or from Bristol and Bath, may travel either via Didcot, Swindon, and Chippenham, or Hungerford and Devizes, as they may elect. Passengers holding Return Tickets may return by either route.

Extract from the GWR timetable for 1890.

Drawings of Structures and Buildings on the Devizes Branch

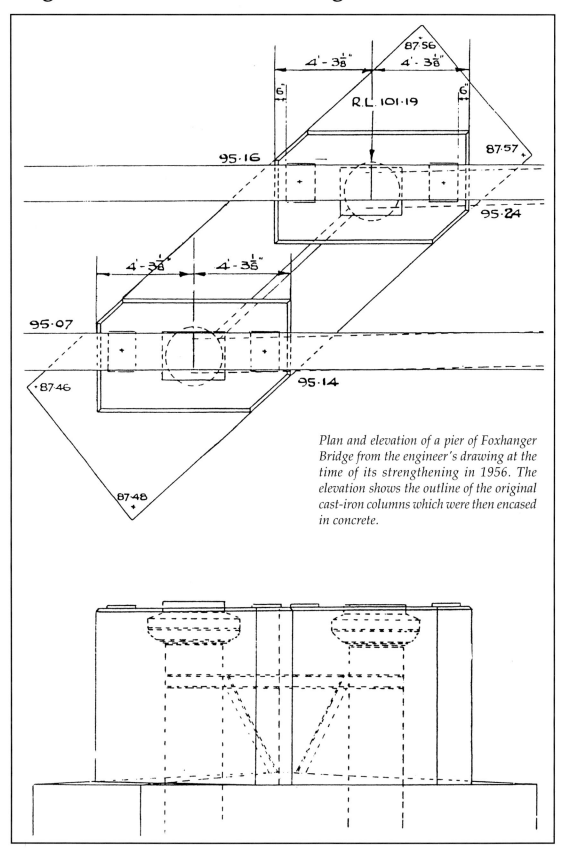

Plan and elevation of a pier of Foxhanger Bridge from the engineer's drawing at the time of its strengthening in 1956. The elevation shows the outline of the original cast-iron columns which were then encased in concrete.

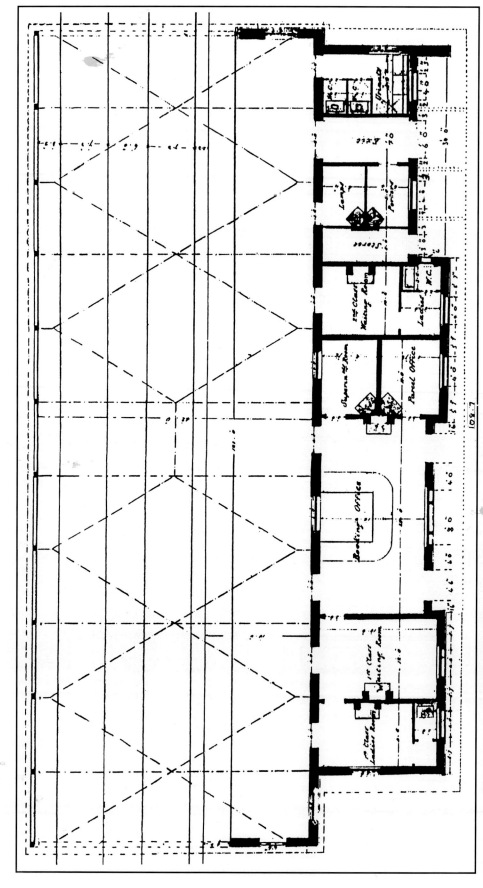

The original Wilts, Somerset & Weymouth Railway plan of the layout for Devizes station, dated 1856.

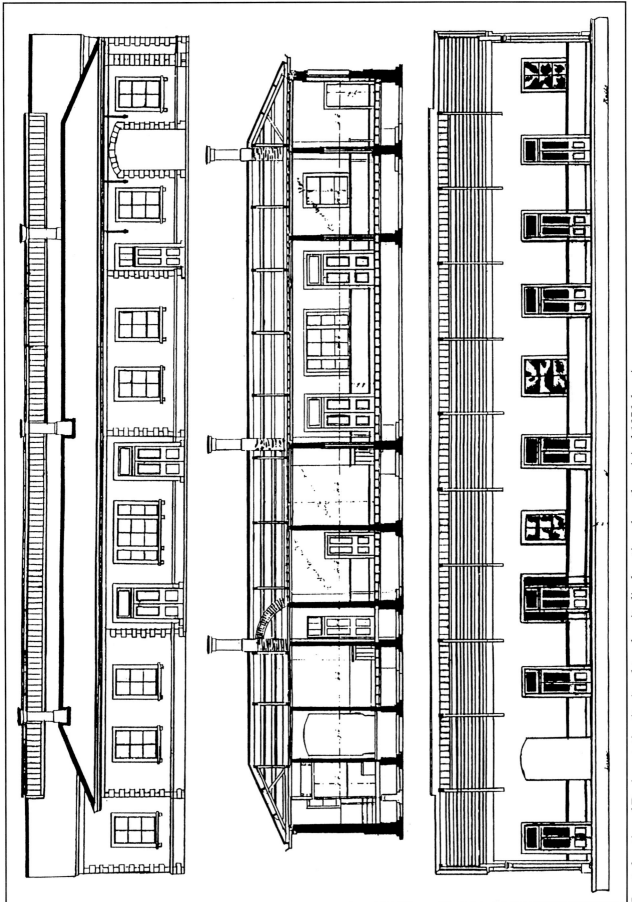

Front elevation of Devizes station (top) and two longitudinal sections from the original 1856 drawing.

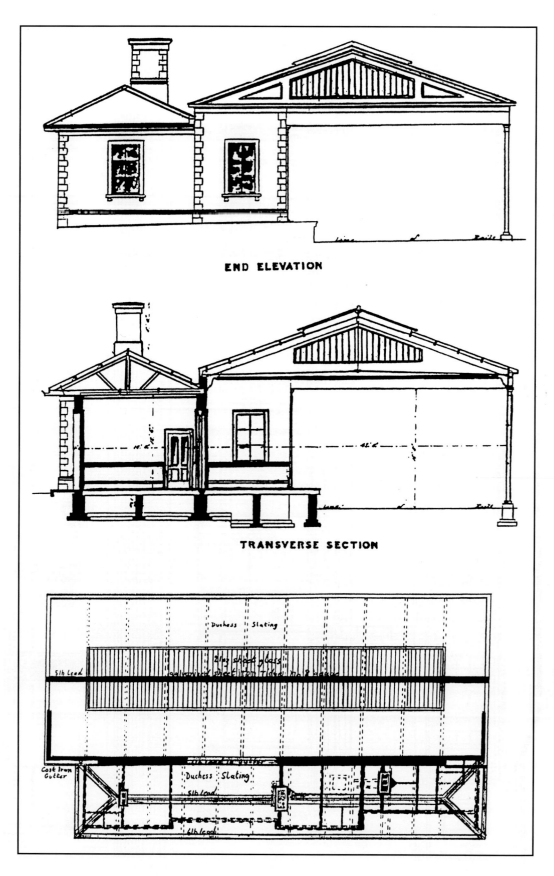

END ELEVATION

TRANSVERSE SECTION

End elevation and section of Devizes station and plan of the overall roof from the original 1856 drawing.

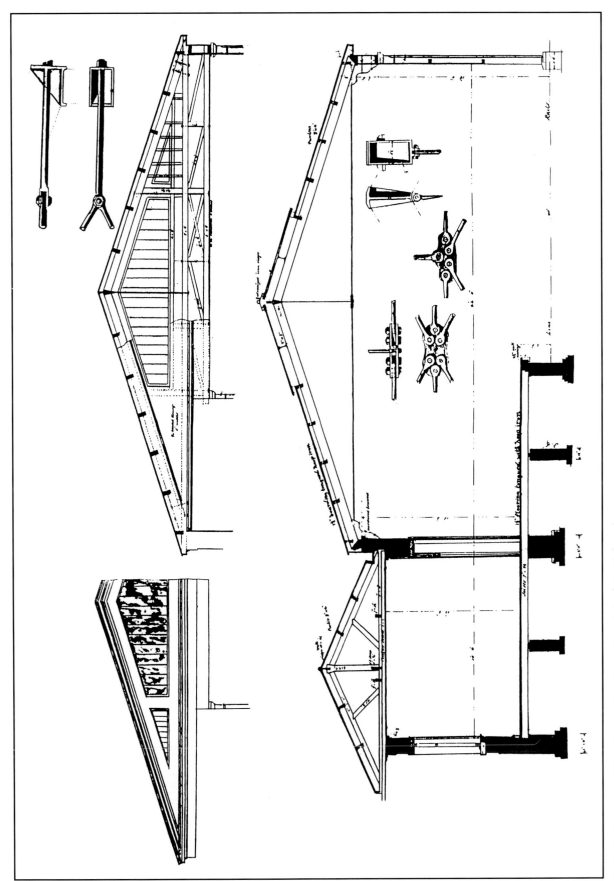

Details of the roof of Devizes station from the original 1856 drawing.

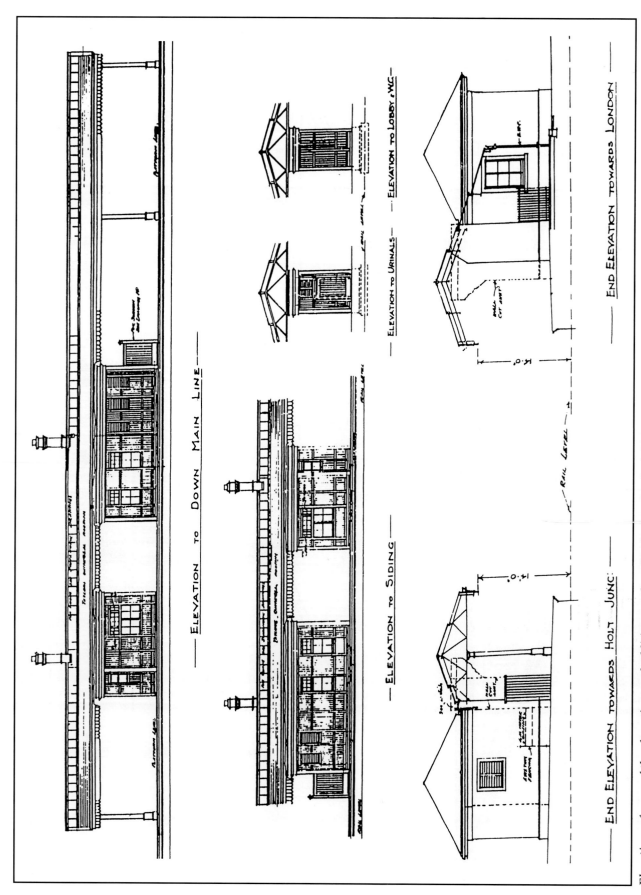

— ELEVATION TO DOWN MAIN LINE —

— ELEVATION TO SIDING —

— ELEVATION TO URINALS —

— ELEVATION TO LOBBY & WC —

— END ELEVATION TOWARDS LONDON —

— END ELEVATION TOWARDS HOLT JUNC: —

Elevations of some of the alterations and additions made to Devizes station in 1909/10.

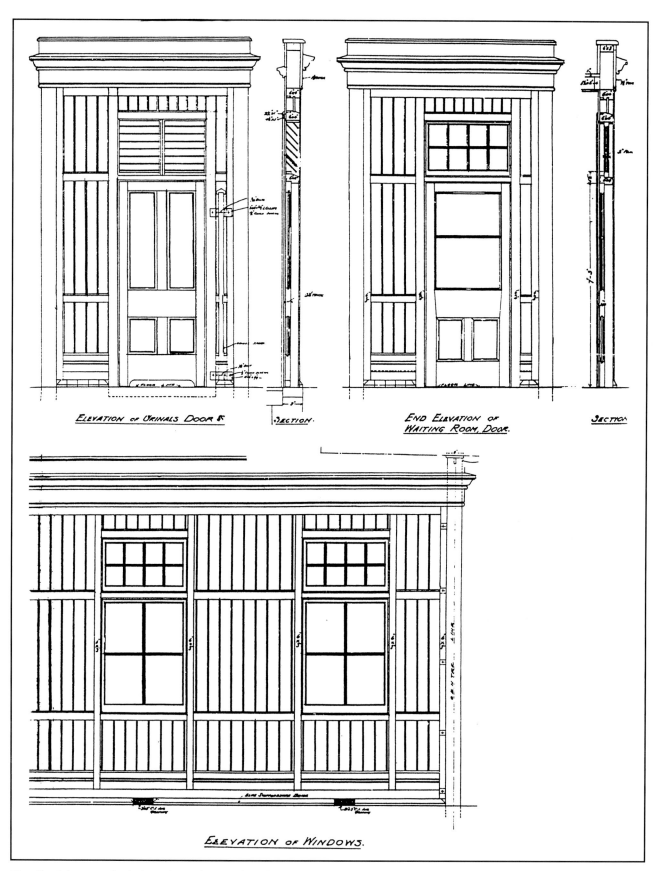

Details of doors and windows from the 1909/10 alterations and additions to Devizes station.

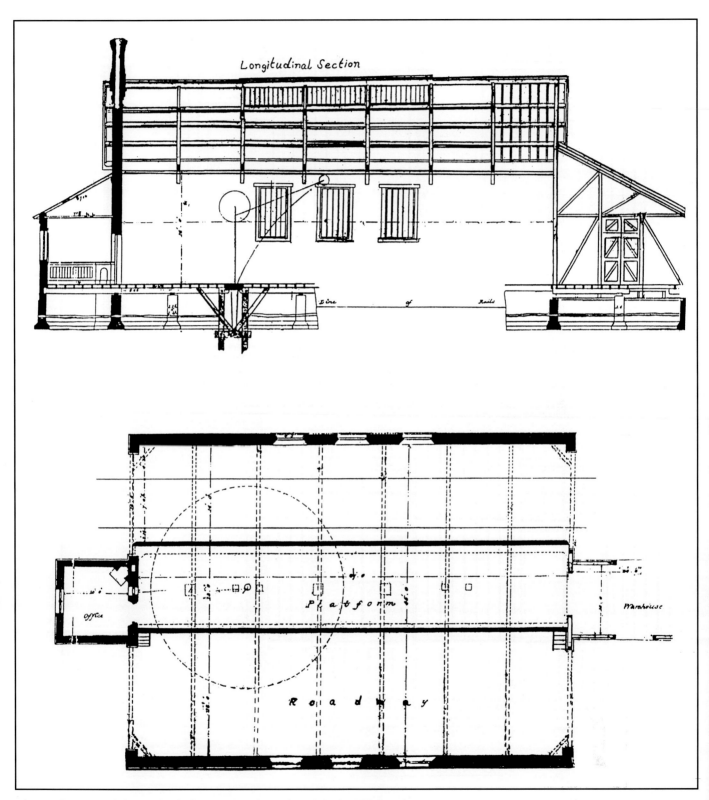

Plan and section of the goods shed at Devizes from the original 1856 drawing.

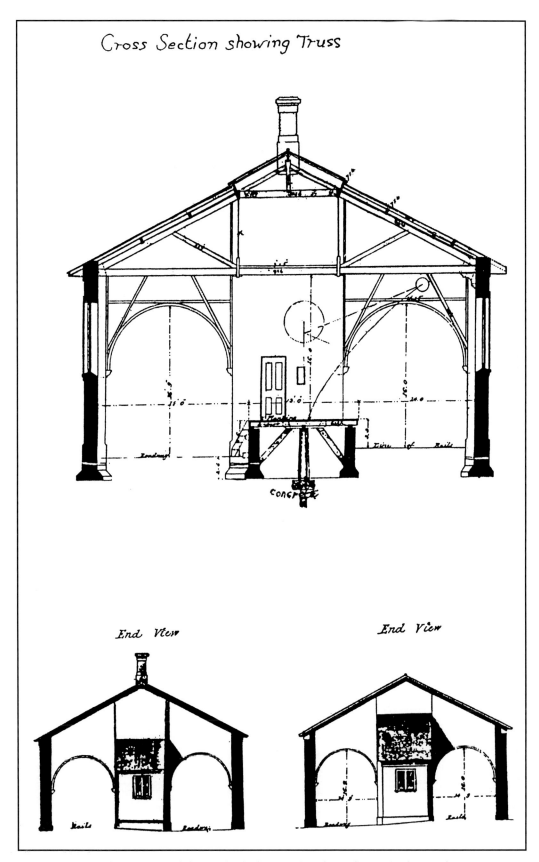

Cross-section and end views of the goods shed at Devizes from the original 1856 drawing.

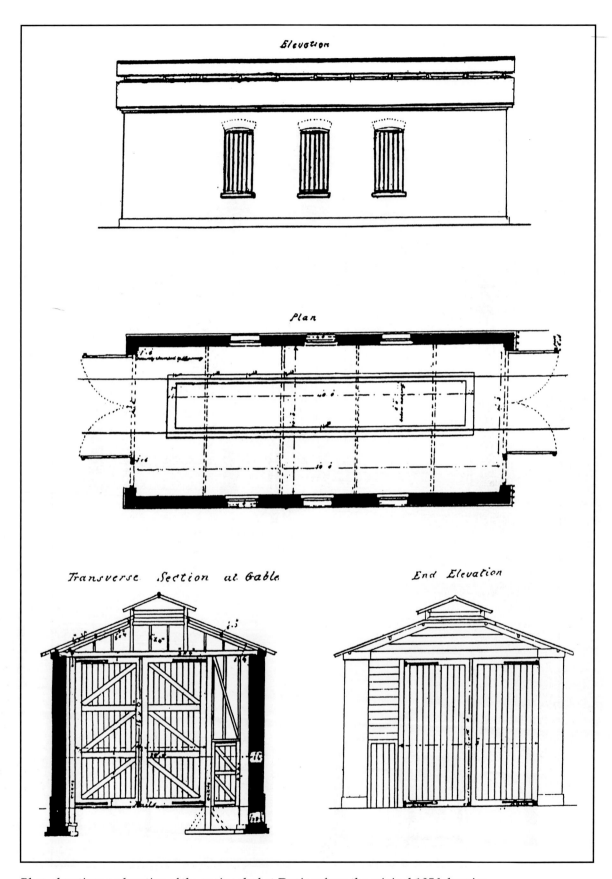

Plan, elevations and section of the engine shed at Devizes from the original 1856 drawing.

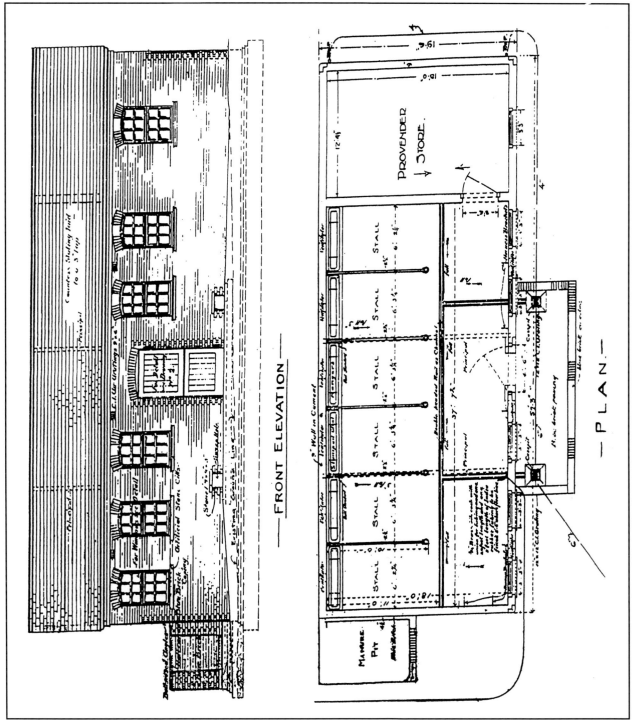

Plan and elevation of the stables at Devizes station, built in 1908.

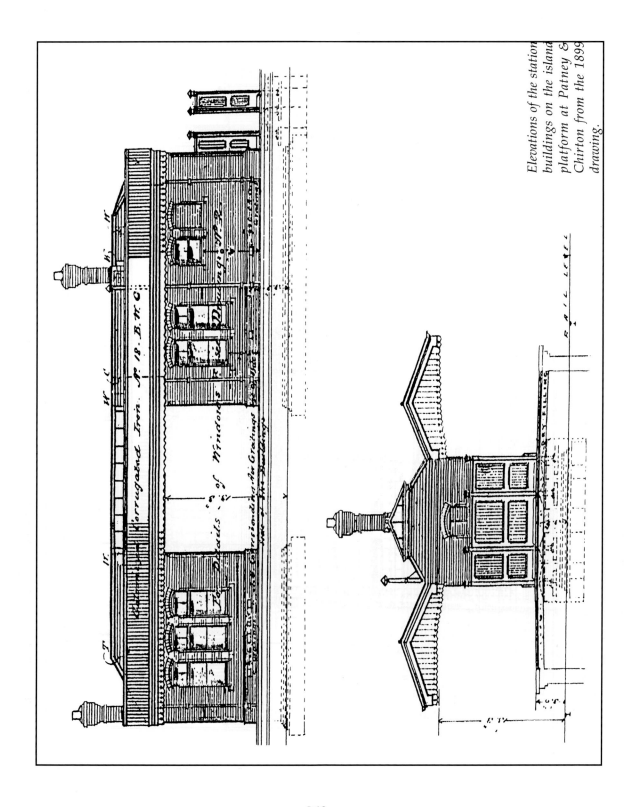

Elevations of the station buildings on the island platform at Patney & Chirton from the 1899 drawing.

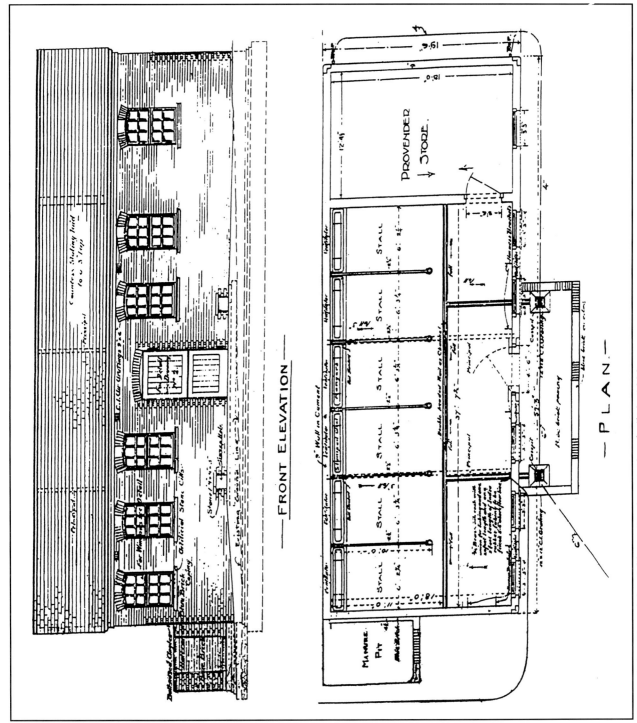

Plan and elevation of the stables at Devizes station, built in 1908.

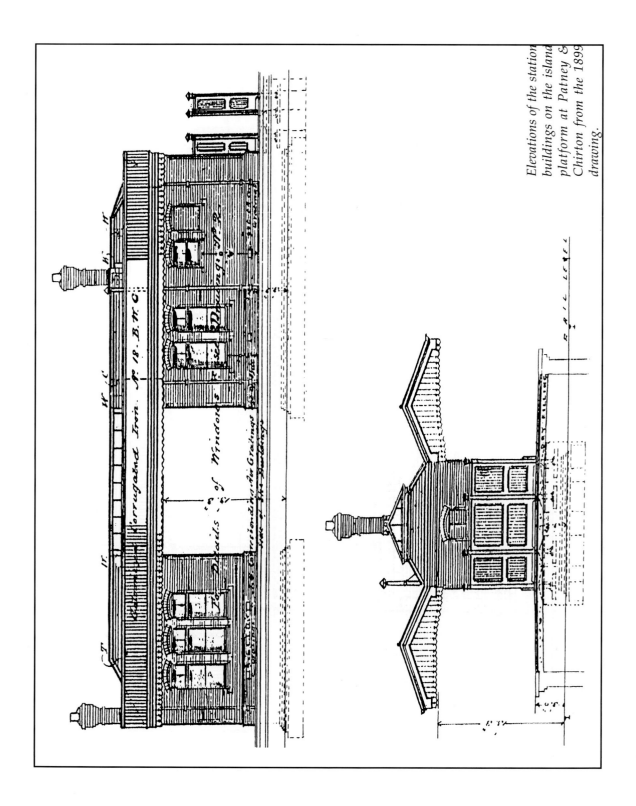

Elevations of the station buildings on the island platform at Patney & Chirton from the 1899 drawing.

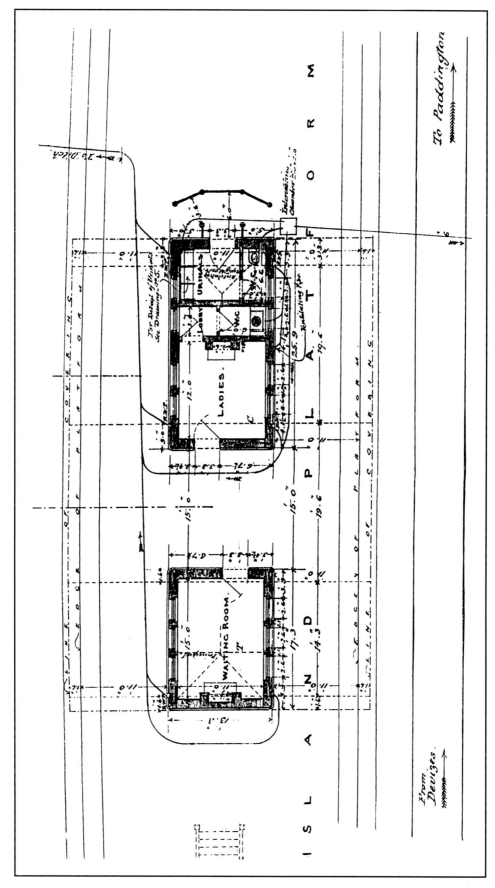

Plan of the buildings on the island platform at Patney & Chirton from the 1899 drawing.

Devizes Branch Staff

The names in this appendix are probably a very small proportion of the considerable number of people who were employed to work on the branch between 1857 and 1966.

It has been impossible to record dates of service accurately in all cases and a dated photograph may be the only indication in respect of a period of service by an individual. This is the date that appears in the listings. Some dates are approximations given by former employees while others appeared in previous articles about this line or in records which we have located.

Many of the staff served in several different posts on the same station during their careers but in the majority of cases names are only indicated once unless transferred to another station on the branch.

Holt Staff

Section Policemen
Robert Thorne 1857
Edward Pyle 1857

Station Master
Edward Pyle c.1874-1881
Samuel Chalke 1881-
Goldsworth Beer c.1912-
Walter Bull c.1930-35
R.Cowman 1935-52
Reg Hopkins 1952-55
Edward Russell 1955-c.64
Jack Hurley c.1964-c.65 (Calne S.M.)
Wilf Clovier c.1965-66 (Melksham S.M.)

Porters
Frank Webb c.1930-c.55
Jock McKinnon c.1955-62
Lew Arlett c. 1962-66
Ernie Darby c.1941-47
Ernie Bishop c.1950
Len Wilkins c.1946 (goods)

Goods Clerk
S.E.Hewett c.1919

Goods Checker
Reg Clarke 1934-48
George Tucker c.1946

Goods Shunters
Reg Clarke 1934-48
C.H.Palmer ?-1941
Ernie Darby c.1941-47
Wilf Drew 1941-
Derek Stowe c.1944-54
Rodney Francombe c.1950-60
Arthur Gillman
Frank Bartlett ?-1955
Albert Callaway c.1950-60
Dave Mitchell
John Hungerford c.1950-60
Stan Tout 1958-66
Eric Eyers
Stan Heyward c.1948
Eric Francis c.1948
N.Kelly c.1948
Danny Tuffin 1956

Signalmen
William Cornish 1879-1923
George Merrett 1879-1923
Mr Cousins 1879-1923
Tom Yeomans 1923-c.55
Ewart Shell 1955-62
John Gould c.1950
George Hunt c.1955-62
Ken Cross 1955-56
Vic Trimell c.1955-62
Arthur Phillips c.1956
Vic Tucker c.1950-55
Charles Millard 1938-45

Permanent Way Gang
Arthur Stone
Oliver Fidler - platelayer
Alf Norris
Len Wootton c.1949-60 - ganger
Bill Woodward

Others
Mr Woods c.1866
Mr Bryant c.1872
Fred King 1912-14 +1930-42
Mr Derham c.1950
Mr Perrott c.1872

Seend Staff

Station Masters
Charles Jackson 1867-75
William Broughton 1875-c.80
John Hodder c.1880-1906
James Hancock 1906-08
Fred Arnold 1908-c.38
Harold Fred Ludgate c.1938-52

Goods Checker
Fred Dollimore c.1920-c.51

Porters
G.Reeves c.1917-
Bert Clack 1918-20
W.J.Drew February-April 1941
Elsie R.Perry c.1940-
Robert Weston 1945-62
Alfred 'Pop' Stapleton c.1930s-40s
Lawrence Buckley 1943-46
Joe Burbidge 1942-45
Percy Vines c.1930s

Permanent Way Gang
George Nash 1922-60 - ganger
Bill Sheppard 1938-66
Fred Abbott c.1940s
Charles Arnold c.1945-
Wally Maynard 1948-50
Arthur Rawlings 1951-59
Ernie 'Jock' McDonald 1953-66
Stan Wise c.1940s-50s
Ralph Butler 1931-38

Signalmen and Signalwomen
Harry Lodge c.1920s-c.55
Bill Brooks c.1927-c.38
Don Chilcott c.1930s-c.40s
Jack Gregory c.1930s-c.40s
Winifred Weston 1942-c.49
Florence 'Duck' Sainsbury c.1941-48
H.A.Viewig 1941
H.W.Powell 1941-

Signalmen and Signalwomen
Bob Bunce ?-1941
Dave Nash 1945-46
Jack Perrett c.1953-June 56
Graham Darby 1952
Sid Perrett 1953
William Wakeham 1953-
Vic Trimell c.1955
Jim Gunthorpe 1950-51

Booking Clerks
Peter Weston 1943-c.46
Miss Bowles c.1940-c.46

Unknown
O.F.Slade ?-1941

Devizes Staff

Station Masters
Francis Verc Holloway 1857-66
John Gurling 1866-75
Claude Pearman 1875-76
George Hyrons 1876-82
Thomas Abrahams 1882-95
J.C.Neville 1895-98
Henry Gerrard 1898-1904
Walter S.King 1904-16
J.J.Eaton 1916-26
S.Evans 1926-34
Denis O'Donoghue 1934-48
Sidney Bray 1948-55
Albert Stowe 1955-57
Edward J.W.Major 1957-64

Crossing Keepers
Charlie Wish 1901-37
Jack Butler c.1930-c.44
Reg Elliott c.1922-c.45
Jack Yates c.1959-60s
Robert Weston 1962-

Chief Clerks
Mr Titball c.1900-c.30s
Tommy Edwards 1921-c.40s
Johnny Gall 1922
Archie Oram c.1930-c.45
Edward J.W.Major 1933-c.44
Mr Harding c.1920s-c.40s
Maurice Brown c.1947-c.50s

Signal Linemen
Frank Brooks c.1914
Harry Dyer 1929-c.40s
Alfred White c.1931-c.40s
Bill Simpkins c.1931-c.40s

Parcels Clerks
Francis Isherwood c.1940s
Gwen Cooper c.1950s

Booking Clerks
P.G.Pyke 1893
Edgar Seth Cross 1913-62
Jack Tottle c.1930s-c.40s
Kath Bishop 1940-64
Mrs Chapple c.1940s
Miss Barkham c.1940s
Maurice Hiscock c.1950s
Ken Welsh c.1950s-66
Alan Mead 1947-64
Gordon Dodge 1953-54
Janet Alexander (parcels) 1953-54

Station Foremen
Frank E.Hill ?-1941
Percy Bond 1934-65
Bill Newman c.1930s-c.40
Ernie Purbrick

Ticket Collectors
George Warren c.1890s
Molly Potter c.1940-c.46
Jim Lane c.1930s-c.40s
William Cox 1921-c.40s

Weighbridge Clerks
Philip Hawkins c.1930s-39
Eric Slade 1939-45
Joan Leaphard c.1940
Vic Grant c.1950s
Ray Shell c.1950s

Shunters
Samuel Stockham c.1890s
Joe Giddings 1942-64
Ernie Ross 1939-40
Reg Chave 1930-66
Stan Hillier c.1950s

Master of the Goods Depot
Mr Knowles 1857-

Porters
Mr Chandler c.1890s
Tommy Truckle c.1890s-c.1920s
William Perrett 1917-36
Bill Brooks 1917-c.27
Jim Nash 1909-46
George Stiles 1905-46
Bill Nutland c.1920s-40s
Dave Nash 1939-43 & 1944-45
Den Slade 1943-44
Doris Ellis c.1940s
Gwen Cotton c.1940s
Walter Tanner (relief) 1945-46
Trevor Brothers c.1944-c.50
Ernie Arnold c.1930s-40s
Colin Clifford c.1940s
Lil Painter 1943-46
Sarah 'Sally' White c.1940-c.46
E.G.Harris 1948
Bob 'Bonzo' Lewis c.1948-c.50s
Sid Guy 1938-41
Arthur Boulter c.1930s-c.60s
Tom Newton 1939-66
Jack Allen 1950-61
Les 'Shack' Wiltshire 1950s-60s
Alfie Wiltshire 1950-61
Bob Diskett c.1956-66
Jack Perrett 1946-c.50
Percy Vines c.1930s
Ernie Bishop c.1930-55
Gerald Taylor c.1950s
Pete Reardon c.1950s
E.S.Perrett ?-1957
Bob Davidge (relief) 1950s
Sam Wilkinson
Pat Salter c.1940s-c.50s
Ken Sheppard c.1940s-c.50s

Goods Checkers
Reg Elliott c.1922
Mr Topp c.1940s

TRAFFIC DEALT WITH

STATION.	YEAR.	Supervisory and Wages (all Grades).	Paybill Expenses.	TOTAL RECEIPTS.	Tickets issued.	Season Tickets.	Passengers (Including Season Tickets, etc.).	Parcels.	Miscellaneous.	Total.
		No	£	£	No.	No.	£	£	£	£
Patney and Chirton.	1903	7	394	2,518	10,124	*	1,291	96	1,131	2,518
	1913	7	524	5,002	8,127	*	740	94	1,978	2,912
	1923	9	1,537	6,988	7,093	9	942	303	2,849	4,094
	1929	10	1,713	5,648	6,224	9	913	173	2,413	3,499
	1930	10	1,687	6,049	5,498	4	823	168	2,608	3,599
	1931	10	1,652	5,040	4,941	8	739	172	2,461	3,372
	1932	10	1,620	5,261	4,045	23	671	145	1,821	2,637
	1933	10	1,594	2,428	3,650	14	698	123	142	963
	1934	10	1,579	2,231	3,572	21	716	150	28	894
Pans Lane Halt. (‡)				Opened March, 1920.						
	1929	Included with Devizes.			83	1,476	—	83	—	—	83
	1930			81	1,247	—	81	—	—	81
	1931			86	1,454	—	86	—	—	86
	1932			63	1,258	—	63	—	—	63
	1933			54	672	2	54	—	—	54
				Included with Trowbridge and Westbury (Wilts) after 1933						
Devizes	1903	26	1,899	40,565	63,609	*	9,876	4,813	3,898	18,587
	1913	32	2,093	40,868	61,423	*	9,164	4,778	3,631	17,568
	1923	39	6,082	52,910	49,135	247	11,551	5,244	4,988	21,783
	1929	36	5,940	50,133	38,897	188	9,684	4,885	4,797	19,366
	1930	34	5,898	47,894	30,743	103	8,217	4,878	4,873	17,968
	1931	34	5,646	44,840	27,894	127	7,729	4,621	5,033	17,383
	1932	32	5,217	40,407	25,679	79	6,862	4,254	3,416	14,532
	1933	30	4,690	37,776	24,013	88	6,750	4,118	1,739	12,607
	1934	30	4,581	37,202	23,042	64	6,411	4,173	1,971	12,555
Bromham and Rowde Halt				Included with Seend.						
Seend	1903	5	235	2,543	13,912	*	801	100	516	1,417
	1913	6	435	5,272	10,790	*	641	129	1,457	2,227
	1923	7	1,135	10,547	9,656	39	679	168	5,407	6,254
	1929	6	1,056	9,717	7,742	14	586	132	4,818	5,536
	1930	7	1,053	9,598	4,060	7	329	124	4,506	4,959
	1931	7	1,003	6,927	4,208	19	323	97	3,000	3,420
	1932	7	997	4,531	3,716	30	345	80	1,520	1,945
	1933	6	931	2,254	3,651	24	351	62	105	518
	1934	6	872	1,926	3,951	21	360	49	39	448
Semington Halt.				Included with Holt Jct.						
Holt Jct. ..	1903	9	573	6,868	12,929	*	669	158	121	948
	1913	11	707	8,366	13,474	*	698	198	380	1,276
	1923	14	2,237	17,433	15,518	121	1,392	229	1,350	2,971
	1929	14	2,158	14,680	15,301	67	1,013	306	1,108	2,427
	1930	14	2,190	14,029	7,174	56	699	244	973	1,916
	1931	13	2,176	13,980	5,523	92	694	226	615	1,535
	1932	13	1,985	17,051	4,642	155	641	240	402	1,283
	1933	13	2,005	15,771	4,024	162	636	195	418	1,249
	1934	13	1,980	18,202	3,511	147	574	216	372	1,162

AT STATIONS.

GOODS TRAIN TRAFFIC.

Forwarded			Received			Coal and Coke "Not Charged." (Forwarded and Received).	Total Goods Tonnage.	Total Receipts (excluding "Not Charged" Coal and Coke).	Livestock (Forwarded and Received).	Total Carted Tonnage (Included in Total Goods Tonnage).
Coal and Coke "Charged."	Other Minerals.	General Merchandise.	Coal and Coke "Charged."	Other Minerals.	General Merchandise.					
Tons.	Tons.	Tons.	Tons.	Tons.	Tons.	Tons.	Tons.	£	Wagons.	Tons.
			Opened	for Goods	Traffic, 1st	October,	1904.			
15	—	1 629	875	3,428	824	624	7,395	2,190	37	164
—	—	1,079	26	1,759	1,144	1,063	5,671	2,894	23	229
—	454	560	84	1,314	1,060	764	4,236	2,149	56	117
—	893	309	81	2,413	846	526	5,068	2,450	76	118
—	201	200	95	792	1,197	627	3,262	1,668	84	109
—	302	690	135	944	1,403	758	4,322	2,624	105	448
—	381	447	104	447	850	529	2,758	1,465	58	574
—	460	165	79	68	1,079	581	2,432	1,337	54	903
9	785	7,508	18,607	12,335	14,051	4,191	57,576	21,078	770	8,219
46	2,087	7,237	10,308	11,439	14,520	5,807	57,453	23,205	861	8,790
111	1,699	5,393	6,017	13,004	11,602		46,377	31,127	659	6,460
186	1,535	3,522	3,937	6,554	18,633	17,398	51,705	30,767	677	6,619
33	1,670	3,517	3,258	9,104	18,101	18,247	53,930	20,926	519	6,321
22	1,166	3,872	2,582	4,183	18,035	18,091	47,051	27,457	436	6,161
30	908	3,790	2,686	3,973	17,583	17,825	46,795	25,875	457	7,402
74	1,211	4,268	2,721	3,144	16,736	17,174	45,328	25,169	376	8,603
—	1,495	3,761	2,051	2,083	15,674	18,182	44,146	24,757	379	9,007
—	263	616	1,351	1,676	1,343	229	5,478	1,126	—	144
14	101	2,522	1,057	6,113	1,804	826	12,437	3,045	0	208
—	1,818	2,015	1,092	3,655	2,057	1,141	11,778	4,293	3	165
7	603	1,861	1,182	2,719	1,332	1,194	8,898	4,181	13	424
8	930	1,957	944	1,052	1,334	1,006	7,831	4,639	13	408
—	326	1,533	946	1,765	1,153	1,045	6,768	3,507	7	492
17	219	911	925	1,012	1,354	1,062	5,500	2,586	13	451
8	410	744	376	376	663	1,431	4,008	1,736	1	358
8	476	503	241	202	632	1,565	3,627	1,478	1	252
7	5,387	2,765	3,912	1,221	2,943	781	17,016	5,920	—	3,394
43	450	2,712	5,668	2,838	5,213	493	16,917	7,090	—	3,415
—	329	6,116	5,576	1,128	3,980	1,291	18,420	14,462	—	5,644
—	200	7,557	2,590	1,694	4,393	5,015	21,449	12,253	—	4,802
—	209	7,630	1,550	1,147	4,723	7,073	22,832	12,113	—	4,838
—	233	7,927	2,834	307	5,069	4,770	21,140	12,445	1	4,857
—	286	10,238	3,000	367	6,505	7,684	28,080	15,768	1	5,911
—	201	10,912	4,426	194	5,084	4,592	25,499	14,522	1	5,457
8	362	11,520	5,551	380	6,291	3,991	28,103	17,130	—	6,248

Locomotives Recorded on the Devizes Branch

GWR Broad Gauge
Fury Class   *Dreadnought*
Hercules Class   *Tityos*
Caliph Class   *Nemesis*

GWR Steam Railmotor No.48

GWR/BR(WR)
4-6-0 Castle Class
4037 *South Wales Borderers*   4073 *Caerphilly Castle*
4075 *Cardiff Castle*   4084 *Aberystwyth Castle*
4085 *Berkeley Castle*   5014 *Goodrich Castle*
5022 *Wigmore Castle*   5029 *Nunney Castle*
5036 *Lyonshall Castle*   5039 *Rhuddlan Castle*
5063 *Earl Baldwin*   5069 *Isambard Kingdom Brunel*
5070 *Sir Daniel Gooch*   5075 *Devizes Castle*
5083 *Bath Abbey*   5093 *Upton Castle*

4-6-0 Star Class
4019 *Knight Templar*   4043 *Prince Henry*

4-6-0 Hall Class
4900 *Saint Martin*   4923 *Evenley Hall*
4924 *Eydon Hall*   4950 *Patshull Hall*
4955 *Plaspower Hall*   4959 *Purley Hall*
4962 *Ragley Hall*   4966 *Shakenhurst Hall*
5922 *Caxton Hall*   5933 *Kingsway Hall*
5937 *Stamford Hall*   5945 *Leckhampton Hall*
5949 *Trematon Hall*   5963 *Wimpole Hall*
5973 *Rolleston Hall*   5974 *Wallsworth Hall*
5993 *Kirby Hall*   6913 *Levens Hall*
6927 *Lilford Hall*   6955 *Lydcott Hall*
6959 *Peatling Hall*   6960 *Raveningham Hall*
6965 *Throwley Hall*   6966 *Witchingham Hall*
6968 *Woodcock Hall*   6982 *Melmerby Hall*
6983 *Otterington Hall*   6990 *Witherslack Hall*
6994 *Baggrave Hall*   6999 *Capel Dewi Hall*
7908 *Henshall Hall*   7914 *Llewent Hall*
7917 *North Aston Hall*   7919 *Runter Hall*
7921 *Edstone Hall*   7923 *Speke Hall*
7924 *Thornycroft Hall*   7927 *Willington Hall*

4-6-0 Saint Class
2906 *Lady of Lynn*   2908 *Lady of Quality*
2913 *Saint Andrew*   2922 *Saint Gabriel*
2931 *Arlington Court*   2955 *Tortworth Court*

4-6-0 Manor Class
7802 *Bradley Manor*   7808 *Cookham Manor*
7809 *Childrey Manor*   7812 *Erlestoke Manor*
7814 *Fringford Manor*

4-6-0 County Class   1002 *County of Berkshire*

4-6-0 Grange Class   6830 *Buckenhill Grange*

4-4-0 Classes   3341 *Blasius*
3363 *Alfred Baldwin*   3364 *Frank Bibby*
3396 *Natal Colony*   3426

2-6-0	4347 5396 6366 7302 7318 7321 9307 9309
2-8-0	2811
2-6-2T	4567 5174 6129 6153 6156
2-10-0	92210
2-4-0	54 483 487 3239 3241 3245 3257
2-4-0T	613
0-4-2T	4832
0-6-0PT	1139 1230 1695 3735 3736 3780 4607 5402 5403 5410 5412 5414 5416 5419 5423 5771 6408 6771 7764 8744 9615 9620 9628 9762
0-6-0ST	1147 1555 1698

0-6-0 Tender Standard and Dean Goods
472   657   672   800   2359 2426 2441

0-6-0 Tender Collett Goods
2208 2217 2250 2261 2299 3208 3217

LMS
0-6-0 2F Tender Locos on loan to GWR in WW2
3096 3603

SR
4-6-0 Tender Loco on loan to GWR in WW2
2329 *Stephenson* (ex LBSCR Class N15X)

ex LNER
4-6-2   4472 *Flying Scotsman*

MSWJR
4-4-0 Tender Loco on troop train use in WW1   7

Diesel Locomotives
D604 *Cossack*   D1010 *Western Campaigner*
D809 *Champion*   D1041 *Western Prince*
D811 *Daring*   D846 *Steadfast*
D812 D817 D822 D837 D983 D7040

Diesel Multiple Units
50165   50870   50923   51052
51080   51093   51383   59424

BR Class 5 73029

Bibliography

Anon., *Holt Junction* (Holt Magazine, 1966)

Anon., *A Last Look at Holt Junction* (Holt Magazine, 1967)

Anon., *A History of Wiltshire, Volume IV* (The Victoria History of the Counties of England, Oxford U.P., 1959)

Behrend, George, *Gone With Regret* (Jersey Artists, 1969)

Bradby, Edward, *Seend: a Wiltshire Village Past & Present* (Alan Sutton Publishing, 1981)

Bray, Nigel S.M., *A Wiltshire Railway Remembered: The Devizes Branch* (Picton Press, 1984)

Carter, Ernest F., *Railways in Wartime* (Frederick Muller, 1964)

Chandler, John, *West Country Landscapes: The Vale of Pewsey* (Ex Libris Press, 1991)

Cornwell, E.L., *The Pictorial Story of Railways* (Hamlyn, 1974)

Crosbie-Hill, William, 'One Day at Devizes', *Great Western Echo*, (Winter 1983/84)

Cunnington, Bernard Howard, 'Pans Lane Halt: The Centre of a former Roman Settlement', *GWR Magazine* (1932)

Departmental Notes, *GWR Magazine* (February and March 1940)

Devizes & District Almanack & Directory (George Simpson, various volumes)

Gaylard, T.J. & Kingman, D.R., *800 Years of the Borough of Devizes, 1141-1974* (no publisher indicated, 1974)

Gillman's Devizes Public Register & Business Directory (G.Gillman, various volumes)

Holden, Bryan & Leech, Kenneth H., *Portraits of Castles* (Moorland Publishing, 1981)

Jackson, Robert, *A Taste of Freedom* (Arthur Barker, 1964)

James, N.D.G., *Plain Soldiering* (Hobnob Press, 1987)

Longmate, Norman, *The G.I.s: The Americans in Britain 1942-45* (Hutchinson, 1975)

Maggs, Colin G. & Beale, Gerry, *The Camerton Branch* (Wild Swan Publications, 1985)

Marshman, Mike, *The Wiltshire Book* (Countryside Books, 1987)

Nicholson, Col. G.W.L., *The Fighting Newfoundlander 1700-1918* (Government of Newfoundland, 1964)

Phelps, Alan, *RAF Melksham: Letters from the Past* (Uffington Press, 1994)

Pigg, James, *Railway Block Signalling* (Biggs, 1899)

The Railway Gazette (10th June 1910)

Ross, Ernie, *Tales of the Rails* (Bristol Broadsides, 1984)

Samuel, Ian, *Doctor at Dunkirk* (Autolycus Publications, 1985)

Saunders, Trevor J., 'Railways to Devizes', *Railway Magazine* (October 1957)

Scotland, Lt.-Col. A.P., *The London Cage* (Evans Brothers, 1957)

Strong, Paul, 'Devizes', *Back Track*, (July/August 1989)

Taylor, John W.R., *C.F.S.: Birthplace of Air Power* (Putnam Press, 1958)

Trigg, Brian, 'Brian Trigg Visits Devizes', *Model Railway Constructor* (September 1965)

Tupper, Harry, 'Devizes (Postcript)', *Great Western Echo* (Summer 1984)

Vincent, Mike, *Through Countryside and Coalfield*, (Oxford Publishing Company, 1990)

Wiltshire (Kelly's Directories, various volumes)

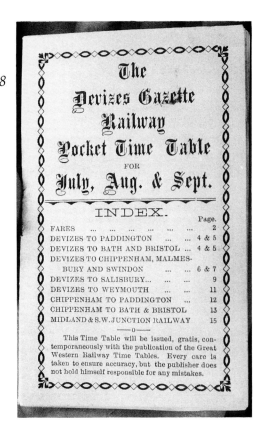

Acknowledgments

We have derived much pleasure from the preparation of this book and the greater part of this results from meeting the numerous ex-railway staff who worked on the line, as well as many of their relations. In every case they made us feel welcome, have greeted the project with enthusiasm, and have freely contributed their experiences and memories. It has been our pleasure meeting them; we thank them all for their help and support, in the hope that they in turn are rewarded by knowing that each contribution has resulted in the promotion of their railway through this publication.

Special thanks are due to the late Bill Perrett, the oldest railway man we met, who at the age of 90 had a remarkable memory for a man of those years; to Eric and Eileen Slade who were visited at their home in Bristol on more than one occasion and in addition to providing answers also generously provided lunches, home-made beer and tomato plants for the garden; to Bob Diskett who was able to identify faces in photographs on our frequent visits to see him; to Dave Nash and his wife Joan, both of whom were related to previous generations of railway men, for their kindness and Dave's much-appreciated tales; to Joe Burbidge who directed us along the right tracks in the early days; and to Bob and Pete Brooks for providing a considerable number of photographs of their father Bill.

There have been many people not associated with the railway who have also contributed. Some of these have done so in the course of their profession or through their interest in other aspects of local history, while others have just been pleased to cooperate when asked. Of these, a special thanks to those men of Holt, John Sawtell and Ian Hibbard, for overwhelming us with photographic material.

Sincere appreciation for the loan of his wartime material is expressed to Clive Seaton whose father Douglas had the good fortune to be able to photograph many interesting trains during the 1940s from the trackside in Hillworth cutting, close to his garden. We thank also Chris Turner for the loan of his research material and notes extracted from the Public Record Office at Kew, and Alan Mead for access to his extensive library of timetables and for his expertise on the subject.

Some material is used from sources which are not identifiable or which originated from individuals who have been impossible to trace. To these we trust that they will accept that the material's inclusion is purely to ensure the retention of a valuable piece of history and not intended as a credit to ourselves. We would be pleased to hear from anybody to whom this may apply.

The passing of some who have contributed serves to remind us of the importance of recording history before it becomes too late. We regret that these indviduals will not see the results of our efforts for which they made such valuable contributions.

We would wish to thank our families for their support and tolerance over the period of six years the book has been in preparation. Our sincere appreciation also to Tim Graham of Millstream Books who, at a time when his business was taking a change of direction, kindly agreed to publish this piece of history, so providing the final chapter of our story.

We would also like to record our gratitude to the following individuals and organisations whose no less valuable contributions have made this book possible:

Alan Alexander
Ian Allan Publishing
Jack Allen
L.H.Arlett & Sons
Mike Arlett
Ernie Axford

Bert Baber
Bob Bailey
Barry Barrett
Ivan Beale
George Behrend
Graham Birt

Kath Bishop
Michael Bolwell
Edward Bradby
Nigel S.M.Bray
Brian Bridgeman
British Rail Record Office
Trevor Brothers
Bert Brown
Charlie Brown
Len Brown
Philip Brown
Tim Bryan
Keith Buckle

Harold Burry
Ralph Butler
Winifred M.Butler

Colin L.Caddy
David Card
R.Carpenter
Jimmy Caswell
Peter Chave
Ron Church
City of Bristol Museum
    & Art Gallery
A.Clarke

Desmond Clarke
Reg Clarke
David Colcombe
R.J.Coles
R.A.Cooke
Jack Cotton
Ian Coulson
William Crosbie-Hill
Larry Crosier
Mrs S.E.Cross
Fred Cundick
Frank Cutting

Graham Darby
Bob Davidge
Devizes Museum
Devizes Town Council
Eddie Dight
Gordon Dodge

Dennis Ellis

Colin Fletcher
Bill Frindall
Peter Fry
Tom Fussell

Jim Gander
Tony Gay
Terry Gaylard
Mr Gee
Reg Giddings
Mrs J.Giddings
Richard Giles
John Spencer-Gilks
Paul Gilson
John Girvan
Pam Gooding
Great Western Society
Tony Green
Jim Gunthorpe
Sid Guy
GWR Museum, Swindon

Judith Hale
Bob Hallam
Duncan Harper
Simon Haynes
Mac Head
Ian Heath
John Heath

Ken Hillier
Reg Hopkins
Roger Hyslop

Reg Instone

David Jones

Paul Karau
Colin Kearley
Bob Keepence
Simon Kennedy
Frank Kimmer

Dick Larden
R.Linsley
Nicky Littlefield
Arthur Lock
Donald Lovelock
Michael F.Luffman

Douglas McGuinness
Colin G.Maggs
John Mann
Brian Matthews
Sid Matthews
Donald G.May
F.May
Wally Maynard
Mendip Minis Ltd
Freddie Merrett
Stan Miles
L.A.Moore Ltd
D.H.Morris
J.Morris
Rachel Moulton

National Monuments Record
    Centre, Swindon
Robert Naylor
Nestlé Co Ltd
Jack Newman
Mrs T.Newton
Jack Nisbet

Richard Packham
Lil Painter
Norman Parker
Jack Perrett
John Perry
Alan Phelps

Richard Pope
Derek Prior

RAF Melksham Historical Committee
Railtrack Records Office, Swindon
John Rawle
P.J.Retter
Timothy Roberts
June Rogers
Ernie Ross
Elly Rowles
John Rowles

John Sainsbury
Maurice Sanger
Trevor J.Saunders
Seend Women's Institute
Signalling Record Society
Ernie Sly
Ben Smith
Betty Smith
Peter Smith
Stella Smith
Stuart Smith
David Snook
Southern Electric (Cotswold Division)
Ray Stillman
Fred Stone
Paul Strong
Jean Summers

Walter Tanner
Albert Tout
Stan Tout

Peter Weston
Gerry Wheeler
Michael Wheeler
Marjorie Willcox
P.J.Williams
Alfie Wiltshire
Wiltshire County Record Office,
    Trowbridge
Wiltshire County Library &
    Museum Service
    (especially the Local Studies
    sections at Devizes,
    Swindon and Trowbridge)
Wiltshire Gazette & Herald
Wiltshire Times & News
Winchcombe Railway Museum

The running-in board on the east end of Devizes station island platform. Photographed in the early 1950s, it was then painted brown with cream letters and mounted in a wooden frame on woooden posts. When the board was originally installed the background was blue enamel with white letters; it was overpainted on nationalisation. The board survives in its original form at Winchcombe Railway Museum.

One of the numerous Devizes station totems which remain in local private ownership. (R.Priddle)